William Graham

The One Pound Note in the Rise and Progress of Banking in

Scotland,

and Its Adaptability to England

William Graham

The One Pound Note in the Rise and Progress of Banking in Scotland,
and Its Adaptability to England

ISBN/EAN: 9783337114374

Printed in Europe, USA, Canada, Australia, Japan

Cover: Foto ©Suzi / pixelio.de

More available books at **www.hansebooks.com**

THE ONE POUND NOTE

IN

THE RISE AND PROGRESS OF
BANKING IN SCOTLAND,

AND

ITS ADAPTABILITY TO ENGLAND.

BY

WILLIAM GRAHAM,
MEMBER OF THE INSTITUTE OF BANKERS IN SCOTLAND.

> " Al is not gold yᵗ glitters, I do feare ;
> And yᵗ with carelesse heat we sette our minde
> On that whose radiance doth but make us blinde ;
> We may perchance attaine it somewhat deare."

EDINBURGH :
JAMES THIN, 55 SOUTH BRIDGE.
GLASGOW : PORTEOUS, BROTHERS, EXCHANGE SQUARE.
LONDON : SIMPKIN MARSHALL & CO.
1886.

TO THE

Members and Associates

OF THE

INSTITUTE OF BANKERS IN SCOTLAND

This Volume

IS RESPECTFULLY DEDICATED.

Contents.

Illustrations.

Preface.

THE following pages were first penned in the form of an Essay upon " The History, Place, and Power of the One Pound Note in Scotland, and its Adaptability to England," which was entered for the competition of the Institute of Bankers in Scotland for 1885.

Having been very hastily written, the writer was agreeably surprised to learn, that the judges for that year —Mr J. F. Stormonth Darling, of the Bank of Scotland, and Mr G. L. Rorie, of the National Bank—recommended that the Essay "bearing the motto ' *Qui honeste fortiter* ' might be printed with advantage to the Institute, owing to the mass of information it contains."

The work has since undergone considerable revision, and now consists of two sections, relating respectively to Scotland and England. In the first are given various leading events in the banking history of Scotland, in so far as these have related to, or been affected by, " the famous sma' note ;" while at the close will be found a few pages upon the law of paper currency, the note exchange system in Scotland, and the manufacture of bank notes. In the second section an attempt is made to prove from experience alone the adaptability of small notes to England; and to shew what are the reasons for the antipathy still entertained in that country against such a currency. To a people so practical as the English mere theory is always unwelcome; and it is hoped that no Englishman, who may be pleased to read the book, will find in it anything which cannot be well attested by the experiences both of England and Scotland.

A few facsimiles of old notes have been inserted to illustrate the Scottish section, which, by their style and workmanship, also serve to strengthen the argument in the chapter upon England.

The writer has pleasure in availing himself of this opportunity of thanking those banks who have permitted the reproduction of their notes; and also of tendering his acknowledgments to the friends who have furnished information, or otherwise aided him in his task.

9 CUMIN PLACE, GRANGE,
EDINBURGH. *March* 1886.

THE ONE POUND NOTE.

Chapter I.—1695-1727.

INTRODUCTORY REMARKS—RISE OF THE BANK OF SCOTLAND,
AND ISSUE OF ONE POUND NOTES.

> "Of writing well, these are the chiefest things:
> To know the nature and the use of things."

THE Institute of Bankers in Scotland could scarcely have chosen a more fitting subject for their Essay competition, or one more in harmony with the spirit of Scottish Banking, than the History, Place, and Power of the One Pound Note. By its means the Scottish banks have so completely adapted themselves to the wants of the greatest number of their countrymen, and so essential an element has it been of our banking system, that in dealing with its past history it is impossible to dissociate it from the history of the system of which it forms a part.

A history of the Scottish banking system, in its widest extension, is simply an evidence of the power of the one pound note; whatever may be its place in the future of Scotland, whether its usefulness will extend still further with the nation's growth, or whether it is being superseded by other agencies, time alone will show; but we may be assured, that it is not without reason that the place and power of this "Promise to Pay" have between them furnished materials for such endless books, pamphlets, and newspaper articles, as our appreciative ancestors have favoured us with in the course of the last hundred years.

A

With so much to guide, therefore, in a study of these points, it seems a pity that so little should be known of its history. Whether it be that this part of its story has been overshadowed by the greater importance of the banking system in general,—the historical aspect being lost sight of in the speculative and theoretical,—or that the very familiarity the Scots people have with it has rendered them blind to its interesting career, it is difficult to say; but none the less is it to be regretted that there is no work pretending to give the history of the one pound note, so that a modern student has to grope his way through the dusty fragments which have been thrown out in the past, picking up a fact here and there, and arranging them in order as best he may. Even, when done, such a history must be necessarily both meagre and vague, since, in the scattered references to notes during a long period, it is so impossible to distinguish between "large" and "small," that the writer has to be content with the certainty that some of them at least must have been one pound notes.

Its adaptability to England is a subject for which there is abundant data. Banking in that country, without referring to other causes in the meantime, has undergone such material changes since Lord Liverpool abolished the one pound note in 1826, that the time seems not far distant when it will come within the range of "practical politics," and again resume its place as a factor in English currency.

A disquisition upon the proverbial caution of the Scottish people may seem a little out of place as a preface to a history of one pound notes. It is however remarkable that, while the universal testimony of Europe accords this virtue to our nation, financial history records few more daring, gigantic, and apparently *incautious* enterprises than those which originated with Scotsmen. Can it be, then, that the Scot is not cautious? We think not. It is never said of him that he runs before he can creep, that he leaps before he looks ; on the contrary, he looks long and earnestly, pondering well all his doings. That busy brain, into which no joke is supposed to penetrate, is ever engaged upon the consideration of more practical things. Speculating, theorising, calculating for a time, to a prompt Englishman or lively Frenchman, his action will seem distressingly slow; but once the brain has done its work, and the theory is formulated,—the calculation completed,—the time of action has arrived, and, having carefully thought out all his plans, there is no daring to which the Scot will not aspire. An English writer says of the true Caledonian : " His Minerva is born in panoply ; you are never admitted to see his ideas in their growth, if indeed they do grow, and are not rather put together upon principles of clockwork. He has no falterings of self-suspicion ; surmises, guesses, misgivings, half-intuitions, semi-consciousnesses, partial illuminations, dim instincts, embryo conceptions, have no place in his brain or vocabulary. The twilight of dubiety never falls upon him. Between the affirmative and the negative there is no border-land with him." It is this unswerving singleness of purpose, based upon profound forethought, which makes the genuine Scot first cautious, and then daring ; and it is upon the soundness or deficiency of his reasoning that the success or failure of his projects depend. In the commercial world, perhaps, no two men exhibit these peculiarities of our race more strongly than John Law and William Paterson. These two Scotsmen, whose names were before the speculative public from 1690 to 1725 with special prominence, were both men of remarkable ability and determination of purpose, possessed of good reasoning powers, and having considerable merit as writers on economics, finance, and mathematics. Law had, however, one great hobby ; his views of basing paper currency on twenty years' value of the land were utterly fallacious, but he had thought them out with care, and sincerely believing them to be right, he knew no rest until, with some modification, they were carried into practice in his Mississippi scheme, with a result which Frenchmen best know. The determination of the inventor only increased the magnitude of the ruin.

While the Law theories thus led to ruin, those of William
Paterson were of a totally different nature. We are indebted to Mr Bannister for the details of the life and
writings of this remarkable man. Gifted with even greater
abilities than Law, he based his conclusions upon sounder
premises. In various pamphlets, and in his "Wednesday
Club Dialogues," he strongly advocated a gold standard
as the only safe basis for a paper currency ; denouncing
vigorously the land nostrums of Dr Hugh Chamberlain and
other writers. The Bank of England was founded upon
his proposals in 1694, and has since suffered precisely where
it abandoned the principles of its founder. That he was a
man of commanding talent, is very well observed in his
life. "His admittance as a bank director has the same
significancy to his honour, inasmuch as the wealthier
men of London, his colleagues, were at that time by
no means of a temper to be guided by a native of Scotland, unless his intellectual superiority was well attested."
He did not long remain a director, but he had scarcely left
when the bank's troubles began, and partly through
neglect of Paterson's caution they were compelled to stop
payment.

Much has been said against him on account of the
disasters of his Darien scheme,—disasters for which England
was alone responsible. But for her selfish arrogance in 1696,
England might now have been owner of the Panama Canal.
It is to this man, then, that England chiefly owes the
modern "Bank Note." For thirty years prior to 1692,
goldsmiths' promissory deposit notes or tickets—written,
not printed—had a large circulation in and around London,
being transferable by simple endorsation where payable to
order, or by delivery when drawn to bearer. The common
law of England had generally considered choses-in-action
(in which promissory notes were embraced) to be transferable, until Lord Coke threw some doubt upon the matter,
and finally maintained their invalidity. The custom of
merchants, after the Restoration, had somewhat ignored
this dictum ; but it is evident that there was a feeling of

insecurity, for one writer,* so early as 1677, advocated the adoption of the Continental practice, "making bills payable to bearer transferable without a slow and expensive assignation, or even any endorsement." Three years after the date of this discourse, a decision was obtained, declaring promissory notes legally transferable. Twelve years passed, and the trade in deposit notes went on briskly, until 1692, when a goldsmith's note came before Lord Holt and the Court of Queen's Bench, in the case Buller *v.* Crips, upon which it was decided, after much discussion, that all such writs were quite illegal, and could not be assigned or transferred. This decision was a severe blow to the London bankers and merchants, and a remonstrance was addressed to Parliament, into which Paterson threw himself with characteristic vigour. He appeared before a Committee of the House of Commons in 1693, and offered to raise money for Government use, by means of his influence with City financiers, on the condition that Government should sanction their " Bills payable in Coin on demand " being transferable to *bearer without endorsement*, contrary to Lord Holt's decision. His views were partly embodied in the Act of the following year, founding the Bank of England (5 Wm. and Mary, c. 20), whereby their notes were made transferable by endorsement, in these terms :—" Which said Orders shall be assignable and transferable in such and the same manner as is mentioned in the said recited Act,"—a previous Act relating to Government duties.†

Chamberlain's rival idea was to have notes payable to bearer on demand in land; Paterson's, to pay coin on demand for formal printed notes. In a very short time mercantile custom ignored the statutory requirement of

---

* "A Discourse of the Use and Power of Parliaments, Laws, Courts, &c.," printer and author unknown. See Bannister's " Life of William Paterson."

† Some writers maintain that the Act bears no reference to notes, but only to bills, issued by the Bank. We prefer to take another view, which has the authority of Mr H. D. Macleod to commend it, although the clause in question is certainly very dubious in its sense.

endorsation, and in 1704 English promissory notes were accorded the same rights as bills of exchange. The whole dispute need never have arisen, for in 1875, as the result of the researches of Mr H. D. Macleod, the decisions of Lord Holt and his *confrères* were pronounced by the Lord Chief-Justice of England to be "a blot on our judicial history, and the Court unanimously reversed them and annulled them."

Paterson nobly did his part in procuring that statutory relief which was supposed to be required. The institution he founded issued the first printed notes or orders ; but it is to Scotland we have to look for the first adaptation of the banker's promissory note to the service of the nation. Unlike England, the right of issue, at common law, of notes payable on demand to the bearer without assignation or endorsement, has never to this day been questioned ; the only point of resemblance in the note troubles of the two countries being in the lack of a firm application of the statutory remedies for enforcing payment, until the Act of 1765 cleared away the doubts upon the subject.

Before entering upon the historical part of our subject, it may be well to glance back a few years, to inquire generally into the condition of the country at that time, and particularly as to the institution from which the one pound note was first issued to the world.

The accession of James VI. to the throne of England in 1603, was an event of the greatest importance for the ultimate welfare of both countries. For a time, however, it was difficult for the Scots, and especially for Edinburgh, to see anything in the good fortune of their king but misfortune for themselves. The expenditure of the Court, with that of the nobles and gentry who surrounded it, was transferred from Edinburgh to London, where heavy expenses compelled mortgage of more than one fair estate in the far north ; violent disputes arose between the two countries as to their customs regulations ; many offices of state, which had given support to numbers of the gentry, were abolished ; and the very peace which ensued between

those who had scarcely known peace for four hundred
years, temporarily threw out of employment crowds of
youthful spirits who had been trained to make war their
trade. With such changes in a small and extremely poor
country, it is not to be wondered at that trade languished,
and that many of our countrymen sought employment
abroad, some in commerce, and others as soldiers of fortune
under the different powers of the Continent. In the wars
that followed, it was no uncommon event for Scot to meet
Scot at the pike's point ; and the story is told of one brigade,
storming up the steep side of a redoubt, being hailed in their
mother-tongue from the walls above, " Come on, loons ; this
is not like gallanting in the High Street of Edinburgh ! "
As years went by, notwithstanding, trade began to expand.
The wanderers returned, with their pockets full of gold, and
with their views enlarged by foreign travel and intercourse
with the keen merchants of the Continent. Much of the
old antipathy died out, or was killed out in the civil wars
of King and Commons, when both nations were sharply
divided amongst themselves into the two great parties of
Puritan and Cavalier, each being in sympathy with their
friends irrespective of nationality ; while the common revolt
made by both against the folly of James II., enabled them
to make a unanimous choice of William of Orange as their
king. A new generation arose that knew of the ancient
Court of Holyrood and the old warfare as a tradition only ;
and although the Scottish spirit was furiously roused by
such events as the end of the Darien scheme, the massacre
of Glencoe, and the Union of 1707, yet the effects were
only temporary ; the utter failure of the Chevalier in 1715,
with the want of support accorded to his gallant son in
1745, proving that the old *hate* had passed away, giving
place to a kind of irritability, which, though greatly lessened,
shows itself occasionally even in our own day. For this
irritability there was sometimes too good cause in the
unfairness or carelessness of England. Much credit has
been given to the " Union " for the prosperous condition to
which Scotland has since risen, but those who have studied

the Articles of that Union, and are acquainted with the kind of trade and customs duties then in force, can scarcely help thinking that Scotland has flourished in spite of the Union, solely through her own indefatigable exertions. One enormous benefit, the value of which cannot be over-estimated, lay in the *peace* that ensued, and in this the North of England equally shared. The "debateable land" on both sides of the Border may date its prosperity from the Union. Middlesex, Wessex, and the South Midlands were the England of long ago, the North being a region of insurrection and alarm. The treaty of 1707 changed this entirely, and by introducing a profound peace, gave alike provision for industry, and that security necessary for its continuance. However, all this was yet to come.

The banking system of Scotland owes not a little to the neglect with which English statesmen treated it in its infancy. North Britain was thought to be then little improved from the time when the Romans "turned back with contempt from gloomy hills, assailed by the winter tempest, and from cold and lonely heaths, over which the deer of the forest was chased by a troop of naked barbarians." * The contemptuous language of the great historian precisely indicates the opinion Englishmen enter-tained of Scotland, even so late as his day. Scottish pride and poverty were proverbial ; England cared not to stir up the one, and had nothing to gain from the other. Scottish merchants had no need to say, as their French brethren said to Sully on his asking how he could assist them, " By leaving us alone,"—they were left alone, to stand or fall according to their strength. Rebellion in Ireland and Louis XIV., the wars of the Spanish succession and Jacobite plots at home, gave Dutch William and his successors such ample employment as effectually prevented interference with Scottish commerce.

From Bannister's " Life of William Paterson" (Edinr., 1858), is taken the following piece of doggerel, written about

---

* Gibbon's " Decline and Fall."

1697, in the full enthusiasm of the Darien and other schemes, which, speaking of Scotland and her laws with pardonable pride, endeavours to illustrate the superior freedom of the Scots law :—

> "Scotland was like to thrive ; 'twas very plain
> They'd got a law, and could that law maintain,
> A law that set all sorts of trading free ;
> No land a wiser law did ever see ;
> No mighty power it needs, no fertile lands,
> No gold, no silver mines, it *all* commands ;
> All that our nature needs or can desire,
> All that for pride or pleasure we require,—
> Free trade will give, and teach us how to use,
> Instruct us what to take and what refuse."

Thus safe in her poverty, Scotland began her first bank. It was assuredly the day of small things. The stamp duties which were remitted to London by John Coutts's house (afterwards Sir William Forbes & Co.) amounted for the first year after the Union to £800! The excise and customs were little better in proportion,—the " Mercantile System " and organised smuggling, both products of the Union, effectually combining to reduce trade and revenue alike. For a reliable history of the early days of the Bank of Scotland, we are indebted to the unknown author of a valuable and scarce work, published in February 1727, entitled, " An Historical Account of the Establishment, Progress, and State of the Bank of Scotland, and of several attempts that have been made against it, and the several Interruptions and Inconveniences the Company has encountered." The author has evidently been connected with the bank in some official capacity, as he speaks with familiarity of all the private meetings of the bank authorities, stating their views with a vigour and frankness peculiar to the times in which he lived. The pamphlet was published in the first year of the Royal Bank's existence, with the view of giving a statement of the old bank's superior claims to public support. From this work we learn that the bank

was founded in 1695,* under an "Act for Erecting A
Public Bank," dated the 17th July of that year, whereby
there was allowed "a joynt stock amounting to the soume
of twelve hundred thousand pounds money" Scots, equal
to £100,000 sterling; the total shareholders not to be less
than sixty, and not more than twelve hundred; two-thirds
of the whole stock to be held by persons residing in Scotland.   Contrasted with the English legislation of 1708, this
may afford us some idea of the number of partners the *Scots
Parliament* had in view as proper for a joint-stock company.
There appear to be two clauses only which have a bearing
on our subject, and one of these is somewhat indirect.   It
is as follows:—"And for the better encouragement of the
said Company and Adventurers, It is hereby statute that
the joynt-stock of the said Bank continowing in money
shall be free from all public burdens to be imposed upon
money for the space of 21 years after the date hereof.   And
that during this space it shall not be leisom to any other
persons to enter into and sett up ane distinct Company of
Bank into this Kingdom, besides these persons allenarly
in whose favours this Act is granted."   We see in this
clause the hand of John Holland, the well-known London
merchant, who drafted the original Act, and whose name
—with those of six merchants in London and five in Edinburgh, all Scotsmen—appears on the list of adventurers.
Imbued as these gentlemen would be with English protective theories, it was natural that they should seek to
bolster up the new Scots bank, as had been done in the
previous year to the Bank of England.   Fortunately for
Scotland, no renewal of the privilege was sought for at the
termination of the period in 1716; and, so far as can be
judged, little harm was done by the restriction, as the Royal
Bank did not begin business until 1727, or eleven years
after the legal monopoly had expired.   On the other hand,
the rivalry which at once sprang up between the two banks,

---

* It may be of interest to mention that the bank's first accountant
was George Watson, the founder of the hospital which bears his name.

shows strongly the danger of such legislation as enables
any institution to establish itself in power sufficient to
endanger the promotion of a kindred company, although
in the present case it must be admitted that the old bank
had decidedly the worst of the fray.   If, however, the Bank
of Scotland had succeeded in its effort to maintain a
monopoly of banking, similar to that enjoyed by the Bank
of England, we should probably have had the same results
exhibited in the North as were in the South, viz., a total
absence of national joint-stock banks powerful enough to
withstand the shocks of financial crises; their place being
taken by a crowd of small private bankers, unknown beyond
the locality in which they dwelt, with a separate note issue
for each county, or perhaps for each town, as once existed
in Northern Italy,—firms of whom every panic that arose
would sweep dozens into bankruptcy, to the certain loss of
those who lent them money or accepted their notes.   To
this extent, therefore, the lapse of restrictive legislation in
1716 has aided in creating that confidence which is yet
accorded to the note issue of Scotland, whether five pounders
or ones.   The dangers of no restriction will be referred to
further on.

The only infringement on the bank's rights during the
years of the monopoly was made by the Darien Company,
who began banking as a means of recovering what they
had lost in their unfortunate colonisation scheme.   The
national sympathy was entirely with the company, or doubtless they would not have ventured on ground forbidden by
a special Act of Parliament.   Reckless trading, advancing
notes on bonds and discounts, rapidly brought their career
to a close in 1698, to the relief of the Bank of Scotland,
who had not cared to contest the legal position, or " quarrel
with that mighty company."

The other clause referred to, maintains the right of
summary diligence for payment of notes, which then, more
than now, bore the character simply of mercantile bills or
promissory notes.   This vigorous remedy had only recently
been introduced,—primarily for foreign bills under Act of

16th September 1681, c. 20, Charles II., but afterwards
extended so as to include inland bills by 1696, c. 36, King
William.   It has been most effectual in assisting merchants
and bankers in Scotland to "getting their own again"
during these two hundred years.   The clause runs : "And
siclike it is hereby declared that Summar Execution by
Horning shall proceed upon Bills or Ticquets upon or
granted by . . . the said Bank, and the Managers
and Administrators thereof for the time."   The word
" Ticquets " used here might embrace writs meaning at that
time cheques, drafts, and similar documents, as the word
" voucher " does now, but it was also in common use
amongst economists and lawyers of the eighteenth century to
imply any token for money of the nature of a bank note ;
and in its present connection may be freely translated as
the " bank notes " of a later age.   The stern measure of
" Summar Execution " was apparently inserted, *first*, to prevent the new bank from imagining that its promissory notes
could not be enforced against it as speedily as the acceptances of any private merchant ; and, *second*, for the purpose
of strengthening its note issue in the estimation of the
public, who would naturally be more ready to accept paper,
of which they had such a prompt and powerful means of
recovering payment.   One instance of the use of the word
" Ticquets " may be seen in the Act of 1797, whereby the
banks were permitted to grant " Notes, Bills, or Tickets, in
the nature of bank notes, payable to the bearer on demand,
for any sum whatever under the sum of 20s. sterling."
Without this authority, however, the violent dispute which
arose between the Bank of Scotland and the Royal Bank
places the meaning of " Tickets " beyond dispute, and at
the same time shows the disadvantage the old bank worked
under, compared with other banks, inasmuch as its " Promises to Pay " were enforceable by summary diligence,
while those of *no other bank* in Scotland were so until 1765.

The subscription lists for the capital were speedily filled
up, the Lord High Commissioner, the Marquis of Tweeddale, setting the example by signing first, followed by his

son, Lord Yester. For some years a very limited business was done, and that chiefly in issuing notes. To run out a large issue seems to have been the one leading idea in all bankers' minds at the time, the possibility of banking without a power of issue being something utterly beyond their imagination ; and it is well to observe the confident fearless way in which the right of issue was then spoken of, for not only was it universally maintained, but no one appears ever to have dreamed of questioning either the right or the public advantage following upon it. The way in which many old-fashioned writers speak of a note issue, may appear to the nineteenth-century economist as more of the nature of monomania than of rational opinion ; but a consideration of the total absence of experience in banking science, with the want of mercantile facilities, should lead us to the more charitable conclusion, that notwithstanding mistakes, made again and again, the foundation of the Scottish banking edifice was then laid, in the main, solidly and well.

As no *deposits* were taken by the bank, its business was exclusively confined to lending its capital, and issuing notes of £100, £50, £20, £10, £5. After the African Company had closed its "bankeering career," the bank, desirous of preventing the establishment of a rival, and hoping to "carry the circulation of their notes through the greater Part of the Kingdom," created four offices, "to wit, Glasgow, Aberdeen, Dundee, and Montrose," their chief hope lying in the profit anticipated from the *increase in their issues* by their exchange business. In this they were disappointed ; trade seems to have been bad, little business was done, heavy charges incurred, and accordingly the directors, finding how "unsafe, troublesome, and improper" the exchange trade was, closed the branches, and brought their money "to Edinburgh by Horse Carriage," at no little expense. Their rules of doing business at this time were, to lend "Money upon Bond, both heritable and personal ; also upon Bill at short usance by way of Discompt, for a month or two, under certain regulations . . . alterable as the Company found convenient."

The issue of a small paper currency was something so entirely novel and experimental, that our author speaks of it with much modesty, not to say dubiety. For a few years no attempt was made to circulate notes of a smaller amount than £5. The greater wealth of England might enable it to be content with this as its lowest denomination, —though we are not aware that any private firm then issued such notes, and the Bank of England certainly did not do so for nearly a century,—but the poverty of Scotland, and its sore need of small coin, required a medium of less bulk, and capable of meeting the smaller transactions of the nation. To meet this want the Bank of Scotland issued their first 20s. notes in 1699. It has been alleged, upon what ground we are not aware, that these were 20s. Scots money, and therefore only equal to 1s. 8d. sterling ; and that the issue of £12 Scots in 1704 was the first issue of £1 sterling notes. The authorities of the Bank of Scotland at the present time give 7th April 1704 as the correct date ; and Mr Kinnear, one of the directors, in evidence before the House of Commons Committee of 1826* stated, that notwithstanding repeated requests to issue "tokens" for £1, the novelty of the experiment made them hesitate until 1704. On the other hand, the author of the "Account of the Old Bank " pointedly mentions, just before he details the burning of the bank in 1700, that in January 1699 notes were issued of the value of twenty shillings, for the expressed purpose of making the "circulation of bank notes more extensive and easy, even in small sums. They were found to be very convenient not only in the country, but also in the City of Edinburgh, though scarce any hopes

---

* Previous to 1704 the directors and proprietors of the Bank of Scotland had received several proposals for the issue of "Tickets," "Stamped Brass Coins," or "Wooden Tallies," for remedying the want of a circulating medium of coin below £5 in value. The proposals were all rejected by the proprietors. They were probably conscious of their want of experience, and refrained for a time from so novel an experiment. . . . In 1704, however, the measure was again brought forward, and £1 notes were issued for the first time. *Parl. Report*, 1826.

were entertained that they can obtain a currency to any considerable value in our public Markets and Fairs, . . . for nothing answers there among the common people but silver money, even gold being little known amongst them." Assuming the writer to be correct in his date, it is very evident from this paragraph that 20s. sterling was meant, and not Scots money ; besides, it is incredible that the bank which hesitated, up *to 1704*, to issue notes so low as £12 Scots, should, *in 1699*, come at one drop from notes of the value of £5 down to notes for 1s. 8d.   In the absence of authentic information, we would suggest—that both parties are correct so far ; that notes for " 20s. sterling," and so designated, were issued in 1699 ; but that, circulating as they did amongst the ignorant lower orders, they were not readily received, from their being drawn in *English money*. Our own fright at the metric system, should lead us to have a fellow-feeling for our poor ancestors, in their confusion over the value of things expressed in a coinage twelve times the value of that to which they had been accustomed. On the same supposition, the bank, possibly seeing how unpopular (amongst the lower orders) such a value of foreign currency was, called them in after a few months, for at the end of 1700 they had only five denominations of notes, namely, those of £100, £50, £20, £10, and £5.   The larger notes, circulating amongst the mercantile classes, would not be so liable to the same disadvantage, as sterling money was perfectly well known to them, most of their account books being adapted to it ; and a few years later, in 1707, Scots money was abolished by law.   There are further evidences in the " Account" referred to, leading to the supposition that the notes of 1699 were sterling money, as, save when the capital of the bank is named, there are no references whatever to Scots money, and even the capital towards the end of the pamphlet is expressed in sterling money.   In 1725 a forgery took place of " *twenty shilling notes*," but there is no indication that these differed in value from those issued in 1699 ; while the notes of the denomination of £12 Scots, down to 1723, bore no trace of the equivalent in sterling money, such as they afterwards did. The point is an interesting one in connection with our subject, and involves a difference of five years in the life of the national note. We hope the Bank of Scotland will put the matter to rest, as it is possible, though we think improbable, that their first historian may have been incorrect in his date.

Annexed we give a sketch of one of these £12 Scots notes, copied from an original in the Antiquarian Museum, Edinburgh. The paper seems poor, compared with modern notes, and wanting in fibre, but bears a good water-mark, evidently produced during the process of manufacture, and not the result of mere pressure, as in the case of many of the forged notes. It has been cut away from the counterfoil in a waved line, for purposes of identification, the cut running down the middle of the cheque at the side of the note. The printing is supposed to be Scottish workmanship, while the paper probably came from France or the Low Countries.

In February 1700 the great fire in Parliament Close occurred, when Lord Leven, with a party of soldiers, was on duty all night keeping the stair and passage clear, while the books, bank notes, cash, and papers were hurriedly removed from the burning building to a place of safety. Scarcely had this disaster passed over, when the bank had their first experience of trouble with their notes, a man, Thomas Macghie, having altered a £5 note to £50. Before doing much mischief the crime was detected, and the "rogue was forced to fly abroad." New copperplates were engraved of all the bank's notes, in different characters, which, it was fondly hoped, would put it out of the "power of man to renew Macghie's villany." In 1710 another "unfortunate," named Robert Fleming, "a very poor man," a teacher in Hamilton, was arrested, and condemned to death, for imposing on some simple people a number of 20s. notes, all written by himself, and having "a dark impression made like the seal of the Bank." In gracious contrast to the brutal code of later days, Queen Anne granted a

No 88 / 54231

Edinburgh June 24 1723

The Governour & Company of ye Bank of Scotland constituted by Act of Parliament do hereby oblige themselves to pay to David Spence or the Bearer Twelve pounds Scots on Demand

By order of ye Court of Directors

BANK OF SCOTLAND NOTE OF 1723.
FROM AN ORIGINAL NOTE IN THE ANTIQUARIAN MUSEUM
EDINBURGH.

reprieve several times, until after her decease he received a remission of his sentence. In January 1723 a third forgery was detected, although the criminal was never discovered : on this occasion the 20s. notes were those practised upon. Again, in November 1726, another forgery of the same notes took place, on account of which John Currie, a bookbinder, was arrested, and confessed to having committed the crime entirely himself, having attempted to imitate the water-mark of the 20s. notes. Various tools and utensils were found in his house, affording additional proof of guilt, if that were required. In their endeavours to trace the culprit, the bank, by warrant of the Lord Justice-Clerk, searched every engraver's office in Edinburgh, besides the premises of those who had tailliedouce printing presses in and about the city ; but all was in vain, until, on Sabbath evening, the 25th December, the secretary of the bank learned that a bit of paper had been picked up in the workshop of the man Currie, by his servant, on which were printed in characters similar to those on the bank notes, the words, " Bank of Scotland." Only a bit of waste paper, a turn of the graving tool, a simple letter or line displaced, no matter how small the defect may be, it seems impossible for forgers, with all the care and laborious scrutiny they must give to their wretched work, to escape these tell-tale evidences of their crime. In both of those forgeries the art of the engraver had been called in, though apparently to very little purpose, the graving being poorly executed. The notes were again all called in, and new designs prepared, " with special cheques against forgery."

The further progress of the bank has little cognate to our subject until the year 1704, when a second issue of £1 notes was resumed, this time under the denomination of £12 Scots. Small as the bank's transactions had been hitherto, the issue of these notes was a vast public benefit, the old metallic currency being then quite insufficient for everyday necessities. At the " Union " the Bank of Scotland took charge of withdrawal of the old coin, when it was called in to be re-coined, and the total of the silver so received amounted to £411,117. 10s. 9d. sterling, of which only £239,036 was Scots coin.* So far as is known, no account was kept of the gold received; but from old records of the Scottish Mint, Mr Adam Smith supposes the annual quantity coined must have slightly exceeded in value that of the silver. Adding these items, and accounting for the amount which must have remained in the hands of a suspicious people, the total metallic currency of Scotland has been variously estimated at from £800,000 to £1,000,000. The smallness of this amount, at a time when there was only one bank office in a country with one million inhabitants, when *metal*—one-half silver—had to do nearly the whole work now done by cheques, drafts, bills, and demand orders, and at a time when paper money was almost unknown, is self-evident, and must have seriously retarded the growth of trade. Sir Wm. Forbes mentions, that in looking over the books of Provost Coutts, even so late as 1740 he " saw many notices of the difficulty at that time of effecting money transactions of any considerable extent, in the county towns of Scotland."

It is somewhat curious, that in the same year in which the bank first issued its £12 Scots notes, it should have stopped payment. So far as can be traced—for our unknown author is singularly reticent as to this "stoppage"—there does not seem to have been much connection between the two events. What effect the small notes had in this crisis, or how many one pound holders " ran " with their neighbours, will probably never be known, until the treasures of the Bank of Scotland's vaults are opened to the light of day; but certainly, in themselves, the " small notes " had not acquired sufficient importance to be the

---

* From Preface to Anderson's " Diplomata Scotiæ " we quote : –

Foreign silver money, sterling, .	£132,080 17	0
Milled Scottish coin, . .	96,856 13	9
Coins struck by hammer,	142,180 0	0
English milled coin,	40,000 0	0
	£411,117 10	9

predisposing cause, unless we consider that they may have been current amongst a lower and more ignorant class, who would be open to alarm. Such a supposition is rather a source of strength to the one pound note, as a prudent bank, knowing this, would always keep more gold on hand to meet possible excitement amongst the lower orders. However, in the present case, it is probable that the advances granted by means of these notes were trifling, and therefore the common English accusation against small notes will scarcely hold. We cannot believe they had acquired sufficient volume to affect the bank's position of themselves, had a reasonable amount of bullion been kept.

In accordance with the theory then very prevalent, that land was the basis of all credit, the bank seems to have locked up most of its *capital* in advances on heritable securities and bonds ; the remainder being chiefly lent upon bills of exchange, leaving too small a sum as cash on hand. It had no *deposits*, and therefore did not require to maintain a large reserve on that account. Its whole indebtedness to the public thus consisted of the amount of the *note issue*, together with a few bills of exchange.* The latter could not be pressed for payment until the due date, and may therefore be dismissed from notice, leaving the notes alone to be accounted for. The total sum of these was always said to be very trifling, until the bank began to receive deposits, at 1707 ; yet, trifling as it was compared with figures of modern times, the bank, in their endeavour to *use all their money to the best advantage, failed to keep up a proper specie reserve.* By a coincidence, the country's resources were severely taxed at that time to meet Government requirements for the Continental wars. Specie was scarcely to be got, and a rumour getting abroad that it was proposed to increase the nominal value of the coinage, a run began upon the bank, which, in its weak condition, had no resource but to close its doors on 18th December 1704. It was the first reading of the lesson which since then has

---

* Used here in the sense of the modern bank draft.

been so often read in vain. The total absence of such
institutions as now furnish banks with "money at call,"
combined with the distance from London, reduced the
assets available as a reserve to the single article of *silver
bullion;* and when the stock ran low, bankers of last century
had a much better excuse than their modern brethren for
hesitating before bringing a new supply from London.
Then it was no case of stepping leisurely at 10 P.M. into
a comfortable "Pullman" at the "Waverley," to wake up
next morning, 'mid "the roar of London town," at a total
cost for the whole expedition of about 2s. per cent. The
very language of travel is changed. They "set out;" we
"start;" they "performed the journey in a week;" we "do
it" in nine hours. The traveller who went to London two
hundred years ago was accustomed to prepare his will
before setting out, and bid an affectionate farewell to the
friends whom he might never see more. The weary journey to and fro in the lumbering mail-coach, with the time
spent in searching for the specie in London, usually occupied the best part of fifteen days, and cost sometimes on
the remittance between £7 and £8 per cent.,—somewhat of
a contrast to 2s.

In a print published by the bank, entitled, "Memorial
and Intimation from the Governor and Company of the
Bank of Scotland, concerning the present state thereof,"
dated 28th December 1704, the bank states the causes of the
run were,—"The scarcity of money all over the kingdom,
which has gradually increased by a tract of export of
money for some time past ; and a report that the Privy
Council was to cry up the value of species, raised about
the beginning of December instant, which, though it was
wholly groundless, and without any shadow of reason, yet
being industriously spread, and kept up by some persons,
occasioned a very great, unexpected, and unaccustomed
demand upon the bank, which at last had such effect, that
on Monday the 18th of the instant December, the money
in the bank was wholly exhausted, and thereby payments
stopt."

From contemporary records it would appear that the bullion then kept by the bank to pay its notes, was almost wholly *silver*, and that of this no great amount was kept, one writer remarking, "that y^e Bank has specie (*i.e.*) silver money for a $\frac{1}{4}$ or $\frac{1}{3}$ pairt of y^e value of y^e Notes out ; if y^e demand is greater y^n y^e specie in Bank, y^e Bank fails,"[*] which it did in the case under notice. Their 20s. notes, and the £12 Scots notes, were necessarily payable in silver, as no gold pieces of these amounts existed.

The character of the silver had also taken its part in bringing on the crisis. If the currency of England had been bad, that of Scotland was so much worse, that "according to our standard an ounce of bullion is worth 5s. 6d. sterling, and according to that of England only 5s. 2d. Thus a hundred pounds of money is worth about our £106. 10s. sterling ; but in respect we put a higher estimate upon all foreign money than our own, most of it, specially the new coin, has found a way to go out of the kingdom."[†]

In view of such a state of things, much sympathy should be felt for the early struggles of the old bank ; it lived in troublous times, politically and financially ; it was working out a wholly new experiment, and surrounded as it was by the land bank and land credit delusions of the time, the wonder is that upon the whole it behaved so prudently and well. Silver might be obtained from London at great cost, but it was only safe so long as it remained in the bank's vaults ; once in the hands of the public, there was little chance of it ever coming back, and the whole labour had to be gone over again, with its attendant expense.

An examination was made of the bank's books and papers by the Marquis of Tweeddale, and other members of the Privy Council, to consider of "the sufficiency of security to the nation for all the bank notes running, and

---

[*] MS. Pamphlet by Mr Patrick Campbell of Monzie, upon a Land Bank, 1708.

[†] "The Crying Down of the Money considered," circular, 1704.

to take such course as in their wisdom they should think fit
for the satisfaction of those who might have bank notes in
their hands." The examination was held the day following
the stoppage, when it was found that the bank's assets
exceeded its liabilities by about one-fourth. From the
balance-sheet placed before the committee of inspection
(of which we give a copy from Mr J. A. Wenley's "Historical
Development of Banking in Scotland," 1882), we see the
amount of their outstanding debts, £50,847, consisted solely
of notes, a fact which shows most strikingly how completely
the note issue was looked to as the prime means of carrying
on a banking business. The whole statement exhibits
banking principles in their crudest form. To meet notes
of £50,000 only £1600 of silver were held, the great bulk
of their remaining assets being quite inconvertible. A
modern bank granting advances on heritable and movable
bonds to the extent of three-fourths of its liabilities, would
be simply courting failure, and we have to thank the old
bank for giving the first proof of the danger of such a
course, and warning to its successors. One good item is
the "first coast" of their banking-house, which with "al
reparations" costs only £694.*

At the adventurers' meeting held on the 27th of December it was agreed that all the company's notes should bear
annual rent from the 18th instant to the 18th of April following; power being given to the directors to postpone the
resumption of cash payments for two months if necessary.
A call of £10,000 was made upon the partners, and it is a
sign of the bank's evident sense of security that the call was

---

* The bank's first office was on the second flat of Paterson's Land,
a tenement down the Parliament Close; from this they were burnt out
in 1700, and removed up the High Street to the close named after Sir
Thomas Hope, Charles I.'s famous King's Advocate. Mr Chambers,
in his "Traditions of Edinburgh," gives some interesting particulars
of the Auld Bank Close, as it came to be called, and also of the Bank
itself, which closed in the bottom of the Close. The whole range of
building was cleared away about 1830 to make room for Melbourne
Place and George IV. Bridge.

Bank of Scotland.

1704.   *Debit.*

Dec. 19th. To Bank Bills charged
        upon the Treas-
        urer p. accot. in
        Ledge. d. fol. 3 . £146,735 0 0
      Deduct for so much
        thereof in the
        Treasurer's hands
        at this day .   .   95,888 0 0
      Remains nett of Bills running through-
        out Kingdom £50,847 0 0
      Ballance due to the Adventurers .   . 12,352 0 8½

           Summa .   £63,199 0 8½

Bank of Scotland.

1704.   *Credit.*

Dec. 19. By Cash in the Treasurer's hands, re-
        mayning in old Merks .   .   . £1,600 0 0
  „ Debts due upon Heritable Bond, per
        particular a/c, besides interest
        thereon 21,968 6 8
  „ Debts due upon movl. bond p. par-
        ticulars, besides running interest as
        above 27,682 8 5½
  „ Inland Bills due thereby p. particular
        list besides running interest .   . 11,253 16 8
  „ The Bank office, for the first coast of
        their house besides al reparations .   694 8 10⅔

           Summa .   .   £63,199 0 8½

not made payable until Whitsunday, or a month after the
date fixed for repaying the notes.

From this date on to 1726 little can be gathered from
contemporary history bearing directly upon the bank,
except that the entire note issue received a slight stimulus
in 1707, the year when deposits were first accepted.

Probably the hope of attracting a portion of the money
due to Scotland in respect of the Treaty of Union, concluded
in that year, induced the bank to take this step, with a view
to increasing its profits by having a larger fund to work
upon. Their profit would necessarily be larger, since no
interest was allowed on the deposits. This, as it turned
out, was a short-sighted policy, for the largest beneficiary
in the Union payments (which amounted to £398,085. 10s.)
was the African and India Company of Scotland, the bank's
early rival. If, as may be supposed from such a patriotic
institution as the Bank of Scotland, they objected to the
terms of the Treaty of Union,* this would account at once
for its known unpopularity with the Hanoverian party in
1715, and also for the malignity with which it was attacked
some years later by the Whigs of the Equivalent Company,
who, after the failure of their negotiations for a union of
capitals with the old bank in 1719, must have suspected its
endeavours to get control, in some way, of the very fund in
their hands, which afterwards formed the capital of the
Royal Bank of Scotland. Mere rivalry scarcely accounts
for the violent opposition of the old bank to the establishment of the new, which has more the appearance of chagrin
at a lost opportunity, combined with the disappointment of

---

* The Jacobite *fama* was strongly denied by the bank, who resented
the suggestion as an insult ; and any dislike the bank might have
against the Union would be from that event having been pressed on
by the African Company, in the hope of recovering some of its lost
capital. William Paterson was strongly in favour of the Union ; and,
strange to say, he had no great opinion of the bank, having written
about it in 1695, that it "may be a great prejudice (to the African
Company), but is never like to do any matter of good to us nor to
those who have it."

defeat in a past attempt, than fear of future competition ;
though no doubt the latter feeling was strongly aroused
after the Royal Bank was fairly launched.

Several attempts, based on current notions, were made
to share in banking profits, though only two of them came
before Parliament. The first of these was that of the
famous Dr Hugh Chamberlain, who—styled Chamberland
—unsuccessfully petitioned the Scots Parliament to erect
a land bank in 1700. The other was that of John Law.
In an overture to the Scots Parliament, dated in 1705, he
proposes the foundation of a land bank, in which notes
would be payable in land instead of in bullion ! and " that
forty Commissioners, appointed by Parliament, should coin
notes to be received in payment when offered." The
scheme gave rise to considerable excitement and discussion
in the House, but was finally rejected, with the remark that
an " issue of paper or bills, without an obligation to pay
coin, was not consistent with the welfare of Scotland."
Speaking of the old bank, Law says, " Its Notes went for
four or five times the value of Cash in Bank, and that so
much as the amount of their Notes exceeded the amount
of Cash in Bank, was a clear addition to the money of that
nation." Besides, it was " more national or general than
either the Bank of England or that of Amsterdam, because
its Notes pass in most payments throughout the whole country,
whereas the Bank of Amsterdam serves only for that one
city, and that of England is of little use but in London."
" Many of the Notes were so low as Twenty Shillings." It
is observable here that Law accounts for the bank's popularity and soundness solely by the circulation of its notes,—
a characteristic piece of reasoning from the Mississippi
schemer.

Another project was mooted by Mr John Campbell of
Monzie, though we are not aware of its having become
public. In an elaborate pamphlet, dated 1708, he works
out a project for a land bank, or a " Land Mint," as he
calls it, in which there is so much good reasoning and
sound sense on some points, that it is difficult to see how

he could have gone so far astray on others. In addition to the notes proposed to be issued against land, he argued for an issue of £1,000,000 in notes, against which the same amount of gold would be kept for change. Freedom of inspection and audit by members of Parliament were amongst the sensible parts of his programme, and no dividend to be made account of but out of profits. Admitting that his project might *seem* an encroachment on the monopoly granted to the Bank of Scotland, Mr Campbell tries to prove that there would be no encroachment at all, as the two banks would be essentially different. " Y^e Banknotes are a credite upon silver pledged, ye Notes of ye Land Bank are a credite upon land pledged ; ye bank pays in silver, ye land mint pays in land. Y^e bank has specie (*i.e.*) Silver money for a ¼ or ⅓ pairt of ye value of ye Notes out ; if ye demande is greater y^n ye specie in bank, the bank fails. Y^e land mint has specie (*i.e.*) land equal to the Notes out, and a million more to make good a year's deficiency, so y^t to all appearance ye Land Mint will not fail." Mr Campbell apparently could get none to help him, and contented himself with placing his document amongst the archives of the Advocates' Library, where it remains a memorial of his prudence in action and his folly in theory.

The bank was again compelled to stop payment by a "run" for gold, caused by the Rebellion of 1715 ; when the deposits and £30,000 Government money which was lodged in the Castle for safety, had a marked effect in shortening the time during which the drain was endured. In the first stoppage, when notes only had to be met, and the amount of these not large, three weeks elapsed before the bank was affected. In the second, they had to close their doors in eleven days,* and remain so for nearly four months ; their notes again being called in, in May, June, and July following, to be paid by a new issue, with interest from the date of stoppage. It has been stated that the directors privately

---

* Arnot's " History of Edinburgh," 1788.

encouraged the run, lest the money might fall into the hands of the enemy.

The French proverb, "*qui s'excuse s'accuse*," is strongly suggested by a perusal of the Bank of Scotland's defence at this period ; they seem to have been conscious that they were scarcely meeting public requirements as they ought, but were in a short-sighted way looking more to payment of a *high dividend* on a *small capital*. Three separate proposals for extension were made to them, between 1719 and 1727, all of which were plainly refused. The first was on behalf of the Equivalent Company, and was handed to the bank in December 1719, without any name attached, by one describing himself as "A Gentleman of Distinction, a well-wisher of his country and of the Bank of Scotland." It was suggested to join the £250,000 of Equivalent Company's debenture bills to the bank's subscription of £100,000, making a total capital of £350,000. Of the profits the Equivalent Company were to get five-sevenths and the old bank two-sevenths. But as the whole of the debentures were paid up, while only a tenth of the bank's capital was so, it was hoped that the latter would see its way to repay the Equivalent Company £225,000, or nine-tenths of the total amount, with other arrangements as to interest. Something might have been made of the scheme, crude and unworkable as it must have appeared to the bank authorities, but, unfortunately sheltering themselves behind the actuarial absurdities of the proposal, the bank declined the opportunity of running out "£225,000 in bank notes" on such terms, and accordingly returned a civil answer in writing to the "Gentleman of Distinction," who by this time was quite well known. On receiving the bank's deputation, the "Gentleman" was so angry at the refusal of his offer, that his interruptions completely prevented the "answer in writing" being handed to him. So far as it dealt with details of the scheme, the directors' reply was able and acute on all points ; but it did not touch the broad question of the bank's position with the country. It is possible, of course, that the Equivalent Company would

not have agreed to terms had they been proposed, but the
defect in the old bank's apology is, that they exhibited no
desire whatever to meet the company in any way,—a slight
which was duly remembered when 1727 came round.

The second proposal came in 1720 from a less credit-
able source. "The Edinburgh Society for insuring Houses
against loss from Fire" was not, as the reader might inno-
cently suppose, a *society for insuring houses against fire*,
that business having fallen through in the first months of
its existence. Being disappointed in their hopes of gain,
the society got into bad humour, and, after sundry secret
meetings, resolved to make a run on the bank, with the
hope of compelling it to shut its doors, when they could
set up in its place. A sum of £8400 of the bank's notes
was expended in this foolish design, the treasurers of the
Equivalent Company aiding it by withdrawing all their
money in gold, and lodging it in the Castle. It is needless
to say that the contemptible trick ended in complete failure ; notwithstanding this, the society had the audacity, a
short time afterwards, to make proposals for amalgamation,
—proposals which the Bank of Scotland rejected with more
politeness than they deserved. Still another "braw wooer"
turned up, in the end of 1721, all the way from London
town, in the person of Mr James Armour, a writer in Edinburgh, representing the "Royal Exchange Company at
London." Upon first consideration of his desires, the bank
declined to open negotiations, whereupon Mr Armour, in
1722, published a pamphlet containing an elaborate account
of his proposals, addressed to Lord Leven, the bank's
governor, and printed with capitals, German text, and
Italics sprinkled amongst the Roman characters with a
taste peculiarly his own. "The sum of the proposal is
this : The Royal Exchange Assurance Company was to
send down to the bank £20,000 sterling (in specie), for
which the said company were to be entitled to one-half of
the whole free profits in the bank, after setting aside £2500
sterling to the bank's proportion." Other proposals were
made as to exchange, but these are suspected to have been

inserted only with the view of diverting " the reader from too narrowly examining his main project."

In all its disputes with English companies, the bank had an unhappy way of invariably styling them " Foreigners," and asking, with patriotic indignation, if it were for the nation's advantage that they should borrow money from a foreign country, which they could easily get in their own ? but perhaps this was only the Scottish return for the manner in which Englishmen spoke of Scotland. It was objected by Mr Armour that the bank could not strengthen its position by calling up more capital from its proprietors, as these would pay their calls, not in specie, but in the bank's own notes ; to which it was retorted, that the bank's position would be strengthened even by such a payment, inasmuch as its liabilities would be lessened by the amount of the notes paid. The point of receiving £20,000 in gold was evaded, by insinuating that it would not be so paid ultimately, but would be settled by bills of exchange, or the bank's own notes. Thus this disconsolate lover was compelled to retire like his predecessors, much grieved that his efforts to induce " Jenny to birl her bawbee" had been in vain. Details of these various proposals have been given at some length, as the same features appear prominently in each : *first*, the desire to share in the banking profits ; and, *second*, to increase these profits by a corresponding increase of credit to the public, granted by means of a larger issue of notes ; the latter, according to the narrow notions of the time, being the most profitable and extensive way of giving accommodation. The amount of notes issued bore an immensely larger proportion to the entire floating paper obligation than it now does, cheques being only used to draw the notes direct from the bank, and not being handed in payment of accounts, as in later times ; so that all accounts, large or small, were settled by bank notes.

While stating these facts, it would be unfair not to admit that the bank had some reasons for declining to increase the scope of its business, for the most indignant outcry against its position undoubtedly came from those who

would only have accepted greater facilities to further their
own private views in stock-jobbing. The South Sea Bubble
was a thing of the past, but the speculative spirit was by
no means at rest. Where the bank failed to discover the
signs of the times, was in not sufficiently appreciating the
difference between the selfish demands of speculators, and
the deeply felt need of the honest trading community.
Mr Macleod, in his "Theory and Practice of Banking,"
quotes their own words, " For the quota of credit in a Banking Company must be proportioned to the stock of specie
in the nation, learned and understood by long experience,"
as a proof of the soundness of *some* of their theories. In the
same pamphlet from which he quotes occur the following
sentences, giving the opinions of the blind prophets of
1727 :—" It is impracticable to support and carry on *two
Banking Companies in one country.* No nation did ever
attempt it. England, where banking is as well known as
in any part of the world, did never try it." " No set of
Scotsmen, who had the nation's welfare at heart, would
ever attempt to disquiet the bank. A proposal for a new
bank would never obtain favour in a Scots Parliament."
The bank's monopoly lapsed in the year 1716. Indeed
the bank did not ask for a renewal, deeming the probability of another bank being originated an impossibility.
Fortunately the monopoly was not renewed. We say
fortunately, apart from any questions of economic principles
as to restriction, for their entire policy at this time stands
out in marked contrast to the energetic, clear-headed way
in which the bank was conducted after 1730. During this
early period of its history it seems to have lacked a more
vigorous management, which could have enlarged the scope
of its business, augmented its capital, and generally enabled
it to afford these increased facilities for banking which were
so much required. Trusting, apparently, to the current
belief that more than one bank was not safe, they do not
seem to have thought of a rival, and, from the want of an
inventive genius in their councils, plodded on in the old
tracks. " If two banks were authorised in England, there

would be a constant hustling and interference betwixt them, till one, or probably both, came to ruin." History proves very distinctly the incorrectness of their opinion. This limited style of banking clearly could not be tolerated much longer, and at last " came the deluge."

Much as that " ill-faured Union" has been reviled, its indirect effects upon Scotland have been marvellous, and not the least of those was produced by the " Equivalent Fund," out of which came to be created the Royal Bank of Scotland. With its establishment in 1727 a new era began. Credit was no longer to run with feeble stream in former narrow channels. Competition, with its good and evil attendants, had begun. New methods of banking were invented. In short, when the first flame of jealousy was burnt out, the two banks settled down to their work, about 1731, in a manner as distinct from that of 1707 as the steam-engine is from the mail-coach. What all this had to do with one pound notes we shall presently see ; but, for a few pages it will be well to look back at the first years of the new bank, and the warfare that ensued,—a warfare all the more interesting to modern readers, since the weapons of destruction were largely one pound notes.

Chapter II.—1727-1750.

THE CONTEST BETWEEN THE BANKS.

SHYLOCK—"Thou call'dst me dog, before thou hadst a cause—
I'll have my bond, I will not hear thee speak—
I'll have my bond, and therefore speak no more."
—*Merchant of Venice.*

THE Royal Bank of Scotland obtained its charter on 31st May 1727; but while in chancery, and before the sign manual of King George I. had been adhibited, his majesty died suddenly at Hanover on 11th June of same year. Some delay took place ere George II. gave the necessary authority, on receiving which, the charter was presented to the Deputy-Keeper of the Great Seal in Scotland on 6th or 7th of July; and regardless of the last effort of the old bank, who lodged a *caveat* against putting on the seal, the charter was returned to the Royal Bank completed on the following day.

To get it passed had been no easy task, and required all the efforts of its supporters by fair means and foul,—an equal amount of the latter being carried on by both parties. The old bank learned that the promoters had placed a draft scheme before the Bank of England directors for their approval and patronage; banking operations being limited to Scotland, the directors cautiously answered that for the present nothing in it appeared to them prejudicial to the Bank of England. After a vain attempt to obtain a copy of this charter, the old bank lodged a *caveat* against its passing; and after consultation with their "Doers" in London, determined to petition the king, which they did in no gentle terms. Seeing that all their efforts would probably be fruitless, they protected themselves by calling up £10,000 of their capital, and waited in angry impatience the further operations of the new bank.

The Equivalent proprietors on their side had not been idle. Villainous rumours about the Bank of Scotland were set afloat. They were accused of disaffection to the Government, a serious matter to the jealous House of Hanover; of sending a gentleman to London with £5000 for purposes of bribery; of having too small a capital; that the " Directors were far too narrow in extending their loans" and requiring security; of not lending on pledge, nor dealing in exchange, foreign bills, or lending money to its own partners; its transfer fees were too high. In short, everything was wrong, and it was impossible that anything could be right. The Bank of Scotland were shrewd enough to point out, that the Royal Bank having a capital consisting solely of national debt, would have no fund to bank with; but on the publication of the charter it was found that due provision had been made for this, the capital consisting of £111,347. 19s. 10$\frac{5}{12}$d. sterling of Government stock, with 20 per cent. additional as a banking fund, the proceeds of calls on the proprietors.

During the time spent in preparing for the start, a sum of £20,000 was paid to Scotland by Government, to be laid out at interest for improving the fisheries and manufactures. Hearing of this sum, the Bank of Scotland determined to apply for one half of it, hoping that the Royal would be content with the other half; but reckoning without their host, they soon found they were in an evil case. The chairman and a majority of the Trustees and Commissioners of the Board of Manufactures were all Equivalent proprietors, and after a scandalous display of jobbery, the whole sum was deposited with the new bank, when it opened in a close off the High Street; affording proof that public men in 1700 were as prone as the "carpet-baggers" of 1865 to "convartin' public trusts to *very* private uses." Not content with this injustice, the chairman of the Trustees ordered his underlings to refuse all Bank of Scotland notes offered in payment of "rates or taxes," and to demand gold or Royal Bank notes.

With this year the Bank of Scotland "Defence" ceases,

and the concluding words are interesting historically :—" I
shall therefore sum up all in one comprehensive Truth—that
those of the Royal Bank have exerted the utmost of their
Power and Strength, and racked their Wit and Politicks, to
bear all hardships on the Bank, to discredit the Company and
encumber the circulation of its Notes, with no other view
but to occasion a Run upon the Bank ; oblige the Directors
to make demands on their debtors ; create national disasters, and (as they hope) to raise clamour against the
Bank—the Royal Bank in the meantime hording up all the
specie they can be masters of, without affording any relief
to the country under the present great scarcity of money ;
while the Bank of Scotland stands passive, or rather on the
defensive, only, trusting to the affection of the country, and
for support from the favour of all who have been accommodated by the bank, and found the conveniency and advantage of the circulation of the Company's Credit and Notes
in the Nation."

The first notes of the new bank were issued, dated 8th
December 1727, apparently in exchange for as much of the
Bank of Scotland's paper as could be got for the money.
With remarkable promptitude the Bank of Scotland at
once endeavoured to make a similar collection of its rival's
notes. The modern exchange clerk might naturally suppose that his occupation then began, as indeed it did in
one sense ; but nothing was further from the old bank's
notions of banking propriety, than that its notes should be
returned to it in thousands by a rival institution, and peace-
ably paid for, as is done in our enlightened times. In those
days it was regarded as an offensive innovation, which was
not to be tolerated ; and accordingly the old lady of Bank
Street began in the most vigorous manner to stop the
offence by destroying the offender. Unfortunately for the
accomplishment of this amiable design, the Royal Bank
proved to be more than a match for its elder rival. It was
the favourite bank with the Government, as well as a considerable portion of the Edinburgh people ; and, above all,
it had the entire support of the Glasgow merchants, who

hoped to extend their credit by its aid. In addition to these, the Royal Bank had other two distinct advantages : it was possessed of a *much larger capital* than the Bank of Scotland, and could therefore endure a heavier blow ; and, being a new bank, it had very few notes in the hands of the public, and was therefore less open to the particular mode of attack. The financial position of the Bank of Scotland was almost exactly the opposite ; its capital was *small*, and being an old bank, would probably be " out " in advances, while its note issue had attained to a considerable amount, having been in fair repute for over twelve years, and now forming a recognised portion of the currency. Thus, without any *extra effort*,* the Royal Bank, in ordinary course of business, became possessed of a number of Bank of Scotland notes ; and then came the defect in *their* exchange system. Instead of presenting these at once, and getting them paid daily in small quantities, they carefully hoarded them up until they reached such an amount as would give the old bank considerable trouble to pay : trouble was what was intended, the more the better : they were then suddenly presented, with a demand for gold. This went on for about three months, the Bank of Scotland vainly trying to scrape together Royal Bank notes wherewith to do likewise in its turn. The end of the squabble was, that the new bank reduced the old to such extremities, that it was compelled to refuse payment of a packet of about £900 of notes to a patron of the Royal Bank, Mr Andrew Cochrane, the Lord Provost of Glasgow. Thus within four months of its first appearance the new bank forced its rival to stop payment on the 27th of March. The whole story of the legal proceedings which ensued is very well told in the print of the appeal, which was brought before the House of Lords in May 1729, by the Royal Bank and Andrew Cochrane as *appellants* against interlocutors of the Court of Session, *versus* the Bank of Scotland, *respondents*.

---

* Although it may not have been required, extra effort does seem to have been made by the Royal to buy up the Bank of Scotland notes.

The appellants' case opens by referring to the Bank of
Scotland's perpetual power of banking, and twenty-one
years' monopoly.   It then says :—" And to give their Notes
or Bills the greater credit, and enable them to recover
money due to them, they are empowered to sue and may
be sued *summarily*,—and therefore the said Act [1696]
declares, That *Summar Execution by Horning* shall proceed
upon *Bills* or *Tickets* drawn upon or granted by, or to, and
in favours of the said Bank, and protests thereon in same
Manner as is appointed to pass upon Protests of Foreign Bills,
by the 20th Act of Parl. 1681, and that no suspension pass
of any charge for sums lent by the said Bank, or to the
same, but only upon Discharge or Consignation of the sum
charged for."   At this point the appellants can no longer
restrain themselves, they swell forth like the frog in the
fable :—" But as the Rules laid down by the Respondents
were too narrow, and that it would be of great Service
to the Country if Credit were made more extensive,—His
Majesty was graciously pleased . . . to incorporate the
Appellants by the name of The Royal Bank of Scotland,
with Power of Banking upon a Fund *much* more extensive,
and *more certain* than *That* of the Respondents."   How the
respondents must have quailed before these sentences.
They are then accused of having made a call upon their
proprietors, with sundry other offences, which had the effect
of " occasioning such an Interruption to Credit that they "
were obliged to stop payment of their notes ; but by an
" Advertisement, promised to pay 5 per cent. Interest till
their Notes would be paid."   " The Possessors of these
Notes finding by this Stop that what had in Commerce
been formerly equal to Specie, was become meer Paper,
applyed to the Respondents for Payment of their Notes,
and upon Refusal, protested against them for Non-payment."   Mr Cochrane, on being refused payment of the
packet before mentioned, went to the Royal Bank, who, at
once, as they said, " in order to prevent an entire Stagnation
of Credit, advanced the same to him."   Thereupon Cochrane, grounding upon the Bank Act of 1696, presented a

petition for letters of horning against the Bank of Scotland ;
but the Lord Ordinary, believing that the whole course of
action was intended purposely to distress the old bank,
instead of at once granting the letters, ordered the petition
to be seen and answered by defenders, and afterwards
delayed it a few days for the decision of six of the judges.
They, in turn, postponed it for nearly three months, and
finally refused to pass it on 25th June 1728.

Seeing that summar execution was denied them, the
pursuers endeavoured to secure themselves by inhibition
and arrestment ; and accordingly, having brought two actions,
one in name of Thomas Peters and Michael Wallace, and
the other in their own name, for payment of £10,255 of
notes, payable to David Spence or bearer, the appellants,
upon depending suits, offered to the Lords bills of inhibition and arrestment. Contrary to usage, these were not at
once granted, but were referred to all the judges, 11th July
1728, who, as in the former action by Cochrane, "refused
to pass the same." An appeal to the whole Court was
decided in a similar way on 26th July, neither horning,
inhibition, nor arrestment being competent against the
Bank of Scotland upon their notes, the diligence being
done *in emulationem.* Meantime the Bank of Scotland had
not been idle. Knowing that further actions would certainly
be brought against them, and that letters of horning were
"frequently passed of course," they petitioned the Court of
Session to withdraw from the Clerks of Court the power of
writing upon any such papers until they, the Bank of
Scotland, had seen them. This the Lords also granted,
and, *contrary to all precedent*, ordered such bills to be delayed
twenty-four hours, in order that the bank might have the
opportunity of answering the same. Immediately after this
the principal sum sued for was paid over, being received by
the Royal Bank under protest, that their acceptance of payment did not affect their right to demand damages and
costs of their proceedings.

On the 19th February 1729, the Royal Bank, now
furious beyond discretion, again resumed the attack, re-

questing the judges to withdraw their previous interlocutors, and find that the defenders (the Bank of Scotland) had no other rights than those common to the " Pursuers, and all others His Majesty's subjects." *No notice was taken of this petition*, while one put in on 25th February was superseded and delayed till the following June. But there was no rest for the unjust judges of the Court of Session ; they might style the petition "disrespectful, indecent, and injurious," as they did, but the Royal Bank was determined on having its " pound of flesh." The appeal to the House of Lords was accordingly prepared, insisting that as the Bank Act of 1696 gave the right of summary execution to the bank, so it also gave it to others against the bank ; to which it was objected by the Bank of Scotland, that notes issued by them as a company were not referred to in the Act, but only bills for money borrowed as private individuals. The Royal replied, " this seems a Distinction without a Difference," and in clear vigorous language proceeded to take the old bank's arguments to pieces, concluding thus : " As the Interlocutors appealed against are not only against the express words of an Act of Parliament, but establish a Privilege in favour of the Respondents different from all other subjects, the Appellants hope that the said Interlocutors shall be reversed, and such other Relief given, as to your Lordships shall seem meet." One of the four names adhibited to the document is that of Duncan Forbes, probably the famous Forbes of Culloden whose statue now adorns the Parliament House in Edinburgh.

The writ for the Bank of Scotland makes the most of a bad case, at the very outset adroitly exhibiting its rival as the *Upstart Institution*. In its opening paragraphs the bank tries to show that its notes or tickets could not come under the Summar Diligence Act of 1681, which only applied to bills of exchange, " but not to cash or *promissory notes* payable upon demand ; " while there is no provision in the bank's Act of 1696 on this point, because to give a charge of horning upon cash notes " would have entirely defeated the institution of a bank,"—how, it does not explain, but endeavours to cover its weakness under protestations of the manner in which "the Company ever since their Erection have executed their trust, with the greatest candor and caution *to the universal satisfaction of this country*, and with the strictest Fidelity and Affection to the present happy Establishment to which they owed their Existence."

Complaint is then made of the Royal Bank (spoken of as "*some* of the Creditors on the Scots Equivalent") "having got a sum of Money into their hands,—became possessed of several of the Respondents' notes, and therewith made for some time a continual demand upon the Respondents, which, with the scarcity of Money in the country, brought them under the necessity to stop payment for a little time." The Bank of Scotland re-opened its office on 27th June 1728, two days after the Court of Session decision in its favour, but there is reason to believe that cash payments were not resumed until 14th November of the same year, when the full sums, with interest at five per cent., were paid to the parties. The clause in the Summar Diligence Act of 1681, requiring protest to be recorded within six months of due date of bill, is taken advantage of, it being maintained that the bank notes, *sub judice*, were due several years before they were protested and registered ; further, that letters of horning could only be obtained by the person specially named in the bill, or in its endorsement, so that in this case David Spence, the bank's own officer, was the only one who could properly pursue ; but apart from these grounds it was insisted that it was neither known nor intended to make bank notes subject to immediate execution. Whatever hopes the Bank of Scotland had of success were soon doomed to grievous disappointment. The case came before the House of Lords on 1st May 1729, who gave the following decision on the 9th :—" It is ordered and adjudged, that the several interlocutory sentences complained of be and are hereby reversed,' and it is hereby further ordered, that the Appellants be at liberty to apply to the said Lords of Session to cause their costs and expenses in the proceedings above mentioned to be taxed according to the course of their Court."*

There is now little doubt that the House of Lords were right, and that the Court of Session were wrong in their view of the case. It may possibly be doing injustice to the old Jacobite Lords of Session, to insinuate that they would naturally have a leaning to the old bank, and wish to repress the new Whig Company on political grounds, as well as on account of the obvious malice which prompted its action ; but the Royal on their side could urge, that had it not been for the antipathy of the old bank at the very outset, the bad feeling which led to the actions would never have arisen.

On the merits of the case, it was fortunate that " Bank Notes " were placed thus early on a clearly defined legal footing as to the steps to be taken for their recovery. At the risk of being tedious, the account of these proceedings has been given at considerable length, since no subsequent action has ever been raised of so much importance in connection with one pound notes. We shall have more to say further on as to this right of summary diligence on bank notes. As before mentioned, the Bank of Scotland resumed payment towards the end of 1728, and do not appear to have suffered much from the Royal Bank's attacks, until after the decision of the House of Lords, in May of the following year, when the old tactics were resumed ; without, however, any more serious result than that of making the directors of the old bank consult as to the surest way of outwitting their opponents by staving off the evil day. Strange as it may seem to us, payment of *specie* on demand was the supposed objectionable point in their note issue, as it was even down to the present century, when the writer of a series of letters in the *Courant* declaimed strongly against the absurdity of supposing that notes should be paid in gold! Except the feeble resort to paying in six-

---

* Reports of Cases Decided in House of Lords, upon appeal from Scotland, from 1726 to 1757.

pences, the only remedy the directors could think upon was the famous " Option Clause ; " and accordingly, " to avoid such distresses in future, the Bank of Scotland, on the 19th November 1730, began to issue £5 Notes, payable to bearer on demand, or £5. 2s. 6d. six months after being presented for payment, in the option of the bank. On 12th December 1732, they began to issue £1 Notes with a similar clause. The other banking companies in Scotland found it convenient to follow the example, and Bank Notes were universally framed with these Option Clauses. They were issued for most trifling sums, and were currently accepted in payment, insomuch that Notes of Five Shillings Sterling were perfectly common ; and Silver was in a manner banished out of the country." *

As a temporary remedy this measure was successful, and it is understood that the bank did not require again to avail itself of the option clause, although it was inserted in the notes for many years afterwards. The lapse of years helped to exhaust the virulence of the two banks, their peace being effectually made about 1749 or 1750, when Messrs Livingston, Mowat, Bremner, and Dingwall, who had begun the first Scottish country bank, in Aberdeen, under the name of the Banking Company of Aberdeen, excited the jealous monopolists of Edinburgh by doing a good business in note issuing, which soon displaced those of the southern banks. Unfortunately no proper care was taken to keep sufficient reserves ; and as the Edinburgh banks were at this time *beginning their own system of note exchanges*, they had good reason to demand of the Aberdeen bank that they should redeem their superfluous paper. In their attack they were only too successful ; drained by unexpected demands for gold, and dragged into an expensive lawsuit, the Aberdeen bank succumbed in 1753. The lawsuit referred to arose in connection with a demand for summary diligence by a holder of Livingston & Co.'s notes ; this was refused by the Court of Session on the ground that

---

* Arnot's " History of Edinburgh," 1788.

these notes were not of the nature of bills, and therefore
did not come under any statutes for summary diligence.
While partly printed and partly written, they were neither
holograph nor legally attested, and besides were not signed
by all the partners. The decision therefore was, that
according to the law of Scotland they were quite valueless,
and should neither have been issued to the public, nor
accepted by them, one eminent judge remarking that they
were " no better securities than a nick-stick."

This procedure of the two banks received a vigorous
check a few years afterwards from the Glasgow merchants.
These gentlemen had invited the banks to open branches
in their city, only to have their overtures declined, until in
1749, the Bank of Scotland, dreaming of the possibility of
destroying its rival's splendid western connection, and increasing its own business, founded a bank there under the
name of the " Ship Bank," of Dunlop, Houston, & Co.,
known at the time as the " Old Bank." Next year the
Royal, thinking only of retaliation, replied by setting up its
old friend, Provost Andrew Cochrane, with John Murdoch,*
under the style of the " Glasgow Arms Bank," then called
the " New Bank." Led away by mutual dislike, they little

---

* " The partners whose names appeared in the firm were Provost
Andrew Cochran, and his brother-in-law, John Murdoch. The former
was an extensive merchant in this city [Glasgow] upwards of half a
century—Cochran Street is named after him. Mr Murdoch, like Mr
Cochran, was elected Provost three several times ; his town mansion
was what is now the Buck's Head Hotel, the oldest edifice extant in
Argyle Street, and giving a good idea, altered though it be, of the style
of residence of the tobacco lords who ruled Glasgow in the days of
these old banks" ("Banking in Glasgow during the Olden Time," p. 11).
The tobacco lords referred to by Dr Buchanan aided greatly in making
Glasgow what it now is, and by their extensive corporations and companies had afforded fair banking facilities to the west for many years
prior to the establishment of regular banks in that quarter. Indeed,
had these wealthy mercantile corporations not existed, the want of
banks would have been felt much earlier ; so that although the first
Glasgow bank only dates from 1749, banking facilities were afforded
there for fifty years prior to that date, which were almost unknown in
Edinburgh.

dreamed of the result, for the dragon's teeth were sown, and in due time the armed men sprang up. Finding, when too late, that their so-called agents were only "fighting for their own hand," the Edinburgh banks endeavoured to stop their business, and withdrew their credits. Their threats and measures were alike unavailing, and at last, about 1758, the strength of the common enemy brought the two old rivals to a second truce,—a reconciliation said to be as uncharitable as the first, and one which brought them little credit, since, according to the Glasgow banks' assertion, it was induced less by mutual regard, than by enmity to their new competitors.

Thus far the tale has been told as by all writers on the subject, and it may, no doubt, be partly true ; but it is an entirely *ex parte* statement, met by the direct denial of the bank's agent, Mr Trotter, whose employment by the banks might be rather traced to an honest endeavour on their part to carry out the *system of exchanges* which they had arranged for themselves in 1752, and thereby lessen the excessive amount of bank paper which was put out by their neighbours. If they themselves took up their notes regularly, there could be clearly no proper reason for other bankers not doing the same ; the latter, however, objected to such an application of the homely proverb, "What is sauce for the goose, is sauce for the gander," and, as will be seen, resisted it to the utmost.

On their first issuing notes, Murdoch & Co. made a pretence of keeping a factor in Edinburgh to retire them on demand, but he was soon withdrawn when they found how troublesome he was according to their way of thinking ; and when this became known to the Edinburgh banks, an agreement was made, as in the Aberdeen case, to send an agent through to Glasgow to harass the new bankers. This gentleman, Mr Archibald Trotter, had been a partner in the firm of Coutts & Co. (then Coutts, Son, & Trotter), and is described by Sir William Forbes as "not possessing liberality of thinking and acting in business," nor "were his person and manner at all calculated to command respect ;" besides, "he was subject to a species of religious melancholy." His employment in Glasgow might afford him ample food for reflection, but would scarcely be a proper cure for religious melancholy. His first duty consisted in calling upon and informing the Glasgow banks of his intentions, and inviting them to take up their notes,—a piece of politeness which was quite thrown away upon Messrs Murdoch & Co. Beginning his operations, he collected notes of the Glasgow banks (making regular journeys to the west, and eventually living there for some years), and presented them, asking payment in gold or Edinburgh notes. A man of Mr Trotter's ability was, however, no match for the Glasgow bankers ; the experience of the Bank of Scotland and the Aberdeen bankers had not been lost to them, and distress sharpened their wits. Accordingly, we find that during thirty-four laborious days the unfortunate Trotter had only obtained payment of £2893 of his notes. On presenting his bundle day by day, Murdoch & Co., with profound deliberation, proceeded to dole out the money in sixpences, regardless of protests or threats of legal procedure. Mr Trotter's own words are too entertaining to be passed over :—" When their Notes (Murdoch & Co.) were presented at the office for payment, a *Bag of Sixpences* was with great Deliberation produced and laid upon the table ; the Teller then proceeded with ridiculous Slowness to open up the Bag and Count the Money. He would first Tell over a pound sterling, in *single Sixpences* ranked upon the Table, and then affecting to be uncertain about the Reckoning, he would gather this small money, and count it over again from One hand to the Other, *sometimes* letting fall a Sixpence for a Pretence to begin anew and count it over again ; on other occasions he would make Time by ridiculous discourses upon the *odd size* or *shape of Particular Sixpences*, SOUND another upon the Table, to try if it was sufficient coin. And *sometimes* he would quit his occupation altogether upon Pretence of some sudden Errand or Call out of the Room. Very often they employed one Coggill, by his ordinary occupation a Porter, to act the Teller, and he lost time and blundered with great alacrity—being instructed to do his worst." On 16th October 1758 Mr Trotter presented £600 of Murdoch & Co.'s notes, offering to receive in exchange Edinburgh notes or gold as they pleased; but it cost him and a clerk no less than nine days' attendance to receive £475 of this sum. From 7th November to 4th December he received average payments of £36 per day, at end of which time he had £2821 Glasgow notes on hand, which Murdoch & Co.'s cashier obligingly offered to pay, £1000 in Edinburgh notes, £821 in silver, as usual, and £1000 by bill on London, payable at thirty days' date! Melancholy Mr Trotter's flesh and blood could endure this treatment no longer; and, accordingly, we find him in Murdoch's telling-room on the 23d January 1759, solemnly accompanied by a notary and two witnesses. Utterly abandoned, the shameless Coggill was again set to work " in the usual manner of payment" in sixpences. Some noteholders were not so well treated as Mr Trotter, being called " scoundrels" by the tellers, and otherwise abused. Sometimes a beating was threatened, and one man was said to have got both a beating and payment in sixpences. The instant the clock struck five all troublesome parties were " thrust out of doors by the shoulders,"—a mode of satisfaction of which there is little doubt Mr Trotter had experience.

An action was raised, before Lord Woodhall, concluding for payment of £3447, the amount of notes in Mr Trotter's possession, with interest from the date of demand, and £600 damages. From the "information" prepared for Mr Trotter's case, in 1760, Murdoch & Co. seem to have had a large circulation,—Mr Trotter asserting that he could have taken up from £80,000 to £100,000 of their notes at any time in Glasgow; and in another place he says, they cannot deny having " issued notes to the extent of above two hundred thousand pounds," although their capital was only about £10,000 or £15,000. The character of their business as merchant bankers, gives an opportunity for the pursuer stating the dangers and distress to trade of bankers engaging in mercantile speculations. The form of the notes was again discussed at great length, as in the Aberdeen case, special reference being made to the option clause, which had been inserted during the controversy. With shocking disregard to their comfort, he calls them "a Bubble and a public Nuisance," and demands that they should remain open for payment of their notes from seven in the morning to nine at night!

The defenders plead that Mr Trotter had acted in *mala fide*, being the agent of the two Edinburgh banks, and paid by them to live in Glasgow for the express purpose of distressing them, and causing a stoppage to their business, as had been done with the bank in Aberdeen. In spite of Mr Trotter's repeated denials that there was any intention to distress, the case was not decided, but was made *avizandum* of again and again, being suspended on every pretext by Murdoch & Co., until June 1760, when Mr Trotter presented a petition, complaining that the defendants were trifling with justice. The Lords remitted the case back to the Lord Ordinary, "to adjust the facts—and especially the fact of Mr Trotter's being a mere hand for the banks, and his intention to distress, which several of the judges thought obvious. Lord Kames observed that Mr Trotter should not have taken the notes. Lord Affleck thought the case of Mr Trotter like that of a man's buying up another's debts *in malitia*. The Lord President and Lord Coalston dreaded paper credit, and thought banks dangerous. A great variety of proceedings again took place before the Lord Ordinary, who again ordered pleadings to the whole Court."* Again and again Mr Trotter returned to the attack, and as often did Messrs Murdoch & Co. draw the Court away from the point by cleverly arranged side issues. Thus the matter meandered on through the mazes of Court of Session practice for other two long years, until in April 1763, the Glasgow bankers, having thoroughly worried Mr Trotter, and discomfited his employers, settled the matter out of Court by paying £600 by way of damages.

The scandalous delays in this case must have been chiefly caused by the hazy notions then prevalent as to note

---

* *Scotsman*, 5th April 1826.

issues and bank notes. Lawyers are notoriously creatures of precedent, and the judges of the Court of Session were only magnified lawyers. Seeing no precedent for a system of note exchanges, and being doubtless imbued with ridiculous contemporary theories, they were too willing to lend an ear to Murdoch & Co.'s frivolous objections. Had they given effect to what was afterwards embodied in the Act of 1765, that all notes should be payable on demand, on pain of summary diligence, they would have given a more comprehensive meaning to the phrase "bank notes," and the records of the country would not have been marred by such a miscarriage of justice.

If the Glasgow banks, or rather that of Murdoch & Co. (for the Ship Bank soon honourably fulfilled all its engagements), had kept a supply of gold proportionate to their issue, they would have had nothing to fear from exchanges of notes ; but issuing, as they did, notes far beyond their capital or means of payment, they had no resources wherewith to purchase gold when the notes were presented, and had they been compelled originally to keep gold for so much of their notes, the latter would have been greatly restricted. To do them credit, therefore, the two Edinburgh banks, notwithstanding many shortcomings, seem at this time to have been sincerely searching, in much uncertainty, after better things, and were really trying *to place the banking system of Scotland on a more reliable basis*, it being their own interest to do so, inasmuch as they were wholly looked to for assistance in those times of panic, caused in great measure by the facilities given for speculation in an over-issue of unsecured notes. The whole case must have been specially annoying to the Bank of Scotland, who by their own Act of Parliament had been held liable to summary diligence for payment of *their own notes*.

Apparently the only practical result of the whole affair, taken in connection with the decision in the Aberdeen case, was to cause the Edinburgh banks to refuse to receive any notes in payment except their own. The provincial bank notes having by this time acquired a considerable currency in the capital, towards which the greater portion of them seems to have gravitated, the effect of the banks' decision "was a loss to the people of Edinburgh, who, when they became possessed of notes of private bankers, in which indeed most of their wages were paid, were obliged either to keep them dead some time on hand, or pay 1½d. every 20s. for changing them" at the brokers (*Scots Magazine,* 1727).

We may here give copies of the notes issued by these two first banks of Glasgow, the first, taken from a charming little reprint, "Banking in Glasgow during the Olden Time," is that of Messrs Dunlop, Houston, & Co., the "Glasgow Ship Bank." It bore a vignette of a ship in full sail, but was very plain in its appearance. It is followed by two of Messrs Murdoch & Co., both copied from the Appendix to the print of Mr Trotter's Case, prepared for the Court of Session. The first exhibits the form in use prior to Mr Trotter's demand, while the second was arranged to defeat his attempts, by means of the option clause, which is here inserted.

To meet the requirements of Scots law, as interpreted possibly by the case of the Aberdeen Banking Company, it became customary to insert in these private note issues the name of the writer of the parts not printed, and also to lodge a bond with some city official with full powers and particulars as to their issue. But it was one of Mr Trotter's pleas against Murdoch & Co., that they had neither lodged a new bond, nor altered the style of the old one, when they adopted the option clause, which was a glaring violation of the terms of their bond.

With this case the discreditable behaviour of the banks to each other seems to have ended. The whole proceedings, and the novelty of the expedients resorted to, afford a glimpse of the commercial courtesy of the time ; besides showing very plainly, that though our official fathers did not at once recognise the maxim that "competition is the life of trade," yet that, towards the middle of the century, a beginning had been made by the two old banks in the establishment of a sound and prudent principle to control the issue of bank notes.

£12 Scots.

[*Ship in full sail.*]

No. $\frac{111}{703}$

Glasgow, 2ᵈ January, 1753.

I, JAMES SIMPSON, Cashier appointed by COLIN DUNLOP, ALEXANDER HOUSTON, AND COMPANY, Bankers in Glasgow, pursuant to powers from them, Promise to pay to JOHN BROWN or the Bearer **Twenty Shillings** Sterling; the Date, Number, and Creditor's name are inserted by me, and these presents signed by me and the said COLIN DUNLOP and ALEX. HOUSTON.

James Simpson

Colin Dunlop
Alexr. Houston

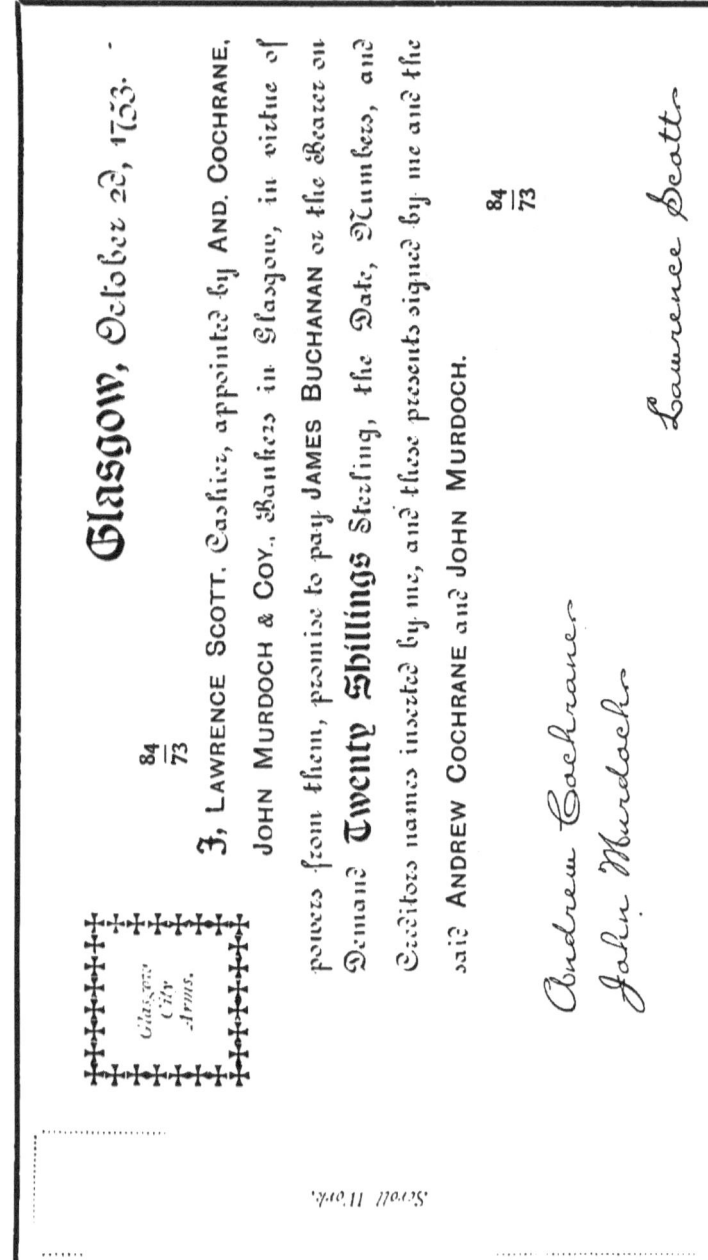

Glasgow, October 2?, 1753.

84/73

I, LAWRENCE SCOTT, Cashier, appointed by AND. COCHRANE, JOHN MURDOCH & COY., Bankers in Glasgow, in virtue of powers from them, promise to pay JAMES BUCHANAN or the Bearer on Demand Twenty Shillings Sterling, the Date, Number, and Creditors names inserted by me, and these presents signed by me and the said ANDREW COCHRANE and JOHN MURDOCH.

84/73

Lawrence Scott

Andrew Cochrane
John Murdoch

Glasgow City Arms.

Scroll Work.

NOTE.—It will be observed that the above bears no Option Clause, that not being inserted until during the contest with Trotter; a specimen is given on opposite page.

$\frac{27}{204}$

Glasgow, ———

3, LAWRENCE SCOTT, Cashier, appointed by AND. COCHRANE. JOHN MURDOCH & COY., Bankers in Glasgow, in virtue of powers from them, promise to pay to JOHN ROSE or the Bearer on Demand One Pound Sterling, or in the option of the Cashier of the said Company, One Pound Sixpence Sterling, at the end of six months after the said Demand, and the Accountant of the said Bank is to ascertain the said Demand and Option, by marking and signing this Note on the back thereof; the Date, Creditors Names, and Sums inserted by me, and these presents, signed by me and the said ANDREW COCHRANE and JOHN MURDOCH.

Lawrence Scott

$\frac{27}{204}$

Andrew Cochrane
John Murdoch

Glasgow City Arms.

Scroll Work.

Chapter III.

" As when some cloud-born torrents from the mountains freed,
Pour headlong downwards, swollen with wintry rain ;
In meeting, overleap their ancient narrow bed,
And journeying seawards fertilise the plain."—Anon.

RETURNING from the foregoing digression to the years immediately following the founding of the Royal Bank, it will be useful to trace the influence on the new methods of banking then introduced, of the note issues generally, and one pound notes in particular. We allude of course, primarily, to the cash credit system, by which those in need of capital were supplied with what they wanted ; and, secondarily, to the deposit system, whereby the superfluous capital of the country was collected from all ranks of life, to be in turn distributed with careful hand to meet the requirements of trade. If in worldly matters it were possible to imagine of an exception to the rule " *Ex nihilo nihil fit*," the Royal Bank might have taken credit for having performed the miracle, on its establishment of cash credits on 12th March 1728.

As each system was dependent on the other for success, cash credits could not have expanded as they did, had the force not been supplied by money received as deposits ; while the latter, in turn, required their utilisation by cash credits, to render them a profitable and attractive means of investment. Few will deny, however, that the cash credit system was the most strikingly original invention,—

the deposit system following upon it as a necessary addition, without which it would not have been complete. It might have been more natural had the banks collected deposits *before* granting credits ; and the fact that they did exactly the reverse, is only another example of the way in which economic principle is set aside by combinations of circumstances. How was it, then, that the advance was granted before money was collected ? and why was it that the Bank of Scotland should be the *first* to place the deposit system on an attractive basis ? thus forestalling the Royal Bank, who had hitherto led the way to reform. The reasons do not seem far to seek.

The Royal Bank had just begun business; it had a larger capital than its rival, and was eager to employ it ; but at the time of which we write the requirements of trade were so very limited that some other means of doing business than lending money on tangible security was found to be a necessity, for such security was rarely to be had from those who could best make a use of capital. Having thus a large capital to lend, it did not urgently require deposits. Besides the employment of its capital, the extension of a note issue was then considered the most important element in a banker's profit.* For both these purposes the credit system was found eminently suitable. It was believed that a good operative credit should be able to maintain in circulation a value of notes equal to its own amount, and of these it was hoped a large number would be one pound notes, as they continued longer in circulation than larger notes ; the latter not filling the same place in the small change currency of the country, and being therefore returned more rapidly against the bank issuing them. Judging from the calculations of recent years, 20s. notes remain very steadily at about 64 or 70 per cent. of the entire issue. The number of transactions represented by this percentage is enormous, especially in view of the time such notes remain in circula-

---

* As indeed it was, since no outlay was involved beyond the cost of preparing the notes ; no stamp duties being charged.

tion. In England two accounts have been prepared to show this, with the following results :—

CALCULATION OF 1818.				CALCULATION OF 1858.			
Notes.	Days.	Notes.	Days.	Notes.	Days.	Notes.	Days.
£1 ...	147	£40 ...	38	£5 ...	72·7	£200 ...	12·7
5 ...	148	50 ...	72	10 ...	77	300 ...	10·6
10 ...	137	100 ...	49	20 ...	57·4	500 ...	11·8
15 ...	66	200 ...	18	30 ...	18·9	1000 ...	11·1
20 ...	121	300 ...	14	40 ...	13·7		
25 ...	43	500 ...	14	50 ...	38·8		
30 ...	55	1000 ...	13	100 ...	29·4		

The defective system of note exchange then and still existing in England, prevents our basing any theory applicable to Scotland upon these figures; but even taking them as they stand, it is more than probable that at that time the difference in favour of one pound notes in Scotland would be even more striking than in England, inasmuch as in the former country these notes were more readily received than gold. Besides, the greater number of debts the 20s. notes would pay in their 147 days than could the £5 in its 148, leaves small doubt as to the advantage of the smaller note as a medium of exchange.

The House of Lords Banking Committee, in 1826, reporting on these points, says, " Thus, supposing a shopkeeper to have a credit of £50 or £100, if his receipts and payments average £5 per day, he may in 6 months or 150 days, have placed 750 of his banker's £1 notes in circulation." " It is quite necessary in order to render a cash credit beneficial, that there should be repeated and continual operations upon it : that the transactions should be numerous ; that there should be a continual drawing out and paying in of money ; and that, by these means, a circulation of bank notes may be promoted, otherwise the account is withdrawn ; and the great reason of this is, that these cash credits are not intended to form dead loans, but to be productive of circulation to the bank."

This profitable business went on during the year of 1728, the Bank of Scotland meanwhile looking on with envious eyes. Unfortunately its power of attracting a share of the gains was small. Its note issue was already considerable, and required some new energy to increase it ; while the idea of calling up more of its capital was contrary to its traditions, as suggesting the possibility of a decreased dividend, and therefore only to be thought of as a last resort. In this predicament the old bank, thoroughly aroused to the necessity of a struggle for existence, behaved with remarkable astuteness, and adopted the enemy's cash credit tactics in 1729 ; but being then in the thick of the fight as to its notes, and apparently feeling its inability to launch the new system without extraneous aid, it at the same time took a step in advance of the Royal, by receiving deposits on its Treasurer's Bond at the rate of 5 per cent. per annum, the forerunners of their deposit receipts of 1810. The effect of these measures seems to have been to restore the old bank to its historic place in public estimation. On several occasions, during its long career, rivals sprang up, who rushed ahead as if threatening to leave the bank of 1696 hopelessly in the rear ; but their speed was not kept up. Some fell back, others failed, and the public favour returned to the Bank of Scotland. Though the policy of the latter had in it nothing strikingly original, it had the same important elements of success as marked that of Queen Elizabeth,—at first not over scrupulous, yet throughout displaying a shrewdness and prudence that never failed to profit by the example and experience of the enemy, until it had regained the position it still worthily maintains of *Primus inter pares.*

Chapter IV.

PRIVATE BANKERS AND THEIR SUPPORT BY THE NEW JOINT-STOCKS—THIRD NEW METHOD.

"A various horde they came, a nameless crew,
Forgot but in the brighter lustre of a few."—CARGILL.

AFTER two years' experience of these reforms, the Bank of Scotland guarded itself in 1731 by commencing to accept deposits for fixed periods, instead of payable on demand, as formerly. This defensive measure was, no doubt, prompted by the same salutary dread of the Royal Bank which had first driven the old bank into the pathway of reform ; and now, in addition, led them again to open branches in Glasgow and the North, only, unfortunately, to be once more withdrawn in 1733. In partial compensation for this lack of support in the provinces, both banks soon afterwards had their note issues increased,* and their profits enlarged, by a business which cannot but be looked upon as a wrong application of the cash credit system, —we refer to the *private bankers*, who then began to establish themselves in Edinburgh and elsewhere. Many, if not most of these, were simply merchants, who besides their usual business carried on the negotiation of bills of exchange, but who, attracted by the profits of banking, and the facilities afforded by the old banks in the shape of cash credits, gradually drew away from merchandise to adopt the profes-

---

* If we can credit information received from external sources, the note issues were enormously increased through the agency of the private bankers ; but in absence of official records such as this century affords, such statements have to be received with caution.

sion of banking. The first and most famous of these has a history little less ancient than that of the old bank itself, while in prudence and uprightness it had few equals amongst its cotemporaries of last century. It was that of John Coutts & Co., in later years to become more famous under the guidance of Sir William Forbes. Of this celebrated banker a well-known author of thirty years ago * writes : " One would need to have lived through the last fifty years in Scotland to be fully aware of the excellencies, of various kinds, which made people speak with such veneration of Sir William Forbes, and maintain a faith in his modest private bank such as is now scarcely given to the joint-stock of large copartneries."

This firm, under its different names, continued to do business with the Royal Bank for nearly a century, sending large numbers of its notes into circulation, although Bank of Scotland notes were also given if asked for. Mansfield, Ramsay, & Co., in 1738; Kinnears & Smiths, in 1748; Fairholme, Cumming, Hogg, Alexanders, and a host of lesser firms,—all had credit with, and issued the notes of, the two joint-stock banks, although some of them in later years issued their own. In this way the old banks became less directly connected with the general public, and were looked on more as the Bank of England now is,—as the bank of bankers ; the Bank of Scotland and the Royal Bank granting credits to, or taking deposits from, the private bankers, who in turn afforded similar facilities to the public. The extent to which this was carried on, may be judged from the facts supplied by Sir William Forbes in his " Memoirs of a Banking House" (pp. 60, 61). His firm had a credit with the Royal Bank of £4000 ; but latterly, instead of requiring to use this, they had deposits with the same bank seldom or never below £40,000; and as interest was only allowed on £20,000 of this, and that at 4 per cent. (after 1781 only 3 per cent.), the profit may well be judged to be, as Sir William states it, " not less than £3000 per annum."

---

* Robert Chambers.

This probably includes the profit received in the circulation of its notes, for it should be kept in mind that, in addition to the notes kept by Sir William Forbes & Co. as till money, and for which they had to pay in the usual way, they were the means of placing many thousands of Royal Bank notes into circulation.

The sanction of cash credits to private bankers, who acted at the same time as merchants, has already been referred to as a misapplication of the system. In no trade or profession is the intervention of middlemen less desirable than in local banking; yet this was practically what the old banks encouraged, when aiding the establishment of private banking on such terms. Blinded, apparently, by the prospect of embarking at once upon a large and easy business, the banks could not look far enough into the future to see the ultimate effects on their own position with the outside public; nor did they consider that banking facilities afforded to the greatest number, formed a method so profitable and simple as dealing with a few large firms. There may be some plausibility in their argument, and so long as these firms worked in a legitimate way no great harm might have been done, though the principles on which they were assisted were wrong. But it is notorious that they *did not* carry on a legitimate business, but indulged in various mercantile and stock-jobbing transactions, which, though then deemed quite fair trade, were entirely outside the sphere of a banker. Thus in many cases the money which was *withheld* from the public by the old banks to be handed over to the private firms, never ultimately reached the public, as it ought to have done, being used instead for speculative purposes by the new bankers. One example may be given of the kind of traffic then too common. The refining of sugar had begun in Edinburgh in 1751, and, being highly lucrative, a number of Edinburgh bankers promised themselves huge profits could they but start a similar trade in Leith, then beginning to rise to considerable importance as a seaport town. The Leith Sugar-House was accordingly built in 1757, and in five years *the whole capital was lost.* The reader can infer *whose* capital was lost. As years went on, and private bankers multiplied, the old banks almost entirely lost touch of the mercantile class, who looked chiefly to the private houses for that accommodation which the latter in turn received from the joint-stock banks. Under such conditions the spirit of prudence and independence was lost sight of amongst the smaller bankers, who recklessly traded up to the full extent of their means, keeping no proper reserves to meet the credits with which their various connections flooded the country, but selfishly looking for assistance to the big banks, who alone could carry them through their difficulties. The joint-stocks, in turn, while bearing the brunt in times of panic, had practically no knowledge, in ordinary times, of the nature of many of the undertakings which their notes and credits were used to foster. During the speculations of 1760-65 private bankers' cash credits were considerably restricted by the old banks, who at that time required all their resources to meet the heavy demands made upon them ; superior attractions for depositors being held out, in all probability, for the same cause.*

Towards the end of the century another and more serious difficulty arose in the management of the joint-stock banks themselves. Many of these private bankers having risen to affluence in the city, were looked upon as fit persons to be entrusted with the direction of the large banks,—an office which they only too eagerly coveted. As directors, they had the pleasure of helping themselves in various ways to the bank funds ; sometimes even, according to a common rumour, refusing an advance to an old customer of the bank, at the board meeting, in order that his business might be secured for their own banking houses. For many years the progress of the banks, especially of the Bank of Scotland and Royal Bank, was retarded for these selfish ends; and it was not until about 1810 that they got strength to throw off this "old man of the sea," who, we shall see, did not accept his downfall without much wailing and vituperation at the meanness and jealousy of those who refused any longer to supply him with legs.

* On this subject see concluding remarks of Chapter VII.

Chapter V.

> " Blest Paper Credit ! last and best supply,
> That lends corruption lighter wings to fly."—POPE.

HAVING treated thus far of cash credit, deposits, and the irruption of private bankers, there is still one more novelty to speak of in the banking begun about 1727,—the Option Clause. Although introduced as a temporary expedient by the old bank in its struggle with the Royal Bank, the right the clause bore on its face seems seldom afterwards to have been abused until about 1756, when the Glasgow banks revived the practice. As 1760 approached, the restless feeling of advancing prosperity forced the postal authorities to increased diligence. The fact is small in itself, but it throws light on the increased hurry of the time. Instead of the three posts weekly between London and Edinburgh, taking 87 hours coming north and 131 going south, there were five deliveries weekly to almost every town in the kingdom, the old system of foot messengers being abandoned and horses used, instead. Some years later the ready means afforded for raising money by notes of bankers were taken advantage of by a number of extremely impecunious individuals in the capital, their example spreading like wildfire through the surrounding country, in a manner which has no parallel save in the North American note issues of 1780. Adam Smith, in explanation of the wonder how these notes were accepted in payment, says : " A person whose promissory note for

£5, or even for 20s., would be rejected by everybody, will get it to be received without scruple when it is issued for so small a sum as sixpence. But the frequent bankruptcies to which such beggarly bankers must be liable, may occasion a very great inconveniency, and sometimes even a very great calamity, to many poor people who had received their notes in payment." Not bankers merely, too numerous as these were, but all classes of people, tradesmen, shopkeepers, coffee-house keepers, employers of labour, and corporations, from the highest to the lowest, adopted with eagerness this new and delightful way of not paying old debts. On next page is given a specimen of a skit published in Glasgow about this time, which is not more absurd than were many of the real notes themselves. Notes payable on demand, or, in the option of the grantor, six months after the date of presentation, or for a certain amount of food, work, drink, or other commodity, were poured out upon the country for 10s., 5s., and down even to 1s. Scots, to an extent which ate up the feeble metallic currency as thoroughly as the rats picked Bishop Hatto's bones.

Numerous forgeries were set afloat, and, miserably executed though they were, did not tend to help matters. A few specimens of genuine notes are still to be seen in the Antiquarian Museum in Edinburgh. One of these, drawn by the Mason Barrowman Company of Edinburgh, states its intention at great length of paying the sum of one shilling Scots (one penny sterling) to the bearer upon demand, or in the option of the directors at six months after the date of presentment, adding, with extreme minuteness, that the legal interest accruing thereupon would be met at the same time.

At a meeting of the Town Council and citizens of Aberdeen with their County Committee, held about 1755, it was unanimously resolved to refuse every note of the Glasgow banks that might be offered in payment, as the town was perfectly inundated with the infamous " inconvertibles" of Murdoch & Co. Some warm discussion ensued as to paper money in general ; and though the expressed

No. 32.

Glasgow, January 16th, 1765.

WE SWARM.
[*Figures of three Wasps.*]

3, JOHN BRAGG, Cashier for ANDREW WHITECOCK, DUNCAN DICK & COMPANY, Bankers in Glasgow, having power from them, Promise to pay to THOMAS TAILOR or the Bearer on Demand **One Penny** Sterling, or in option of the Directors THREE BALLADS, six days after demand; and for ascertaining the Demand and Option of the Directors, the Accomptant and one of the Tellers of the Bank are hereby ordered to mark and sign this Note on the back hereof. By Order of the Court of Directors.

John Bragg

Andrew Whitecock

A border, of eleven Wasps, ran round the Note.

opinion was anything but complimentary, it is only fair to state that the notes of the Edinburgh banks were excepted from the condemnation. One writer, in a very sensible "Address to the Town and County of Aberdeen," dated in 1755, complains of the condition of trade, and points out that the chief cause of depression is "the currency of paper money or bank notes, which by increasing the quantity has sunk the intrinsic value of our money, without the smallest advantage to any individual but the bankers themselves. I may venture to affirm that there is at least twice the value of bank notes as there is of real money circulating in Scotland (if I had said six times the value perhaps I had spoke within bounds), so that here is the whole cash of the kingdom tripled by a fiction. Labour and goods rise or fall as money is cheap or dear. In times when money is really cheap, the disadvantages attending a rise in prices are mollified by the increased riches of the country; but when the plentifulness of money is induced by a huge volley of paper money, such stagnation is lasting so long as the money paper lasts, and thus trade is reduced and commerce languishes by a mere paper fiction."

The city of Perth made itself notorious by the manufacture of these notes, no less than six banking companies springing into existence at this time, all trading in these small fish. "The first bank established there was called The Banking Company, and commenced business 4th June 1763, the notes signed John Stewart & Coy., and Perth arms at the head. In the course of little more than the next twelve months no fewer than five banking companies were established, namely, The Tannerie Banking Company, erected 4th June 1764, the notes signed Stewart Richardson & Co., an oak-tree being at the head; The Banking Company, erected 20th June 1764, the notes signed Wedderspoon & Co., the thistle and crown being at the head of the notes; The Banking Company, erected 17th July 1764, the notes signed M'Keith, Rintoul, & Co., the king's head being at the top; The Craigie Banking Company, erected 20th August 1764, signed John Ramsay

& Co., bearing a garb on their notes; The Banking Company, erected 3d September 1764, the notes signed by John Bruce, and having the Bruce crest and motto at the head."* Five banks in four months were surely too many; yet the wonder is, that they all seem to have been conducted so prudently that they had the good sense to amalgamate (after the passing of the 1765 Act) into the Perth United Company, afterwards the respectable Perth Banking Company, now merged in the Union Bank of Scotland.

Similar houses sprang up in Dunkeld, Auchtermuchty, Montrose, Linlithgow, Kirkliston, Falkirk, and elsewhere; but Dempster & Co., of Dundee, who came into existence in 1763, excelled them all in iniquity, by postponing legal payment for twelve months,—offering to pay, as they chose, either on demand or at the end of six months, in gold, or *in notes of the Edinburgh banks*, the latter bearing a second option clause of six months. A facsimile of their one pound note is given opposite.

A number of these banks were able to go on for some years, their issues being paid out partly by means of hired agents,—who received a quarter per cent. to travel about the country,—giving them in exchange for gold and notes of other banks, and partly by means of imprudent advances made to a much greater extent than the bank had either capital to warrant or reserves to meet. The inevitable loss fell, not on the banks, unfortunately, but largely on the people, who were often compelled to keep large numbers of notes in their possession, from the want of any means of obtaining payment except under a charge for commission. Edinburgh suffered very severely from this, as well as such centres as Aberdeen and Dumfries. Public attention was at last aroused to the nuisance, and at the meetings of the heritors and gentry of Aberdeenshire, Roxburgh, Selkirk, Haddington, and other counties, the matter was discussed, and various remedies suggested,—all except Renfrewshire resolving to take no other notes than those of the Edin-

---

* "History of Perth." T. H. Marshall, Perth, 1849.

No. $\frac{0}{111}$ 793

Dundee 8th Augt 1763   £1..—

I Robert Jobson Cashier to George Dempster Esqr &
Compy: Bankers in Dundee, in Virtue of Powers from
them, promise to pay to Andrew Pitcairn or the Bearer
on Demand at the Companys Office here One Pound
Sterling, or, in the Option of the Directors, One Pound &
Six pence Sterl: at the End of Six Months, either in Cash or
in Notes of the Royal Bank or Bank of Scotland, and
for Ascertaining the Demand & Option of the Directors,
the Acomptant is hereby ordered to mark and sign this
Note on the Back hereof. And these presents are signed
by me & by   John Haliburton   Wm Alcarry

R. Jobson Cash:

£12 Scots N.° 199

79378

Edinburgh 5th April 1762

The Royal Bank of Scotland

pursuant to Act of Parliament & Letters
Patent under the Grant-Seal is hereby obliged to pay
to [   ] Dowglas, Or the Bearer, One Pound
Sterling on demand.   Or in the Optium of the
Directors, One pound Six pence Sterling at the
End of Six Months after the day of the demand &
for ascertaining the demand & Option of the Directors
the accomptant & two of the Tellers of the Bank are hereby
ordered to mark & sign this Note on the back of the same

By Order of }   Alex. Simpson own
the Court of } Thos. James Lockhart
Directors.

burgh banks, and to get the option clauses abolished. The western county maintained that many of the Scottish banks were quite as sound as those in Edinburgh, and that restriction to the latter would only help to give them a monopoly of banking.

In October 1763 the Linlithgow justices proposed that all notes below £1 should also be swept away at the same time as the option clauses. The writers in the *Scots Magazine* in this year on the subject are legion, but one is specially deserving of attention, who insists that *private bankers* should only have the right of issue granted to them on proper inspection being made by Government officials, and upon advertisement twice every year, in the public papers, of a full statement of their assets and liabilities,— a writer who has evidently been ahead of his time. None of the Edinburgh private bankers added to the evil, as in the capital bankers were too busily engaged in the profitable work of retiring the country banks' paper, who all made some show, for a time at least, of having an agent to retire their notes.

Two of the large banks struggled hard before submitting to the objectionable clause. The Bank of Scotland had been the first to adopt it in 1727, and still bore the clause on their notes ; but the Royal and British Linen Company banks had not availed themselves of it. The demand for specie from them was therefore so specially severe, that the Royal, in self-defence, was compelled to give way about 1761, and adopt the odious precaution.* The British Linen Company bore the drain only a short time longer, for in the same year they state, that " the very great scarcity of silver, and the unwarrantable methods taken to carry it off, having induced the directors of the Royal Bank to issue notes with the like option clause contained in those of the Bank of Scotland, and all the private banking companies ; this measure of the banks has occasioned an unusual demand for specie for the company's notes, and made it not only

---

* A facsimile is given of one of the Royal Bank notes bearing the optional clause.

advisable, but necessary, to take the same precautions the banks and other companies have done."

Some authorities will have it that the coin was carried out of the country by this deluge, others, with more truth, plead the want of coin as the cause of it. As the exchanges were always more or less against Scotland, the pseudo-remedy of an increased paper currency only aggravated the disease, by raising the exchanges still further in favour of London, with the inevitable result that the small amount of coin remaining was carried off faster than ever. The metallic currency was certainly shamefully deficient both in quantity and quality ; * nearly half a century having elapsed since its renewal, and the usual causes having been at work during that time to reduce the scanty stock. Concurrent with this want of a circulating medium, there arose a violent fit of the speculative mania ; every one, regardless of the means, hasting to be rich along the road leading to the ruin of 1772. The legislation of 1765 gave this a temporary check, which only continued until new ways were discovered into which the speculators at once ran, to find themselves at last face to face with the collapse of Douglas, Heron, & Co.

We can easily trace the effects of the two old banks' operations in all these events. The evil example of the option clause is of course directly attributable to the Bank of Scotland, though the Royal Bank was not blameless in the matter. But it is through the cash credit system that we can best follow their workings. To enlarge the profits of this system, credits were at first granted to any one, private bankers or otherwise, who cared to ask for them, the note issues being correspondingly increased. The private bankers in their turn determined to make a profit for themselves by issuing their own notes, an example which was finally communicated to the lower trading com-munity, who, tormented with a wretched metallic currency,

---

* One package of £192. 3s. light gold weighed only 45 oz. 9 dwt. ; was sent to London, and at £3. 17s. 10½ d. per oz. brought £177. 8s. 2d. Loss, £14. 15s. 10d. = £7. 14s. per cent.

and taking advantage of the perfect freedom from all restriction as to issuing of notes, saw a means of doing so with immunity, by means of the option clause. At no part of our banking history does the want of legislation appear more pressing than at this. The essential principle of a note issue—prompt convertibility : payment on demand—was utterly lost sight of by those who ought to have known better, as well as by the crowds who were perfectly ignorant of any principle in the matter. We know of no more fit comparison to the total lack of legislation in Scotland at this time, than the excess of it in England. The systems of the two countries were as far removed from each other as extremes can be, but, as is often the case, the extremes produced the same common weakness and confusion. England floundered on with its difficulties for another half-century ; in Scotland, fortunately, the trouble was speedily dealt with. The county meetings had not been without their effect. The shrewd men of the old banks saw through and through the mischief their own hands had helped to create. The fall in the exchanges was a serious item against their profits ; as, apart from the depletion of their specie reserves,* it involved the issue of so many small notes, placing their own larger notes (for once 20s. notes were "large") at a disadvantage, cutting them out of circulation, and replacing them with worthless paper, all bearing the unworthy option clause.

The remedy obtained from Government by the Bank of Scotland and the Royal Bank, through the good offices of Lord Advocate Miller of Barskimming, son-in-law of Provost Murdoch, of the Glasgow Arms Bank, is another example of the manner in which Government has often dealt with these questions,—mistaking the effects for the cause, legislating for the former, and leaving the latter out of sight. No regard was paid to who ought or ought not to issue notes,

---

* About 1762 the British Linen Company were so short of gold, that they paid a Mr Walter Elliot £2. 2s. for collecting £350 in gold for them at Stagshaws Fair.

the right was still left open to all and sundry who cared to exercise it. Had some efficient law been passed, allowing such a right only to responsible parties, who could prove their right to be considered responsible by the publication of their accounts, a vast amount of evil would have been averted; but, as usual, to stave off the pressing need of the moment, was the primary thought. The measure granted was excellent so far as it went, but the original cause of the grievance, the right to issue notes, was not touched. We are far from disputing the benefits which have accrued to Scotland from this common law right, but what was required was, that some means should be adopted of ensuring convertibility, by gauging generally the ability of the issuer to pay.

Notwithstanding this radical defect, the Act V. of George III., c. 49, remedied four matters of detail in a very thorough way. The optional clause was swept away, no one being allowed from and after 15th May 1766 to issue any "note, ticket, token, or other writing for money of the nature of a bank note, circulated or to be circulated as specie, but such as shall be payable on demand in lawful money of Great Britain, and without reserving any power or option of delaying payment thereof for any time or term whatever." Section IV. reasserted the law of summary diligence, which, though plainly laid down in the statutes of Charles II. and William III., 1696, c. 36, as to bills, had been nevertheless either hazily understood or wilfully misinterpreted by the Court of Session in the notorious cases of Royal Bank v. The Bank of Scotland, and Trotter v. Murdoch, so that promissory notes were not included. The dread of diligence was completely put to rest by the case of the Aberdeen Bank, as bankers had only to continue issuing promissory notes—*i.e.* documents not of the "nature of bills"—to make themselves perfectly secure against summary diligence; while they were always assured of their right of diligence against the unfortunate Bank of Scotland, who had been held liable to it by the famous decision of the House of Lords in favour of the Royal Bank. Thus the

old bank for nearly forty years after 1727 was the only
bank in Scotland* whose notes were payable on pain of
summary diligence.   Notwithstanding this security, the
ignorant public did not confine their patronage to the old
bank, for, as a writer in the *Scots Magazine* of 1770
remarks, "Country people, who are not clever at perceiving
distinctions, see a mixture of print and manuscript, with
some flourishing, and they inquire no further."   The uncertainty upon this important point would aid materially in
increasing the number of worthless note issues of 1750 to
1765, as had their grantors known their liability to be put
to the "horn" when payment was not made upon demand
or at due date, they would scarcely have been so eager to
launch their inconvertible paper on the public.   So far,
then, the Act of 1765 did good by stating distinctly the
liabilities of the note issuer.

In event of non-payment, a protest could be taken
between the hours of nine in the morning and three in the
afternoon, which was to be registered in the competent
judicatories, within six months after the date of the protest,
"letters of horning upon a charge of six days, and the
other usual execution of the law of Scotland to pass
thereupon."

To avoid such delays as disgraced the cases before
mentioned, no suspension or *sist* of the charge to pay was
to pass except upon discharge of the notes by the holder,
or tender of the full sum contained in them by the grantor,
in the form of an instrument duly signed by a notary
public and two witnesses, with legal interest and all
expenses of protest, registration, and such diligence as

---

* The Royal Bank, happily, never had occasion to have the
question discussed in court as to their notes, and from their being a
corporation, it is possible that summary execution might have been
enforced upon them, as being signed by an authorised official of the
corporation, and payable on demand, without the uncertainty introduced by the option clauses. But even in their case, from their notes
being promissory notes, it is more than questionable if summary
diligence could have been obtained, this right not covering promissory notes until 1765, under the Act referred to above.

might have followed thereon. In event of any overcharge in the expenses, the banker was at liberty to seek his remedy in the proper court, by an ordinary action ; while the right of the holder to damages for delay in payment was also specially reserved.

With the same object of preventing delay, in protesting each note separately, it was enacted that protest of any number of notes might be made jointly, by prefixing the full tenor and contents of any one and thereafter adding the dates and numbers of all others of the same tenor.

We now come to the most drastic clause in the Act. The seventh, after narrating the inconveniences caused by the issue of notes of small amounts, declares that from and after 1st June 1765 no notes were to be issued, re-issued, or given out as specie by any person, " for any sum or sums of money less than twenty shillings lawful money of Great Britain," upon pain of a penalty of £500. As might have been anticipated, many of the erring banks heard of this Act with no little anxiety as to its effect. The Dundee bank was a fair example of many others. On 21st February 1765 " the directors resolved to circumscribe the circulation of notes, and to grant no more cash credits till the effect of these alterations in the law is seen." The necessity for some more definite action was speedily forced upon them by the remembrance that their note issue amounted to £34,503 (of which £28,526 were £1 notes), and that they only held £1395 of specie to meet this large sum. Their London agents were hurriedly requested in April to collect, " as fast as they could," £1740 in small gold and silver, half guineas, quarter guineas, 18s. pieces, 9s., 13s. 6d., and 4s. pieces, while Mr Fyffe, their agent in Edin-burgh, was " told to pick up what gold he could under a guinea ; " further, " the directors finding the company dis-tressed by the great demands on Mr John Fyffe, their Edin-burgh agent, for retiring their notes, are unanimously of opinion that the only remedy that can be applied thereto is by abridging the business of the company. The cashier is therefore desired for the future to discount no bills ex-cepting those payable in London, Edinburgh, and Glasgow."

Immediately on the passing of the Act, notes below 20s. steadily declined, while the others did not materially increase ; the exchanges rising slightly as a natural result, the drain of gold stopped, and the better class of banks and bankers began vigorously to increase their metallic resources, so as to ensure instant convertibility when the different sections of the Act came into operation. Notwithstanding all these efforts, some years passed before the exchanges were again in a satisfactory state. More than a hundred years have elapsed since then, but our note issue has never again sunk below par.* (But see page 121, &c., for effect of Restriction Act on Scots notes.)

Throughout these remarks upon the new departures in banking, brought in about 1730, we have endeavoured to show the action and reaction of each upon the note issues of the time. Of the four systems spoken of, only the two grand inventions still exist and flourish in our midst,—cash credits and deposits,—mutually supporting each other, and freed from the impeding clutch of private banking. The latter continued for nearly forty years in great force, and stretched in gradually diminished strength well into the present century, to expire about 1830 ; while, as we have already seen, the fungus growth of the option clause was summarily removed in 1765. Much as had been done by the note issues in all these transactions, the *great* work of the one pound note was yet to be begun, when *branches* were founded throughout the country.

---

* Adam Smith mentions that during the first years of the abuse, while the exchange between London and Carlisle was at par, that between London and Dumfries would sometimes be 4 per cent. against Dumfries, though this town is not thirty miles distant from Carlisle. But at Carlisle bills are paid in gold and silver, whereas at Dumfries they were paid in Scotch bank notes ; and the uncertainty of getting these bank notes exchanged for gold and silver coin had thus degraded them 4 per cent. below the value of the coin.

Sir William Forbes states that the rate of exchanges was sometimes so high as 5 per cent. against Scotland for bills on London.

On the passing of the Act 12 George III., c. 72, in 1772, bank notes were specially excluded from the six years' prescription ~~of summary diligence~~, first enacted in that year, for bills and promissory notes.

Chapter VI.—1745-1770.

THE BRITISH LINEN COMPANY—NEW BANKS—BRANCHES.

*" In the long run the State, or Individual, or Company thrives best which
dives deepest down into the mass of the community, and adapts its requirements to the wants of the greatest number."—W. E. GLADSTONE.*

IN taking a general survey of the banking history of last
century, whether in Scotland or in England, one of the
most obvious defects was the prolonged confinement of
the joint-stock banks to the capitals of the respective countries as the field of their operations.   Two gallant attempts
had been made by the old bank at times when it was in sore
straits, but both alike, from several causes, were unsuccessful.   Upon the first occasion, in 1696, they did not seek for
business in its most attractive form, and failing in the direct
object for which they were intended (exchange business),
the branches were withdrawn in a few months.   Again, in
1731, the attempt was renewed with as little success.
Apparently accepting their failure in too desponding a
spirit, the bank made no attempt for nearly forty years to
allow to the provinces the benefits which had been lavished
on the capital.   The Royal Bank, with singular apathy,
did not open a branch until 1783, when its Glasgow office
was begun, and having accomplished this, they remained
perfectly quiescent for over half a century.

Between the years 1731 and 1763, partly owing to the
disturbed state of the country, but principally from the
defective policy of the Edinburgh banks, the whole banking
system of Scotland was limited to Edinburgh and Glasgow, save during the brief existence of the Aberdeen
bank,—which came to an end not so much from want of

support in the north, as from the inexorable policy of the southern banks, who would neither themselves open branches nor cared for any other doing so, but insisted on the Aberdeen bank retiring the notes, of which it had, as was then customary, issued far too many. It is more than probable, that, had the Bank of Scotland and the Royal Bank instituted an energetic branch system about 1750, working with credits and deposits by the aid of their notes, and maintaining proper gold reserves, the parasitic growths which disfigured their business for so long would not have come, into existence, or, deprived of proper nourishment, would have sooner drooped and died. The congestion of such a large proportion of the capital in two or three towns, necessarily left the more distant provinces in an extremely unprovided condition. Remembering that poverty is the mother of discontent, is it too much to suggest, that had the branch policy of 1860 been introduced in proportionally smaller scale in 1740, the increase in occupation and prosperity north of the Grampians would have been so great that Glencoe might have been forgotten, and the glorious but unfortunate page of "the '45" would never have been written?

With the foundation of branches by the large joint-stock banks, the extinction of the dependent class of private banks was only a matter of time. A house like Sir William Forbes, James Hunter, & Co. was quite an exception to the rule : keeping large reserves of ready cash, in gold, as well as notes of the other banks, they had in addition extensive deposits with the two oldest banks (though at different times), partly payable on demand, and partly with six months' notice ; they were also, excepting the Bank of England, the largest holders of consols of any bank in Great Britain. Such a house was clearly independent of any joint-stock bank, and could safely rely upon its resources both for advances and deposits ; again and again, when many of their cotemporaries were borne down in the panics of 1772 and onwards, Sir William and his partners bore the strain of public demand with apparent ease. The

fact of their granting a cash credit for the large sum of
£100,000, paid out largely in their own notes, to a single
company, may afford evidence of the extent of their
business. But the smaller houses, those who cared not to
maintain independent reserves, but relied on their larger
neighbours, might have read their doom when the joint-
stock banks opened their first branches. They had originally
been encouraged by the Bank of Scotland and Royal Bank
solely for selfish ends, as it was thought that business could
be done in larger sums with them than directly with the
public. The character of business done at the branches
slowly but surely opened the eyes of the banks, to see that
a *safer*, and therefore more profitable, trade could be got at
through them than with the help of the private bankers.
We shall therefore see how, during the next half-century,
the credits and other conveniences of the small bankers
were steadily curtailed, until few, if any, of the older houses
remained, except such as had taken the more honourable
course of making themselves independent.

The wondrous impetus given to various industries,
through the canals, roads, and spinning mills promoted in
England and elsewhere from 1760 onwards, has peculiar
interest to the subject of banking, both in that country and
in Scotland. In England, from the monopoly granted to
the Bank of England, the greater part of the burden fell
upon private banking houses, who were, with some few
honourable exceptions, quite unable to supply the amount of
capital required. In Scotland, on the other hand, it is from
this time that the strong joint-stock banks, led off by the
British Linen Company and the Bank of Scotland, began
to lengthen their cords and strengthen their stakes in every
direction north and south of the Grampians. The results
as to the private firms were only what could be expected.
Unfortunately for England, she did not perceive the cause
of her weakness ; while, by the greater freedom of Scottish
institutions, the cause of weakness north of the Tweed was
gradually removed. In both countries private banking was
the defect. In Scotland it was seen to be so ; while in

England, as the history of 1826 shews, the whole burden of blame was practically laid upon the one pound note.

We have already shewn how the private bankers withdrew for speculation funds which, but for the want of agencies, should have gone to fertilise the provinces. Little or no benefit to general trade accrued from these proceedings; and the only interest taken in provincial matters seems to have been to purchase corn from the farmers, at ridiculously low prices, to be hoarded until sold at the highest possible rate to the consumer; even this was not so universally profitable, as might be supposed. Few efforts were made to encourage manufactures, fisheries, or other pursuits, until about 1735, when the linen manufacture began to expand. The appearance of Prince Charles in 1745 stopped progress for a time, the banks closing their doors and carrying their gold and valuables into the Castle for safety. The Prince proclaimed that no alarm need be felt by the banks, as their treasure would not be touched, and that he was agreeable to receive and issue their notes in payments. Finding that a deaf ear was turned to his charming, he sent to the Royal Bank demanding gold for £857 of their notes, and in a few days for £2307 more. Upon refusal a protest was taken by John Murray of Broughton, the Prince's secretary, who informed the bank that execution would follow in forty-eight hours; and under this threat the bank agreed to make payment if the Governor of the Castle would grant them access to their specie. When this was arranged, the bank authorities passed the Highland sentinels on the Castle Hill, and, advancing to the drawbridge under a flag of truce, were admitted into the Castle. In this visit they carried off £12,000 in gold, and availed themselves of the opportunity to burn £60,000 of their notes, tearing up, for want of time, a large number of others,—an operation which was speedily cut short by the commander, General Guest, who ordered them to be gone without further parley. On returning to town, the notes received from the Prince's secretary were at once cancelled, along with £600 received from the Governor. Of these two sums about £1800 were 20s. notes. In a few days the trouble was renewed, Mr Patrick Smyth, a brother of Smyth of Methven, demanding from the Royal Bank £1819 in gold in exchange for notes, —£1117 more of their notes coming in almost next day. In both cases the usual farce of protest was gone through, followed by the bank telling out the gold, and settling matters amicably over a bottle of wine. On 25th October an exchange was made between the Bank of Scotland and Royal of £4000 of their notes, and soon after the last demand was made on the Royal by the Prince's servants, on this occasion for the small sum of £417 of gold for that amount of notes. To add to their annoyance, a forgery of their notes was mentioned to the Royal Bank, of which, fortunately, nothing seems to have come. The diary of Mr John Campbell, cashier to the Royal Bank at this time, from whose pages we have taken the foregoing story of the "1745" in Edinburgh, finishes off, evidently with a sigh of relief:—"Sent snuff and paper to Earl Breadalbane." Thursday, 14th November 1745.—"2000 foot and dragoons entered the city this morning." Monday, 18th November. —"Wrote to Lord Justice-Clerk about bank affairs, and advised him the old bank had opened shop." Wednesday, 20th November.—"Went to the Castle of Edinburgh with several of the officers of the bank, and got down all the boxes." Saturday, 23d November.—"Got down rest of bank effects from Castle." The banks had been closed from the middle of September to above date ; but it took a month or two to enable them to settle to their work in an efficient manner.

With the battle of Culloden the hopes of the Jacobites were crushed for ever. Immediately afterwards the King was approached by the Dukes of Queensberry and Argyle, the Earls of Lauderdale, Glencairn, and other notables, for the purpose of obtaining a charter for a new company, to be established for the encouragement of the linen trade. The time was thought opportune, as " it was considered to be of much importance, with a view to tranquillise the

country, and call forth its resources, that the attention of
the Scottish people should be directed to the advantages to
be derived from trading and manufacturing enterprise. It
was anticipated that, by affording the direct encouragement
of a Government institution to the linen manufacture, it
would become the great staple manufacture of Scotland,
and would provide ample employment for the population ;
while extensive markets for the produce of this labour
would be found within the United Kingdom and in the
colonies, then chiefly supplied with linen from Germany."

A charter was granted, dated 5th July 1746, in which
the capital was stated at £100,000, of which only £50,000
was to be subscribed for ; the company having power, in
addition to dealing directly in linen, " to do everything that
may conduce to the promoting and carrying on of the linen
manufacture."

The first few years of the new company, and their
manner of business, are deeply interesting, and directly
affect our subject, for in them the foundation was laid of
the widespreading system of branches, which has given
such an impulse to banking in Scotland. It is largely
owing to the branch system that the poverty-stricken Scotland of 1700 has now £80,000,000 lodged in her banks, and
it was by means of the *note issue—the one pound note issue*
—that these branches were established and maintained.
How often is it the case that the greatest improvements in
science and manufactures are due to the discoveries of out-
siders,—men who have not been trained in, nor had any
connection with, the particular study or profession which
their genius has advanced ! The inventor of the spinning
frame was a barber, the victor at Arcot and Plassy a clerk,
Faraday a bookbinder's apprentice ; and now the originators
of the plan whereby note issues, deposits, and cash credits
were to receive the widest extension, were the partners of a
linen company ! Before any idea of banking was enter-
tained, extensive correspondence was held throughout Scotland with the weaving industries. These were chiefly
composed of the lower orders, who, having little or no

capital of their own, were only too glad to commence work
for the new company. " In a very short time accounts
were opened by men in every portion of the land from
Shetland to London." Material was supplied to the workmen, who, on returning the manufactured goods, were at
once paid for their labour. In this way the need of small
amounts of capital by a vast number of individuals was
satisfactorily met. Instead of the congestion and windy
speculation of the first half of the century, a small beginning had been made of more prosperous banking, whereby
the powers that had so long lain dormant were to spring
up into new life,—as

> " Seeds that mildew in the garner,
> Scattered, fill with gold the plain."

Very early in their career an office was opened in London,
and by 1764 agents had been appointed in different parts
of the country, by whom bills were discounted, and to
whom notes or bills were regularly sent for circulation or
negotiation. The accounts for a time were kept merely
in the agent's name, and not in that of his branch, so that
in some cases it has been difficult to trace the exact year
when business was begun. But there are records of the
agents' transactions in Glasgow, Forres, Montrose, and
Dundee in 1767; and gradually, as industries gave hopes of
success, new agencies were opened, until in 1793 the British
Linen Company had eleven branches in full operation
throughout the country,—Montrose, Duns, Cupar, Wigtown,
Forres, Jedburgh, Inverness, Dunbar, Dumfries, Berwick,
Glasgow, and Dundee, and soon afterwards Leith, Haddington, Inveraray, Biggar, Castle - Douglas, and Dumbarton were added to the list. By these means the bank
laid its foundations broadly and securely in such a manner
that any temporary pressure upon one point might be
relieved by the support given at another. By its branch
system the British Linen Company attained a circulation
of its notes unknown to any of the other banks, a position
which in 1845 gave it the advantage of having the largest

Edinr 6th Septr 1754   No 1446

4356 00

The British Linnen Comy Promise

to pay to William Fell or Bearer, on demand.

TWENTY SHILLINGS Sterling: Value

Received in Goods.

By Order of

the Court of

Directors.

Walter Hog for the Manager

authorised circulation of any bank in Scotland, at which time one pound notes formed 73 per cent. of the entire issues of over £3,000,000.

At first the British Linen Company did no banking business, and to this may be ascribed their comparative immunity from the assaults of their two older neighbours; but gradually, as their mercantile affairs extended through the country, the want of any agency whereby money could be readily paid or remitted, compelled them to do a little banking for themselves ; bills were discounted, drafts or bills of exchange granted, and in 1747 their first notes were issued, of £5, £10, and £20, payable on demand ; and for £100, bearing interest at 3½ and 4 per cent. These were not issued by way of banking accommodation, as in the case of a cash credit,—their first notes as bankers not being issued till about 1750,—but were handed out in payment of goods received, and as such they were readily taken by the public, and as promptly retired by the Royal Bank, with whom the British Linen Company kept its account.* The Bank of Scotland at first made some objection to receiving these notes, asking the Royal Bank if they guaranteed payment of them, but were at once told that those who took them did so at their own risk. A dispute also arose with reference to the notes, very similar to that raised by the Bank of Scotland in 1726, before the terms of the Royal Bank's charter were known, regarding the powers of that bank to have an issue. The British Linen Company were authorised by their charter " to borrow money at interest," but were not specially allowed to " issue notes," which, it was asserted, was a means of borrowing money *not at interest*. In both cases, however, the right at common law would have overridden any negative conclusion drawn from possible omissions in the charters; and, in addition, the British Linen Company maintained their ground under cover of the clause permitting them to " do anything that may conduce to the promoting and carrying on the linen manufacture."

---

* A facsimile of one of these notes is given opposite.

During the twenty years 1740 to 1760 a number of forgeries occurred in the United Kingdom, none of them of good execution or importance historically, except one in 1758, when, for the first time, a Bank of England note was dealt with. In their varied operations, as we shall see, forgers generally confined themselves to notes of the smallest denomination current; in this case it was a £20 note, the smallest then in use. The forger, a linen-draper in Sheffield named Vaughan, was found guilty and executed; the unfortunate man having fallen into the snare through his attachment to a young lady of Sheffield, to whom he wished to appear as a man of wealth. The more merciful law of Scotland, in 1764, condemned a man named James Baillie, a Dundee schoolmaster, to stand in the pillory for a day, having a label on his back bearing the words " Infamous Forger," and thereafter to be transported to America, " never to return."

The year 1758 may also be remembered as that in which the first legal decision was given as to the ability to follow and claim a note that has been stolen. A mail-coach having been attacked in England, a number of notes were stolen and put into circulation. The loser subsequently sued a *bonâ fide* holder for the amounts of some, whose numbers and dates he had. Lord Mansfield decided that bank notes were of the nature of coin, and could not therefore be followed by the party losing, while the onerous *bonâ fide* holder was entitled to demand payment from the bank.

Another event happened on 24th March of the same year, when the Royal Bank issued the first Scotch notes for one guinea, the reason assigned for this singular denomination being, that the scarcity of silver rendered such a means of giving change a necessity; and accordingly they were put up in packets of nineteen,—such a packet, with one shilling added, making exactly £20. They ran as follows :—

> " THE ROYAL BANK OF SCOTLAND (pursuant to Act of Parliament, and Letters Patent under the Great Seal) is hereby obliged to pay to *David Baillie, Secretary*, or the Bearer on Demand, One Pound One Shilling."

The words in parenthesis appearing for the first time in their notes, occasioned a little hesitation in their reception amongst the commonalty, which however soon passed away. These notes were only issued during the year 1758, no more being put out until May 1768, when both the Royal and the Bank of Scotland stopped their issue of one pound notes entirely, and replaced them with guinea notes. In a short time the British Linen Company and many of the other banks adopted the same course, so that the one pound note was left solely in the hands of the provincial bankers, who certainly made the most of the opportunity thus given them. From statistics of the Dundee Banking Company,* given in the following chapter, it will be seen that almost the whole circulation of that bank consisted of one pound notes.

Allowing that the Dundee bank's issue of small notes was abnormally large, we have still ample ground for assuming that the proportion of one pound notes, or guinea notes, circulating in Scotland at this time, must have been little short of 80 per cent. of the whole circulation,—a much larger percentage than at present, when it is only about 69 per cent.

A considerable exchange business was done in Edinburgh during the years of the inconvertible note issue (*Scots Magazine*, 1770), by bankers and merchants exchanging the notes of the country banks at 1d. per 20s. note ; as the issues increased, and people became more anxious to get rid of their "dead money," the brokers advanced the rate to 1½d. per 20s. note, equal to 12s. 6d. per cent. In 1766 small houses made quite a harvest, even at the lower rate of 1d. per 20s. note. Larger amounts were exchanged at 5s. per cent. for Glasgow notes, and 7s. 6d. per cent. for those of Perth and Dundee.

On the approach of the years of the small note nuisance, with its attendant high rates of exchange, the respectable banks, and such companies as the British Linen Company,

---

* Boase's "History of Banking in Dundee."

were fully alive to the danger ahead. The note issues in
previous years had been run out to an excessive amount.
Making the mistake of supposing that printed notes lying
in their own tills formed an asset, and ignoring the addition
made to their liabilities by their issue, bankers continued to
discount bills and make advances of their notes to any
extent that the public asked for,—regardless of any proportion of capital, or reserve to floating liabilities (which
were not recognised as liabilities),—no application for an
advance being refused until the vessel was perilously near
the rocks.

About 1751 the two senior joint-stock banks had their
attention forced to the danger of the extensive notes issues,
partly by the serious expense occasioned by the high rates
of exchange on London ; and beginning at once to restrict
their own issues somewhat forcibly, by declining to discount
or give cash credits, they rather increased the distress by
the sudden withdrawal of their paper ; and as gold was not
to be had, the small note nuisance was more helped than
hindered. To carry out this economy in their notes, they
established, as was mentioned before, the first amicable
system of note exchanges. Excellent as were the intentions
and results in later years, the plan was somewhat in advance
of the age, and was not so universally agreeable to other
bankers as could have been wished. Indeed, the determination of the two banks to compel their neighbours to take up
their surplus paper, had no other effect for the time than to
create a determined opposition to their efforts, and cause a
cry from the private bankers as to the jealousy and
pusillanimity of the large joint-stocks ; but as such cries
were generally loudest when some unreasonable request had
been refused, we need not consider them to be of much
historical value.

In 1761 and 1762 cash credits were still further temporarily restricted by one-fourth of the amount, and by the
banks declining to allow private bankers and other firms to
draw out funds in the morning to be re-deposited the same
day. In 1763, from the same apparent distrust of the

mercantile element, two important Edinburgh banking houses ceased to have any connection with mercantile or trading operations. This was the more remarkable, as of the twenty Edinburgh private banking firms only some two or three confined themselves solely to banking, all the others dealing in corn, tobacco, or other merchandise. The two houses were those of Sir William Forbes, James Hunter, & Co., and the British Linen Company. The former, taking advantage of a change of copartnery, resolved, from and after 1st February 1763, "that the house at Edinburgh should totally abstain from dealing in corn, or any other species of merchandise ; confining themselves solely to their regular business of receiving money on deposit, granting cash accounts, discounting bills, and dealing in exchanges on London, Holland, and France,—a resolution to the adherence to which the great prosperity of the house may— under heaven—be mainly attributed." * On several occasions the firm transgressed their rule, and were invariably punished by the heavy losses which ensued.

The same prudent course was followed by the British Linen Company, from the slightly different reason that it "would be of more utility, and better promote the objects of their institution, by enlarging the issue of their notes to traders and manufacturers, than by being traders and manufacturers themselves." Their subsequent history shewed that the "enlarging the issue of their notes" had not been abused, however sinister such a statement then appeared.

Partly owing to these restrictions, and partly from the natural increase of the country, a number of provincial banks came into existence. The Thistle Bank of Glasgow started in 1761, and is now merged in the Union Bank of Scotland ; 1762 saw the beginning of David Watson & Co., as 1832 saw the winding up ; the Dundee Banking Company, afterwards bought up by the Royal Bank ; and John Macadam & Co., of Ayr, purchased in 1771 by Douglas, Heron, & Co.,

---

* Sir William Forbes' " Memoirs of a Banking House."

both opened in 1763. The six mushroom banks of Perth
united in 1766 into the substantial Perth United Banking
Company, afterwards the Perth Banking Company of 1788,
continuing the premier bank in the Fair City until 1843,
when the Union Bank took it over. In the same year
Johnston & Lawson, of Dumfries, commenced the business
which aided so materially to ruin Douglas, Heron, & Co.
The year 1767 witnessed the successful establishment of the
Banking Company of Aberdeen, for eighty-seven years a
highly profitable and independent bank; it joined the
Union Bank in 1854. And, last of all, the grand fiasco of
Douglas, Heron, & Co. came upon the scene in 1769.

Chapter VII.—1769-1772.

DOUGLAS, HERON, & CO.—THE NOTE EXCHANGES, AND RESULTS OF THE ACT OF 1765.

"Get wealth and power, if possible, with grace;
If not, by any means get wealth and place."—POPE.

THE Act of 1765 had only "scotched the snake, not killed it;" the latter event was reserved for 1772. During the decade 1760–1770, the two large banks, knowing the mischief that was being worked in London, determined to do their duty by keeping it, if possible, out of Scotland, and steadily refused to issue their notes to a greater extent than they clearly saw their way to retire. The Royal Bank went the length of withdrawing the cash credit of the British Linen Company in 1766; both banks refusing British Linen Company notes for five years, until 1771, when, it is to be presumed, the British Linen Company proved its good standing. Being also seriously engaged in somewhat expensive methods of reducing the exchanges on London (a matter which called for restriction of paper money *), the banks gave no ear to the vehement outcry of the speculative crew that swarmed and surged round their doors. These virtuous characters were hugely indignant that their loud-tongued complaints were not listened to; and as month after month of the same reserved policy on the part of the banks passed by, without sign of change, their wrath waxed hotter and hotter. "Their own distress,"—for they were in distress, but through their own extravagance,—

---

* "A note of either of the banking companies, established by authority, is a *rara avis in terris*, seldom to be met with but in the bankers' shops in the town of Edinburgh."—*Scots Mag.*, 1770.

" of which this prudent and necessary reserve of the banks was no doubt the immediate occasion, they called the distress of the country ; and this distress of the country, they said, was altogether owing to the ignorance, pusillanimity, and bad faith of the banks, which did not give a sufficiently liberal aid to the spirited undertakings of those who exerted themselves to beautify, improve, and enrich the country."

Adam Smith's scathing words are not too strong to describe the covetous crowd who reaped their harvest of sorrow in 1772. Not content with already possessing considerable wealth, the well-to-do classes began to wish for an increase in their capital at a rate much greater than the fair trade of the nation could supply. Speculations in land, both at home and abroad ; the wish for improvements in agriculture to remedy a bad harvest ; bogus companies in London ; speculation in the government funds ; anything or everything, engaged the minds of the Scots capitalists, as well as those of people who wished to be capitalists with other men's money. "At the same time, those projectors and improvers, flattering themselves with the prospect of the immediate advantage to be derived from their speculations, launched out into a style of living up to their expected profits, as if they had already realised them."* The delusion that, because they were spending money freely, they must necessarily be wealthy, speedily forced many to have recourse to the ruinous circles of bills on London as a means of raising money. These the banks flatly refused to discount ; and thus thrown back upon their own resources, the spendthrifts projected the Ayr Bank of Douglas, Heron, & Co. This "crude panacea" at once relieved them of all their bills,—lending out its credit in *notes* to every one who came to it with a bill in his hand. The proprietors of the company were specially favoured with accommodation, none being sent away empty. The old delusion of printed notes—mere "till money"—being an asset, came again into

---

* Sir William Forbes' "Memoirs of a Banking House."

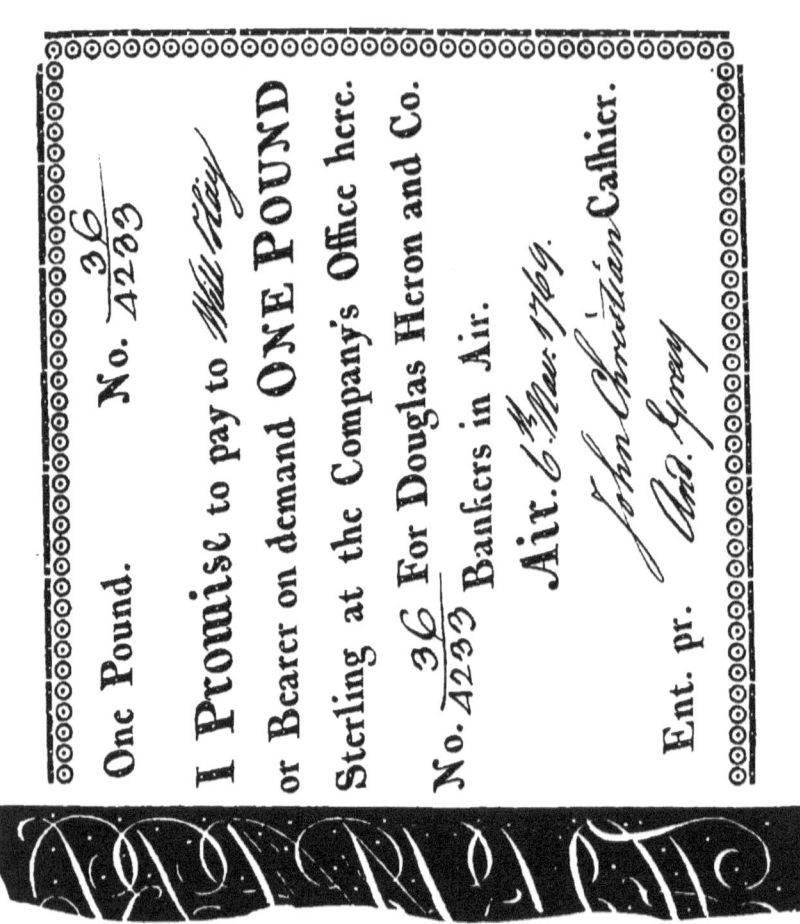

One Pound.　　No. 36⁄4233

I Promise to pay to *Will Hay*
or Bearer on demand ONE POUND
Sterling at the Company's Office here.

No. 36⁄4233 For Douglas Heron and Co.
Bankers in Air.

Air. 6ᵗʰ Mar. 1769.

John Christian Cashier.

Ent. pr. *Geo. Gray*

full swing, *for the last time* in Scotland. When their deposits were exhausted, the bank simply printed more notes, literally *made money*, as they had promised to do, and issued it with amazing generosity on all sides. Their first notes bore the date of "Air, 6 Nov. 1769," and, according to an advertisement then published in the newspapers, were at first of the value of £1, £5, and £10, while a number for one guinea were promised in a short time. Their 20s notes ran as in copy annexed. In a few months the notes issued greatly exceeded £250,000, while their discounts and advances ranged beyond £1,000,000, of which the proprietors had got £400,000. This reckless folly could not last long, and the day of reckoning came soon.

After their plucky but unsuccessful efforts in 1756 and 1761 to broaden the system of note exchanges they had arranged for themselves in 1752, the Edinburgh banks refused to have any connection with provincial note issues ; their reason being, that from the absence of any means for legally enforcing payment they formed no proper security to the holder, and were therefore only a danger. Seeing no way out of the difficulty, the Bank of Scotland and Royal Bank had no other remedy than to wait the course of events, and strictly guard their own issues, which, being always convertible, were eagerly pounced upon by the country banks, and used to demand gold. In this manner ten years of conflict and confusion passed by, the banks all the while being blamed for their niggardly advances until at last the Act of 1765 gave the thorough remedy that was required. The banks appear to have given the Act some years to clear away the litter of notes left by 1763, but in 1770 the Bank of Scotland had the credit of re-establishing the exchanges, by advertising that on and after 20th May of that year it would pay the notes of Douglas, Heron, & Co., the British Linen Company, Johnston & Lawson of Dumfries, the Perth United Company ; having three days previously given notice that it would pay those of the three Glasgow banks,—The Ship, The Arms, and The Thistle. Up to this time, from 1756, they had refused to receive in payment any notes except their own, or those of the Royal Bank. This healthy action at once cleared the Edinburgh market of a large quantity of inconvertible paper, which had circulated there for years.

Not content with taking up the notes of the banks mentioned, the Bank of Scotland seems to have worked most resolutely to enforce retirement of their notes by the other banks throughout Scotland. In 1771 they compelled the Dundee Banking Company to pay £5400 of its notes in gold (91 per cent. of them £1 notes), and at the same time made demands on the Perth United Company. This action excited so much bad feeling in both of those banks, that the Dundee bank arranged to send £5000 Bank of Scotland notes to Edinburgh and demand gold in retaliation. A few months afterwards the Dundee bank had again to pay £9500 in specie to the Bank of Scotland, for its notes retired by that bank. The scare of 1772 had fortunately compelled them to lay in a larger stock of gold than usual, otherwise they might have been as unable to meet the bank's demands as was the Perth United Company, who had to borrow £1000 in gold from their Dundee friends to enable them to meet their engagements. Under this healthy system of exchanges the notes of the Ayr bank came in against them with merciless regularity, and had to be paid in gold, or gold's worth, Edinburgh notes, or London drafts. At all times expensive, the cost of these drafts now became destructive ; to add to their distress, the London agents, Dimsdale & Co., refused to go further, and thus reduced to desperation, the Ayr bank's agents ran over the south of Scotland hurriedly collecting gold, or other banks' notes, from any one who was simple enough to take their notes in exchange.

All was of no avail. On Friday evening, 12th June 1772 (the unlucky day of the week), a horseman from the south galloped into Edinburgh with news of the panic in London, and of the failure of Neale, James, Fordyce, & Downe, with a long list of kindred firms. The paper companies of Scotland heard his tidings with despair. In a few days the information spread in all directions, and a furious run was made upon the banks. On the 15th, Fordyce, Malcolm, & Co. stopped, to be followed next day by Arbuthnot & Guthrie ; on the 24th, Wm. Alexander Sons, with several other firms, joined their bankrupt brethren, But the greatest of all was to come. Douglas, Heron, & Co. do not seem at first to have been objects of public suspicion, until a story being set afloat that their bills had been refused by the London bankers, "the common people ran in crowds to draw specie for their notes, and on Tuesday evening the following advertisement was handed about in Edinburgh, 'Bank Office, Canongate, June 16, 1772.— Whereas, the Branch of Douglas, Heron, & Co. have for these two days past, had an immense demand for specie from the lower class of people in exchange for notes,'" owing, it was said, to some evil-minded persons having raised sinister rumours regarding them, therefore Douglas, Heron, & Co. would pay £100 as a reward to any one who would give information as to the inventor of this pernicious report (*Scots Magazine, 1772*). The expense of this advertisement might have been spared; no doubt it had its small share in hastening the closing scene.

The Bank of England held £150,000 of the bank's paper,—one writer says notes, but this must surely be incorrect, as Scotch notes could not travel to London in such volume. As all further aid was refused from that quarter, the Ayr bank was compelled to shut its doors, and on 26th June it issued the following circular :—" AIR, *June 25th*, 1772.—The Company of Douglas, Heron, & Co., Bankers in Air, taking into their consideration the present state of the credit of the country, and the uncommon demands that have been made upon them for specie, owing to causes sufficiently well known, have come to the conclusion to give over for some time paying specie for their notes. But as the country, who have received the most liberal aids from this Company cannot entertain the smallest doubt of the solidity of its foundation, it is hoped that on occasion of a national emergency of this kind, the holders of their notes will not be under any alarm ; and in order to give full satisfaction to the public, they hereby declare, That they will pay five per cent. interest for such of their notes as remain in the circle, until paid, after 26th June current.—JOHN CHRISTIAN, *Cashier.*" "John Christian, Cashier!" How could the man sign such a name to such a paper? The time was past for any endeavour to conceal their disastrous failure under verbosity as false as it was pompous ; the Air bank was down irrecoverably. At the time of the stoppage the liabilities to the public amounted to £1,120,000, made up of £300,000 deposits, £220,000 note circulation, £600,000 drafts on London outstanding. These figures do not indicate the amount of the note issue during the few bright days of the company, when it must have been much larger, as latterly it had been reduced through being returned to the bank by the medium of the exchange, and the inability of the public to absorb it. As *notes* were paid off, the *drafts on London* had to be correspondingly increased plus charges to meet them. The total loss to the partners, 225 in number, was £663,396. 18s. 6d. ; their Graces the Dukes of Buccleuch and Queensberry, with some other wealthy shareholders, having the privilege of burdening their estates with redeemable annuities to the extent of £457,570.

In September following the bank again tried to face its creditors, and re-opened its offices, advertising the notes payable in gold, at Ayr only, and relieving holders of large notes by exchanging them for £1 notes. Again help was vainly besought to carry them through ; but the Edinburgh banks had already enough of their notes (the Royal having taken up £65,000), and would have no more ; while the Bank of England was equally unaccommodating, receiving in reward the hearty execration of the "embarassed bank and its friends, without a word of acknowledgment of the great sins of the embarassed bank itself." Thus they tottered on until 12th August 1773, when they went into voluntary liquidation, "leaving an amount of destitution

in their wake such as Scotland had not experienced since
the wreck of the Darien expedition. It is said that a large
proportion of the land of the county of Ayr changed hands
in consequence. For the remainder of their lives its shareholders were never done with paying." * On the previous
day the Bank of Scotland and Royal Bank had advertised
that *they* would pay all notes of the bankrupt firm,—the
wise precedent of the policy of 1857-78.

The panic acted with intense force in Edinburgh,
sweeping down every private banker, except Sir William
Forbes & Co., Mansfield, Hunter, & Co., and William
Cumming & Sons, besides ruining many merchants and
traders. Sir William Forbes records, that a "smart run" was
made on all the Edinburgh banks on the Monday following
Black Friday. His own office must have escaped easily, as
it appears that the run subsided on the Tuesday,—which can
be easily accounted for, as it was well known that he was
entirely outside of the circulating bills that weakened his
contemporaries, and, further, he did not at that time issue
notes of his own house. Glasgow suffered very little
compared with Edinburgh, which is somewhat strange,
considering both its speculative tendencies, and its geographical connection with the scene of the Ayr bank's
operations. It would appear that the Glasgow merchants
were engaged in a rising and profitable trade of a *substantial*
character, and not being attracted by the schemes of the
idle capitalists of the east, escaped being drawn into the
vortex of the circle bills. From Mr Boase's " Century of
Banking in Dundee," we note the following, which shews
that his bank had been run upon very severely, and
narrowly escaped a collapse :—

	Circulation.			Specie.		
1772. Mar. 16,	£47,330	0	0	£17,729	0	0
April 6,	37,779	0	0	11,050	0	0
June 15,	33,828	0	0	10,967	0	0
Oct. 19,	15,920	0	0	6,132	0	0
Nov. 7,	16,164	0	0	4,034	0	0
„ 21,	18,812	0	0	3,881	0	0
Dec. 5,	19,544	0	0	5,135	0	0
1773. Jan. 30,	19,015	0	0	3,847	0	0

* R. Chambers.

It is obvious that an institution conducted upon such principles as that of Douglas, Heron, & Co. could have no hope of maintaining itself beyond a very limited number of years, even if all circumstances were favourable to its existence. Had it come into the world twenty years earlier, it would certainly have had a better chance of postponing the evil day for a time ; but in 1770-72 there were two remorseless automatic agencies at work, of whose existence Douglas, Heron, & Co. scarcely seem to have been aware,— these were the Act of 1765, and the note exchange system. Both proved their thorough efficiency during the years of the Ayr bank's life. In spite of the most strenuous exertions on the part of the bank to keep out their issues of notes, the clean sweeping exchanges rapidly collected from the public their superfluous paper, and returned it against them. Here the Act stepped in to do its part with its trenchant remedy. Prior to 1765, what delays, what mean subterfuges were not resorted to, in order to delay payments, which it was not in the power of the bankers to make, and to postpone them even beyond the limits of the option clause! With Douglas, Heron, & Co. all this was impossible. ' Notes payable on demand, failing which, summary execution," was an enactment too simple to be misunderstood, too comprehensive to be evaded ; they had nothing before them but the stern alternative, " Pay, or stop." It is true that the London crisis was the *immediate* cause of the run which brought them down ; but let us consider how the Ayr bank's notes affected the London market. The vast proportion of the advances, whether in bills or credit accounts, or mere overdrafts, had been paid out in *notes ;* for when the bank failed, there were only £300,000 of deposits, against debts due to the bank of £1,200,000. If the Bank of Scotland had at present an issue of notes bearing the same proportion to its paid-up capital, its circulation, instead of being about £800,000, would amount to £2,600,000 ; the same calculation applied to the respective deposits would give the Bank of Scotland a note issue of £8,000,000. Such an amount of paper (even though it were convertible) could not be utilised by the people ; and, as with Douglas, Heron, & Co., a large proportion would find its way back at once against the Bank of Scotland. In the same way the Ayr bank had their surplus paper to meet, but, unfortunately for them, they had not wherewithal to meet it. Public confidence was entirely on their side, and for a time they were enabled to clear their way by drafts on London, of which they had no way of paying even the charges for renewal from time to time as they fell due. As it so happened, the reservoir of the world's commerce (the London market) was already well filled with similar paper, and the Ayr bank's contribution caused it to run over. The immediate result of this stoppage in the discount of accommodation bills was the failure of Neale & Fordyce ; the public confidence was broken, and the rest is already known to the reader. The whole forms a complete circle. Speculators wished advances, which were made by unsecured notes. The latter, however, required payment; and as there was no gold, settlement had to be made in London bills. These no one would discount or retire ; and, as the result, panic arose in London, spreading to Edinburgh, and concluding with failure of the Ayr bank and ruin of the speculators.

Another important result of the Act of 1765 may be traced in the lesson taught by the failure of the Ayr bank. The original copartnery of that bank bore the names of 136 partners, amongst whom were to be found dukes, earls, landed gentry, lawyers, merchants, shopkeepers, tradesmen, but not a solitary banker. In a word, the bank was begun and managed by men who professed to know more of the business of a banker than those who had been trained to that profession. Devoid of necessary caution or prudence, inflated with the importance of unsound theories, their inexperience led them to neglect the commonest precautions, of which the hardly-earned experience of other banks had made them only too well aware. In their desire for an increase of capital, by "leaps and bounds," they paid no attention to the average rate at which it had increased in the past, nor to its possible limits in their own time.   As in 1874, so in 1771, prices were exorbitant, while the exports had never been so high.   The crash came quicker a hundred years ago than in 1874 ; a greater amount of confidence on the part of the public, and fraud on the part of the City of Glasgow Bank, combining at once to prolong its career, and aggravate the distress when at last it was made public.

In both banks, however, the speculative mercantile element was the cause of the ruin, and it is interesting to note how thoroughly that class took the lesson of 1772 to heart.   In the fall of the Ayr bank, nearly the whole system of private banking merchants was dragged down ; and from this period we find that private bankers* (nor indeed joint-stock banks for nearly sixty years, to any extent) did not meddle with merchandise, while the mercantile classes as rigidly abstained from intruding into banking.   A lively remembrance of the disasters of the Ayr bank was probably the direct cause of this change ; but the firm basis upon which the *note exchanges were put by the Act* of 1765, was undoubtedly the original though unseen cause.

The Act had been passed, and the provisions as to notes of less than £1 came of necessity at once into force ; but the effect of the summary execution clause, in combination with a system of note exchanges, *was not for the time realised.* Indeed, judging from present experience, it is probable that the proportion of mercantile men were ignorant of its pro-visions ; for no case having been raised in Court to excite and attract public attention to the danger, they dealt with their note issues according to the old and lax tradition, until the blow fell, and they were unable to tell from whence it came, or why !   Nothing else can account for the evi-dently honest indignation of the shareholders at not receiv-ing assistance from the other banks.   They were so grossly ignorant of banking principles, that they did not know that they had erred, much less how ; for, as their circular shews, they attributed their failure to a national distress of

---

* Except Maberley & Co., who failed.

some kind, for which they could not be held responsible. Notwithstanding all their protestations of virtue (at best decidedly foolish, if sincere), the penalty had to be paid, and while they might be ignorant of the principal instrument of their punishment, neither they nor their descendants forgot the punishment itself.

Speaking generally, this was the last great effort in Scotland of the fallacy *that notes in the banker's till are money*,—that printed paper is as good as gold, and could be freely treated as an asset, without at all considering it as a liability. The real theory of the matter may not have been profoundly established, but the experimental stage had passed, and gradually the writings of Adam Smith, the Act of 1765, and the recollection of the Ayr bank, from this period onward, in so far as they proved that bank notes were dangerous weapons in unskilful hands, each did their part in placing Scottish banking on a firmer and more honourable foundation.

Viewed in its connection with the train of events just narrated,—such as the note exchange system of 1752, the British Linen Company new branches, the stoppage of the option clause, and the enactment of summary diligence in 1765,—the one pound note appears to have been in a *transition state during these thirteen years*, emerging in a capacity wholly distinct from that which it occupied at their commencement, but a capacity which, nevertheless, rightly understood, strikingly indicates the increased wealth and prosperity of the country. So deep had been the poverty of Scotland during the first half of the century, and so small the amount of accumulated wealth, that even their proverbial honesty could scarcely have ameliorated the condition of our ancestors, had the note issue not stepped in to occupy the place of *capital*. Blind and ignorant as they may have been to the modern philosophy of paper money, the Scotsmen of last century keenly appreciated the opportunities which Providence placed in their way. Their credits and their notes were to them capital, not currency merely, but capital with which they could buy and sell and realise a profit on their transactions. Conveniently enough, notes did serve as a currency, but their primary nature, in the opinion of last century, was that of capital. In our economic times it appears a mere till-money delusion; but prior to 1750, before the dire necessity for such an expedient had passed away, it was no delusion, but a most powerful and practical medium for the production of wealth. As this became evident to the general public, the invariable riot of excess occurred in the paper money, leading to the stringent action of the old banks, and, subsequently, to the legislation of 1765; so that when Douglas, Heron, & Co. began business, it was discovered that the necessity for a note capital had disappeared, in consequence of the country's new found riches, which *now* formed its capital, and only required the aid of the notes for its *transmission and distribution*. In short, from 1700 to 1750, the note issue was primarily capital to the nation, while it also served as a currency; and from 1760 onwards its proper function was that of *currency*, so far as the public were concerned,—for, as will be seen, it was, and ever has been, equal to capital to the banks.

In the absence of statistics it is impossible to prove with certainty another effect of this transition in the position of the note; but from the activity displayed by many of the banks subsequent to 1765 or 1770, it is evident that some unseen causes drove them more completely into a channel of business, which hitherto they had not taken advantage of. Up to this time the profits of banking had been largely made up of interest on the circulation of notes. The return on partners' capital was never large, for the excellent reason that the capital was invariably small, only a few of the larger banks having much to boast of. These two items, and speculative profits, produced the dividend; for deposits during the first sixty years of their existence were scarcely reckoned worth the trouble of collecting, inasmuch as interest had to be paid to the depositors, leaving only a *margin* of profit in the bankers' hands, whereas with a good note trade the *whole profit* was retained. With the transition from capital to currency, this one-sided system of banking came to an end ; and it would be interesting to ascertain the fluctuation in profits which must have arisen between 1760 and 1780, when bankers saw their note circulation going out of demand, or shrinking in the action of the note exchanges. There can be little doubt that such fluctuation did exist, and that it was one of many causes which led bankers to increase their facilities, by opening branches and taking in more deposits, for the purpose of recouping themselves for the loss of the *note capital trade*, by working upon a still greater fund than they had hitherto had any experience of.

In the succeeding chapters an account will be found of this new departure in banking ; and it is worthy of notice how, for a time at least, the banks hardly perceived the opening made for them, but endeavoured rather to meet the changed condition of affairs by an increase in their partners' capital, until the lapse of years gradually revealed to them the extraordinary capacity of the *branch* and *deposit* systems.

Chapter VIII.—1773-1793.

NEW POLICY OF CHARTERED BANKS—JOINT-STOCK BANKS.

" The endurance of human institutions is dependent upon their close imitation of the works of Nature, whose plans are ever free, yet deeply laid and strong."—The Pyramids of Gizeh.

THE nine years between 1774 and 1783 were years of continued conflict to the British Empire. The Independence of America; wars with France, Spain, and Holland; tumult and rebellion in Ireland; and the partial conquest of India,—had all to be fought out, with their varied results of defeat, victory, and accumulation of debt.

At no previous time had England so well displayed her tremendous vitality and resource. Driven out of her magnificent heritage in North America by the folly of her statesmen and the imbecility of her generals, she accepted the inevitable with surprising equanimity, and after sweeping her Continental rivals from the seas, turned with resistless energy to Hindustan for new glories and responsibilities.

Notwithstanding her engagements in these gigantic movements, Britain was little affected by them internally; secure within her shores from foreign invasion (though not from its dread), she experienced none of the suffering and misery which war inevitably brings upon the scene of its action. In comparison with the first half of the century, Scotland enjoyed even greater tranquillity than England. The genius of the elder Pitt had found an outlet for the warlike spirits of the north in the formation of the Highland regiments, and in this way a population, which had been at variance with the more settled parts of the country for centuries, found congenial employment in other lands, leaving their native country in a condition of political quiet it had never before witnessed. When after the lapse of years the survivors of the Highland brigade returned to their mountains and glens, it was no longer to live as mere freebooters and disturbers of the Sassenach. Local antipathies had disappeared; *omne solum patria est*,—the world had been the scene of their hardships and of their conflicts, not less wide was the field of their sympathy and glory. Wherever *Britain's* battle had been fought, whether amid the snows and forests of America or under the burning sun of India, their comrades lay silent but not forgotten. Thus in the remembrance of these mightier struggles of the Empire, clan disputes melted away, and the once restless reivers of the Highlands were converted from their petty strifes and Jacobite sympathies to their rightful place in the history of Great Britain. A north of England proverb says that " a Scotsman and a Newcastle grindstone may be found all over the world." What was originally said of the Lowland Scot has since become as true of the Highlander ; the keen perception and vigorous action of the Celt have fitted him to adorn every position in life. By this change in her national life Scotland was materially benefited ; for though the process was both rough and costly, yet in the end it helped to achieve the unity of Celt and Saxon, who, without losing their individuality, were at last welded into one nation, and prepared to embark on the advancing tide of improvement which distinguished the latter half of the eighteenth century.

Naturally Scotland was less directly connected with these wars than England, in whose cause they were fought, the north country being left to pursue her own ways in a quiet back-eddy out of the whirl of imperial politics. Of this quietness one of the Edinburgh banks was not slow to avail itself. Taking advantage of the clearance effected by the crisis of 1772, the Bank of Scotland determined to take up her position as the leader of Scottish finance, and thereby fill up, if possible, the blanks caused by the failure of so many bankers. The double purpose would be served, of giving the benefit of their extended credit, and at the same time preventing the establishment of these insecure firms which had sprung up from the necessities of particular localities.

The increased responsibility they were fortunately quite able to face. The exchange on London in December 1773 had not been so near par for fifteen years, the rate for bills at sight being only ¾ per cent. 1772 had not found the big banks asleep ; they were prepared with considerable stocks of gold to meet the crash which they saw must inevitably come, their demands upon the country banks for exchanges of notes having doubtless greatly increased their specie reserves. Whenever Douglas, Heron, & Co. were off the scene, gold became more plentiful, old defaced coin being bought by the Bank of Scotland at £3. 16s. 6d. per oz., and sold by them in London at £3. 17s. 10½d., leaving a very fair profit after paying expenses of transit. The Dundee Banking Company alone had collected £16,477 of specie to meet possible demands, although their usual stock had seldom been over £2000 since they recovered from the scare of 1765, when they had thought it prudent to purchase £9000.

The opportunity was one not to be missed, and accordingly the old bank again led the way by increasing their capital from £100,000 to £200,000 ; and a few months later, taught by the British Linen Company, they opened branches in Dumfries and Kelso. In the following year, 1775, Ayr and Inverness were chosen, and some years later Stirling, Aberdeen, Dunfermline, Haddington, Perth, and Kirkcaldy. At the same time they took the entirely novel step of publishing a " Quarterly and Annual State of Conduct."

By these means deposits accumulated in such increased volume, that the bank made public announcement that loans would be made on heritable property. Had any agreement been come to with the Royal Bank, so that the same wise policy of extension might have been adopted by them in conjunction with the British Linen Company, it would have had a marked effect in reducing the number of new banks which, attracted by the strides that were being made in the spinning and weaving industries, came into existence in the following ten years. But seven firms in Edinburgh and four in the provinces had all begun, and were issuing their notes, good or bad, as events shewed, before the Royal Bank made any movement to adapt itself to the wants of the time. The provincial banks referred to were those of Hunter & Co. at Ayr, successfully launched in 1773 by the former cashier of Douglas, Heron, & Co.; the Stirling Banking Company, in 1777; the Commercial Bank of Aberdeen, in 1778; and the Paisley Bank, in 1783.

In the latter year the Royal Bank increased its capital from the original £111,347. 19s. 10$\frac{5}{12}$d. to £150,000; while in the following year, and also in 1780 and 1793, further additions were made, raising the total capital to £1,000,000, fully paid, of which £438,652 were entirely out of profits, —a proof that their limited area of operation had not affected their prosperity.

The first increase in 1783 was probably made to meet the *supposed* requirements of the Glasgow branch, which was opened in that year; and the doubling of the capital in the following year, to meet its *actual requirements*.

The race between the two banks to enlarge their capital is somewhat exciting, and appears as follows :—

	Bank of Scotland.	Royal Bank.
1773	£100,000	£111,347
1774	200,000	111,347
1783	200,000	150,000
1784	300,000	300,000
1786	300,000	600,000
1792	600,000	600,000
1793	600,000	1,000,000
1794	1,000,000	1,000,000 fully paid.

The capital of the old bank was not fully paid, which may be accounted for either by their doing a smaller Edinburgh business than their rival, or more probably by their having larger deposits and therefore not requiring so large a capital as the Royal Bank, whose Glasgow connection at

once involved it in considerable advances, from which it
suffered very heavily in 1813, 1814, 1815, and 1816, when its
note issue underwent such a collapse that during 1814 it
fell to one-fourth only of what it had been in 1810, or what
it subsequently rose to in 1820.   The Bank of Scotland did
not open in Glasgow until 1804, although the House of
Commons Report gives 1793· as the correct date.

Any hope of co-operation between the two senior banks
was completely destroyed by sundry pamphleteers, who,
with their bitter pens and false assertions, spread idle
rumours of the old bank's plots to obtain an influence in
the management of the Royal Bank by placing creatures of
its own at the board of direction ; the real fact being, that
the Royal Bank greatly wanted shaking up of any kind
that would throw off the private-banker directors who
controlled its affairs.

One paper in the Advocates' Library,—" Bank Disputes,
Edinburgh, 1778,"—after stating that £87,800 of the Royal
Bank stock had been transferred during two years up to
1778, insinuates that the old bank was the enemy who
desired to sow the tares in its neighbour's field.   Another
blow is struck at the Bank of Scotland regarding its new
stock, which, though issued at £83. 6s. 8d., rose in less than
a year to £125.   The whole pamphlet, from the intimate
knowledge of the Royal Bank's affairs, was evidently put
out by that bank as a *ballon d'essai*, with the view of injuring
the old bank and a certain private banking firm which had
offended the Royal ; from a printer's error regarding these
disputes it has been asserted that the latter made another
" run " on the Bank of Scotland, but there is absolutely no
proof of such an event taking place.*

The increased wealth and enterprise of the country was
not, however, to be guided or sustained by only three banks,
even with their new branches.   The peace of 1783 introduced a number of country joint-stock banks of a semi-
private nature, many of whom had very small partnerships.

---

* See " History of Banking in Scotland," by Mr A. W. Kerr, page 95.

The Merchant Bank of Stirling in 1784, the Greenock Banking Company of 1785, the Falkirk Banking Company of 1787, the Paisley Union Bank of 1788, the Dundee Commercial Bank and the Leith Bank of 1792, each greatly added to the note issues, and prepared the way for 1793 and 1797. The small note issues of these provincial banks were specially large, several of them ranging up to 90 per cent. of their whole circulation, while that of the Edinburgh banks was not over one-half.

The renewal of the semi-private banks, and their unwarrantable issues, does not seem to have been viewed with complacence in all quarters. One writer in the *Bee* of 1792, a valuable little weekly "intelligencer," referring to the note currency of "this critical period," says : "I call it critical, because the unlimited right of setting up private banks, their multiplicity, the obscure characters and doubtful credit of some of the bankers, afford a favourable opportunity for the directors of the chartered banks to offer themselves as doctors to this political malady." After presuming that the directors would simply recommend " amputation," and thus leave the country not merely with a bad leg, but with no leg at all, the author considers that " of all the evils that could befall Scotland, that of reverting again under the power of the chartered banks would be the worst." Allusion is no doubt here made to the constant friction which went on, in greater or less degree from 1780 to 1810, between the old banks and the new bankers ; and it was only when the old banks universally spread their wings over the provinces, that they recovered their ascendancy and removed the reproach which the writer in the *Bee* attaches to them. With considerable acuteness he foresees in a dim way the necessity for branches, or, at least, for provincial banks of a sound character, using the homely argument,— " In truth, bankers, like bakers, are not of great use unless *near the seats* of commerce. Edinburgh might as well pretend to issue loaves for all Scotland as bank notes. What benefit would an Aberdeen merchant derive from the Edinburgh banks, if he wanted a bill that had a short

time to run discounted on the spur of his business? Or
how could an Angus farmer procure credit for a few months,
for the purchase of cattle to eat his grass, or of lime to
improve it?" "The very expense of postages in correspondence with Edinburgh would consume half his profits,
beside the chance of him and his sureties being unknown at
such a distance."

The Bank of Scotland had only begun its office in
Aberdeen a few years prior to the publication of this article,
a fact of which the writer may not have been aware when
he chose that town as one of his examples. That he was
aware of *some branches* being opened is obvious, for a
little further on he accuses the old banks of going into the
provinces solely for the sake of cutting out the new
banks. "Suppress the other banks, and they will soon
shrink back into their own offices in Edinburgh," a predic-
tion which has certainly not proved to be correct. A new
profit was found in the branches, of which the small bankers
had little experience, for they do not appear to have
sought for it. In their neglect of the deposit system these
new provincial bankers were, somewhat after the fashion of
Murdoch & Co. in 1754, relying largely for profit on their
note issues. The Dundee bank gives an example of this.
They did not begin formally to accept deposits until 1792,
the same year in which the article in the *Bee* was penned,
a departure which they possibly learned from the British
Linen Company, who, as early as 1767, had an agent in
that town, Mr John Neilson, who discounted bills, retired
notes, and collected deposits. That the other country banks
were banks of issue but not of deposit is also shown by the
same writer, who does not see why the whole profits of the
note circulation should be confined to Edinburgh. In his
concluding remarks he draws a dismal picture of his country,
if, by any turn of affairs, it should ever be subjected to a
banking monopoly, and hopes "that our Parliament is too
faithful to its trusts to deliver a country into the merciless
paws of monopolists of any kind." Had he lived to see the
forty years following 1845, he might have known that even

the evils of a monopoly are mitigated by multiplying those who enjoy it.

There is a sad want of definite information as to this period,—abundance of pamphleteers with their generalisings and absurd theories, but few reliable facts. No Government returns existed in those happy days to harass the circulation clerk or delight the currency doctor ; all was darkness and mystery. Were it not for the "Memoirs of a Banking House" by Sir William Forbes, and Mr Boase's invaluable statistics of the Dundee Banking Company, there would be so little public information to trust to that we take the opportunity of echoing the Dundee banker's hope, "that the Bank of Scotland, the Royal Bank, and the British Linen Company, may some day be induced to have prepared and printed for general information a similar report of the amount of business they have annually transacted at their head office and at their several branches. When they do so they will confer a very great favour on the community, for they will supply a larger amount of information respecting the commercial progress of Scotland as a whole, and of its several districts, than any other parties are able to afford." Falling back, therefore, upon "A Century of Banking in Dundee," we shall give a few particulars as to banking in that city that may throw light upon the estimation in which one pound notes were then held, as well as upon the ideas the Dundee folks had at first as to the proportion of cash assets and capital to liability.

Occasion may afterwards be taken to refer to the causes affecting the note issues in the nineteenth century, but, briefly, the Dundee bank was principally affected by the bad condition into which it had been allowed to drift, and therefore, after 1810, does not exhibit facts which can be widely applied ; at the same time, the introduction of quicker communication, by means of railways and steamboats, gave a powerful impetus to the work of exchange by cheques and similar vouchers passed on deposit accounts, a process which prevented note issues from increasing in the same proportion as capital and population.

Statistics of Dundee Bank.

(Compiled from "A Century of Banking in Dundee," by Mr G. W. Boase.)

Year.	Capital.	Deposits.	Total Note Circulation.	Amount of One Pound Notes.	Per cent. of £1 to Total.	Gold, Silver, and Mixed Notes.
1764	£1,260	None.	£30,395	£22,066	73	£2,826
.5	1,260	"	33,803	26,072	78	2,808
6	3,480	"	34,503	28,526	82	4,257
7	5,220	"	31,980	31,196	91	9,911
8	5,655	£8,562	32,496	31,524	97	3,689
9	6,090	None.	33,524	32,091	95	3,783
1770	6,960	"	27,482	25,476	92	3,100
1	6,880	"	30,192	28,494	91	2,453
2	6,880	"	43,652	39,425	90	18,296
3	6,880	"	23,367	22,255	95	4,212
4	6,880	"	27,670	26,961	97	2,848
5	6,880	"	35,876	33,928	94	4,177
6	6,880	"	39,932	38,174	96	4,321
7	6,880	"	42,862	39,885	93	4,677
8	8,640	"	46,798	43,158	92	9,999
9	8,560	"	37,909	35,349	93	9,943
1780	8,560	"	40,346	37,241	92	7,798
5	10,700	"	55,416	59,927	92	8,395
1790	21,400	"	43,407	39,793	88	9,321
3	21,400	£55,769	70,288	62,213	88	9,938
4	31,637	48,810	50,254	45,339	90	13,608
5	31,637	73,514	69,064	61,724	88	8,359
1800	31,700	119,385	60,915	42,073	69	18,646
1810	35,725	337,204	58,473	47,555	81	11,273
1820	16,379	332,464	32,217	21,777	68	9,835
1830	25,200	419,580	26,316	17,050	65	4,121
1840	60,000	501,098	31,232	21,912	71	13,770

Remarks.

The amount of one pound notes was increased when the Act of 1765 came into force, smaller notes being then declared illegal. In that year there were £6000 of 5s. notes current.

Cash.—The actual specie included in this head was very high in 1772-1794 and 1797, all years of panic.

Large Notes.—Up to 1776 the notes above £1 only formed 2 or 3 per cent. of the whole circulation.

1793.—The sudden bound in the *notes* this year is remarkable, as deposits were first begun to be regularly received in 1792. Panic at close of year 1800. £5000 5s. *notes* reduced the average, showing how promptly the public would imitate America in its small note issues, were they allowed. Several of the averages after 1810 include guinea notes.

While deposits—capital and cash—were all increased, notes maintain surprising uniformity over 100 years. The highest circulation was in 1809, £84,968, consisting of—

5s. notes,	£6,325	11	0
£1 "	61,317	9	0
1. 1s. "	5,795	9	0
5 "	12,370	0	0
20 "	5,160	0	0
	£84,968	0	0

As showing the rapidity with which provincial bank paper found its way to the capital, it is mentioned that in the first eighteen months of the Dundee bank's existence £55,000 of the bank's notes were paid by their Edinburgh agent, Mr Fyffe, a sum which so distressed the bank to pay that in 1765 they refused to continue the retirements, apparently in the hope that they might still remain in circulation. The Act of the same year stopped this dream, as the notes were simply sent through to Dundee and presented there, and seeing that nothing was to be gained the bank again resumed its Edinburgh retirements in 1766. For many years thereafter a sum of notes, gradually increasing to three or four times the amount of the whole circulation, was yearly paid in Edinburgh alone.

The year 1778 was one of great scarcity of money, London bills standing at a high premium in consequence of dull trade and numerous bankruptcies. The distress had indeed begun in the previous year, a slight run having been made on Sir William Forbes, James Hunter, & Co.'s bank, owing to a loss they made with Mr Fall of Dunbar. The one pound note holders seem to have been the most panic-stricken, as the circulation of these notes fell nearly £6000, though the decrease was more than made up by the rise in large notes, caused no doubt by the wants of the mercantile classes, who felt severely the need of advances to carry them on.

1779 was little better for the Dundee bank, pressing wants compelling them to bring down specie from London by land, a very expensive means of transit. Hitherto the banks had used the Berwick smacks, insuring the cargo during the winter months only, and taking the risk from April to October in each year ; but the dangers of privateering now compelled them to abandon this comparatively cheap and speedy transit, and resort to the slow heavy waggon, at a cost of about 1 per cent. for silver, with ½ per cent. to the London agent for collecting it. Adding to this ½ per cent. over both metals for carriage, the total cost was £1. 8s. per cent. on a mixed remittance of silver and gold.

Gold alone usually cost from $\frac{1}{2}$ to $\frac{3}{4}$ per cent. for carriage;
but in times of scarcity, or under an adverse exchange,
a commission had also to be paid for its collection, the
bullion points in the exchanges of all countries being then
necessarily much wider apart than now, when telegrams
and cheap railways minimise time and outlay.

An important factor in the circulation of the country
came into existence on 1st January 1782, when Sir William
Forbes, James Hunter, & Co. issued their first notes. Had
all the bankers of Scotland imitated the example of this
wealthy house and established a sound business before
issuing their notes, the roll of failures would not have
reached its present length ; but adopting an issue of notes
as the quickest way of getting business by granting
advances, without having regard to the safest way, the
majority of banking houses had sprung up into huge
connections with the rapidity of Jonah's gourd, to wither
away with equal speed when touched by the heat of
adversity. Devoid of any firmer support than the circulation of their notes, these firms appear to have regarded
capital and reserves not so much as bulwarks of safety in
time of need, as unproductive consumers of profit in time
of success.

Sir William Forbes and his partners were induced to
take this step by the restrictions, and possibly the jealousy,
of the Royal Bank, who had begun to look upon private
bankers not only as rivals, but as an unsafe element in the
banking system of Scotland.   In this view they were
undoubtedly perfectly correct, for most of the private
bankers depended entirely upon the two banks in times of
trouble.   Unfortunately, in the case under notice, the Royal
Bank cannot have been fully aware of the resources of this
oldest of the private banks, for, in pursuance of their
decision, they intimated to Sir William Forbes that any
deposits he might in future have with them would have
to be at a much lower rate of interest, otherwise his account
would be closed on 1st July (a Sunday),—thinking, as Sir
William says, that he would have no resource but to comply

with their desires. "This measure, which we could not but regard as ungenerous on their part, led us to consider in what manner we might contrive to render ourselves independent of them altogether;" and after consultation on the matter, "we formed the bold resolution of issuing a few notes ourselves of the nature of bank-notes by way of experiment, for which we thought our credit and character in the world sufficiently established." It was resolved that no agent should be employed to push the notes, as was the custom of other bankers; but if any customer intimated a preference for notes of the joint-stock banks, he was to be at once accommodated with what he desired. Due notice was given of the intention to the Bank of Scotland and the Royal Bank, with intimation that the notes would be taken up once every week, or oftener, if desired. In regular course the banks replied, stating that they would receive the notes in payment, but would expect that exchanges would be made every day, which was at once agreed to.

After all this prudent forethought in the origin of the scheme, it is amusing to read that, falling into the error of the Royal Bank, they had dated their notes on Sunday, 1st July 1781, a circumstance that caused the good folks of Edinburgh to be "much tumbled up and down in their minds" over the matter. The old notes were called in and burnt, and a new plate engraved, dated 1st March 1782, the new notes being handed out to the cashier on the 5th of the same month.

At first only guinea and five-pound notes were issued, the first amount printed of the smaller note being about £55,000, while between 1782 and 1789 £519,330 were printed, a quantity indicating the extensive circulation and wear the notes received before they found their way back to the bank. Twenty-shilling notes were not put into circulation until 1st June 1798, when £45,000 were printed.

The annexed table exhibits the bank's circulation for some years after the first issue in 1782, distinguishing between notes of £5 and upwards and one pound or one guinea notes.

Statistics of Circulation
OF SIR W. FORBES, JAMES HUNTER, & CO., FROM 1782 TO 1827.

Dates.	Total Circulation.	Guinea Notes.	20s. Notes.	Total of Small Notes.	Percentage of Small Notes.
1782, Jan. 1	9,900	Not shewn	None	Not known	...
,, ,, 14	15,100	8,175	,,	8,175	53
,, ,, 28	26,800	Not shewn	,,	Not known	...
,, Feb. 7	37,900	,,	,,	,,	...
,, Apr. 27	48,300	23,400	,,	23,400	48
,, May 28	60,500	32,700	,,	32,700	54
,, June 28	58,900	34,300	,,	34,300	58
,, July 31	63,300	55,800	,,	55,800	86
,, Nov. 20	84,600	44,300	,,	44,300	52
,, Dec. 31	82,750	51,600	,,	51,600	62
1783, June 23	81,270	51,270	,.	51,270	63
,, Dec. 10	89,060	55,360	,,	55,360	62
1784, June...	110,770	68,970	,,	68,970	62
1785	99,400	61,200	,,	61,200	61
1786	96,100	57,900	,,	57,900	60
1787	94,100	58,700	,,	58,700	62
1788	100,700	52,800	,,	52,800	52
1789	90,500	60,700	.,	60,700	67
1790	101,200	62,900	,,	62,900	62
1793	94,100	57,700	,,	57,700	61
1795	99,800	58,400	,,	58,400	58
1797, Jan. 1	115,200	63,900	.,	63,900	55
,, Mar. 1	84,300	51,100	,,	51,100	60
,, ,, 23	63,900	41,300	.,	41,300	64
,, Apr. 15	48,500	31,800	,,	31,800	65
,, ,, 17	47,200	29,800	,,	29,800	63
,. Aug. 8	93,000	51,300	,,	51,300	55
,, Oct. 27	108,100	63,300	,,	63,300	58
1799	136,400	43,880	36,620	80,500	58
1800	142,600	Not shewn	Not shewn	67,270	47
1801	192,300	,,	,,	75,460	38
1803	169,700	38,400	52,800	91,200	53
1805	207,265	38,955	57,020	95,975	46
1807	225,444	37,464	71,515	108,979	48
1809	220,700	29,505	72,650	102,155	46
1810	251,400	52,815	57,730	110,545	43
1811	210,525	47,670	58,720	106,390	50
1812	244,440	Not shewn	Not shewn	107,210	43
1813	170,028	39,123	44,980	84,103	48
1815	142,000	Not shewn	Not shewn	80,500	56
1816	172,351	,,	,,	84,100	48
1817	153,920	,,	,,	77,300	50
1818	208,000	,,	,,	104,720	50
1820	211,312	19,656	85,086	104,742	49
1822	182,785	14,427	85,556	99,983	54
1823	210,000	13,860	89,985	103,845	49
1824	209,150	14,155	74,160	88,315	42
1825	189,257	11,697	80,250	91,947	48
1826	214,056	11,949	85,202	97,151	45
1827	161,430	9,450	69,856	79,306	49

Remarks on Table.

"The amount of our notes has not only far exceeded our utmost expectation, but has been the one cause of the great increase which has taken place in the original and fundamental branches of our business,—the deposit of money with us at interest and the negotiation of bills of exchange between Edinburgh and London, both of which branches have been enlarged to a most astonishing degree ; while, on the other hand, those branches of our business have been the means of facilitating and extending the circulation of our notes, so that they have mutually acted and reacted on each other."—"Memoirs of a Banking House," Sir W. Forbes.

1784.—Increased circulation to meet wants in monetary crisis of 1783-84.

1788.—In this year there was a "run" of poorer classes with small notes, which was more than counterbalanced by increased circulation of large notes to meet necessities of *commercial men* ; in the following year, from the continued depression, small notes were largely used.

1797.—The effects of the tremendous "run" of this year are here shewn in an exaggerated scale, as Sir W. F., from prudential motives, paid all his own notes presented through the exchange, but did not keep up his circulation by issuing any, until he saw what course events were likely to take. To *increase* the *paper* currency was almost impossible for some days, as it was coin that was wanted.

1810-1815.—Want of bullion and commercial speculation increase the circulation greatly at the beginning of this period ; as the distress passes on, the circulation rapidly decreases. The fall in large notes is very marked. The guinea notes with their odd shilling are found useful as change, but begin to disappear from 1811.

1782-1827.—46 years' average of small notes, 54 per cent.

1865-1874 inclusive.—10 years' average of small notes for the Scottish banks, 64.5 per cent.

As the end of the century drew near an extraordinary outburst of crime occurred throughout the country, and a few of these relating to bank robberies and small note forgeries may be mentioned.

On January 26, 1774, an advertisement appeared in the Edinburgh papers regarding an extensive forgery of Bank of Scotland guinea notes :—" The engraved part is well executed, so that at first sight it is difficult to distinguish the forged from the real note. The forged note wants the watermark on the paper which is in that of all the real notes, but an imitation of it is attempted with an instrument, which is discovered by looking at the back of the note." Next day the British Linen Company issued a similar advertisement regarding its one pound notes, dated 6th September 1770 :—" The forged notes are done on common paper. The figure of the woman and ship is ill executed and appears faint, and the strokes of the letters in the copperplate print are less full and broad than in the real notes." The imitation of the watermark had nearly cut the paper by the pressure required to bring it out. In both cases £100 reward was offered by the banks, but without apparent effect. A similar attempt had been made on the British Linen Company in November 1772, in which one John MacAffee was found guilty. From the facsimile notes of the period, reproduced elsewhere, the reader may judge that a very elementary knowledge of engraving would suffice to impose upon the public.

During the night between the 16th and 17th of February 1788, the Dundee Banking Company's office was broken into and robbed of £423, of which nothing was recovered. A singular fatality attended this robbery. Two men were tried, convicted, and hanged at Edinburgh, asserting their innocence to the last. In the same year other two men were arrested, of whom one was sentenced to be hanged but was afterwards pardoned. In 1790 suspicion fell upon a fifth man, who had been convicted of forging a bill. He was shipped to Botany Bay, but was hanged on the way for mutiny. Yet a sixth individual in 1790, on being condemned to death for robbery, endeavoured to get a respite by asserting his knowledge of the bank robbery; his story was disbelieved, but, with the rope round his neck, he repeatedly declared that the three men previously sentenced, two of whom had been executed, were perfectly guiltless of the whole affair.

In 1791, on 29th October, £1600 in guinea and one pound notes were stolen off a cart in Glasgow. The owners, Messrs Andrew, George, & Andrew Thomson, bankers there, advertised a reward of £200, which they paid to a lad in the following month, who had found the box, and its contents untouched, in a dunghill in the Saltmarket which he had been clearing out. In the same month 500 guinea notes of the Paisley Union Bank were removed from a mail coach running between Carlisle and Glasgow. On 14th October 1797 Milesius Roderick M'Cuillin was condemned to be hanged for uttering forged notes in Scotland, a sentence which was carried out on the 21st of that month.

By the Stamp Act, 1791, one pound and guinea notes were for the first time threatened with taxation; but upon the rumour becoming known amongst the Scottish members of Parliament, it met with such decided opposition that the proposal was abandoned for a time.

Chapter IX.—1793-1820.

The French Revolution and War Crises—Cash Payments Stopped—Depreciation of the Note.

> " When all around was danger, strife, and fear,
> While the earth shook, and darkened was the sky,
> And wide destruction stunn'd the listening ear
> Appall'd the heart and stupefied the eye."
> —SCOTT, *The Vision of Don Roderick.*

DURING the nine years' peace—from 1783 to 1792—
the country made rapid strides, the two large banks
advancing with the times in financial prosperity if
not in popularity, Bank of Scotland stock fetching a little
over £300 per cent., and Royal Bank new stock steady at
£240. To increase the prosperity many of the banks
opened branches in different parts ; amongst others the
Dundee bank, on 24th March 1791, minutes a resolution,
"that as the circulation of the bank has considerably
diminished, and probably owing to the number of branches
from other banks which have been opened in this and the
neighbouring towns, it is expedient for this company to
establish branches in other towns." They accordingly did
so in Brechin, Arbroath, Forfar, and Kirkcaldy, carrying on
a good business for some years, until heavy losses, caused by
absconding agents, led the bank to close them all,—a line
of action which might have been avoided by the timely
appointment of a good inspector.

Scarcely had the country time to think upon its renewed
prosperity, when the long pent-up volcano of the French
Revolution burst out upon the world. The cataclysm of
blood, plunder, and war which ensued, the derangement of

commerce, and the inundation of France with millions of assignats,—all combined to produce European disturbance, from which England and Scotland were not free. In the midst of the confusion and excitement which immediately arose, the militia were called out to resist the dreaded invasion of the Revolutionists, an act which at once "checked mercantile credit all over the kingdom." The revolutionary party in Britain did their utmost to increase the alarm, with the view of overthrowing the Government. A serious demand for money set in upon all the bankers (twenty-two of whom failed in England alone), and rose to an extent that caused the stoppage of the old firm of Murdoch & Co., the Glasgow Arms Bank, whose business had greatly declined since Mr Trotter's days. Immediately thereafter James Dunlop, one of the wealthiest men in Glasgow, and the house of Bertram, Gardner, & Co., in Edinburgh, also stopped ; "and to complete the confusion, the four banks in Newcastle, which were known to be opulent, were forced to shut up." Sir William Forbes has left a note of the effects of the run on his house, shewing that while only 60 interest receipts were granted between 23d to 30th April 1793, the number paid was 608. The sum paid of interest receipts from December 1792 to 23d May 1793 was £263,724 ; and the sum on current account as much more. The circulation of his notes* affords a little glimpse into the character of the run, the one pound note holders being the principal actors. As the British navy cleared the seas of the French marine and restored commerce in some measure, trade gradually became better than it had ever been during a foreign war ; but the alarm of the invasion of Ireland, and the scarcity of gold from the war drain, brought about a most violent run upon all the banks in 1797, though fortunately of shorter duration than that of 1793. The lower orders and agricultural population were the most easily excited, and the Edinburgh bankers were beginning, according to Sir William Forbes, to dread a

---

* See Table, page 110.

"still severer demand, when, early in the morning of Wednesday the first of March, an express arrived from London to the directors of the Bank of Scotland from Thomas Coutts & Co., informing them that the demand for gold at the Bank of England had risen to such an alarming height, that the directors had thought it proper to state the circumstances to the Chancellor of the Exchequer, who immediately procured an order of the Privy Council to be issued, prohibiting that bank from making any more issues of specie for their notes." It is chiefly the panic in Scotland that specially relates to the subject ; but as it arose in England, it will be well to consider both cause and effect in that country. From 1794 to 1797 war expenses had drained the Bank of England of gold, a matter which caused the country much distress, as the bank did not make up the deficiency by a smaller note issue, but left that duty entirely in the hands of feeble private bankers, who, being unprovided with specie, were at once compelled to stop payment, when confidence broke down and a demand arose. Nearly a hundred country banks were bankrupt in England during 1797. The bank had tried to keep back the Atlantic with a mop of five pound notes, issued for the first time, its previous issues having been for larger denominations. It is no exaggeration to say, that had the Bank of England at this time issued one pound notes, as it afterwards did in the panic of 1825, the storm would have been prevented. It was purely a scarcity of a *suitably small circulating medium* in which the public could have confidence, and not a commercial crisis in any sense. In the Restriction Act, passed to confirm the action of the Privy Council, it was provided that £25,000 in cash might be advanced to the Bank of Scotland and Royal Bank.

On the news reaching Edinburgh, an interesting proof was seen of the estimate in which Sir William Forbes was held by his fellows in the banking profession. Walking into his place of business at ten o'clock, wrapt in gloomy enough reflections, he found it filled with a jostling crowd clamouring for gold. To the celebrated house in the

Parliament Close the cashier and deputy-governor of the
Royal Bank and the treasurer of the Bank of Scotland
resorted for consultation with the famous banker. Mr Hog,
the manager of the British Linen Company, was sent for,
and seems to have come at once. Sir William, with
characteristic sense of the respect due to the old bank, then
adjourned with his friends to the Bank of Scotland, where
it was agreed that there was no other course open but to
follow the example of the " Bank of England, and suspend
all further payments in specie." A public meeting was
held, at which the decision was unanimously confirmed ;
expresses were sent out in hot haste to the provincial
towns, and circulars were scattered through Edinburgh with
the intelligence. The direst uproar at once broke out, and
every bank in the town, for the remainder of the week, was
crammed with "fishwomen, carmen, street porters, and
butchers' men, all bawling out at once for change and jostling
each other in their endeavours who should get nearest to
the table." Specie was in existence, but no one would part
with it, and as Saturday drew on, the want of small change
exhibited itself in various distressing ways. The banks
were besought to issue smaller notes than for one pound,
but the Act of 1765 standing in the way, recourse was had
to tallies, tokens, and sometimes even to tearing a twenty-
shilling note into quarters, for which the banks afterwards
freely paid the proportional sum. In England an issue of
one pound and two pound notes for the first time by the
Bank of England greatly lessened the inconvenience, while
a large quantity of Spanish 4s. 6d. dollars were marked at
the Mint and circulated along with quarter guineas and
some other small coins. In a short time an Act was passed
through Parliament, 37 Geo. III., c. 32, suspending the Act
of 1765, and authorising specially the three old banks, and
generally other bankers who had been accustomed to
circulate notes on or before 2d March 1797, to issue " notes,
bills, or tickets in the nature of bank notes, payable to the
bearer on demand, for any sum whatever under the sum of
20s. sterling ;" while such of the banks as had already issued

notes in contravention of the Act of 1765 were indemnified for having done so. The duration of this Act was subsequently extended, by Act 37 Geo. III., c. 61, to 5th July 1799, during which time many banks availed themselves of the liberty it gave, the Dundee bank alone issuing over £12,700 of 5s. notes, representing 50,800 notes,—an amount that would imply that the benefit was largely taken advantage of for a time, though from the nature of the panic, which was purely one of scare excited by the necessary action of the Bank of England, the need for notes smaller than one pound soon passed away, as the specie holders, bowing to the inevitable, produced their hoards in exchange for goods or bank notes. Opposite is given a facsimile of a British Linen Bank note for 5s. issued in 1797. Sir William Forbes remarks that he did not issue 5s. notes as the other banks did, "being convinced that there was no real scarcity of specie in the country, and that it would make its appearance when the panic should wear off, as actually proved to be the case." His own note issues were restricted for a time, none being issued for several weeks ; but as large numbers were paid, the circulation fell from £115,200 in January 1797 to £47,200 in the following April, the amounts of one pound and one guinea notes at the same times being respectively £63,900 and £29,800. In *number* the large notes were about 8000 and 3000 at the two periods, so that the area of panic must have been principally confined to one pound note holders of the "fishwomen and butcher men" type described in his memoirs.

The position of the Scottish Banks was now a most anomalous one, and illustrates strikingly the effects of public confidence during a national emergency. The Act of 1765 had given the remedy of summary diligence to all holders of notes who could not get payment on demand. Such payment implied settlement in specie, as no notes were legal tender in Scotland ; and now, in 1797, there was not a bank in Scotland who would give specie for their notes. Yet there is no record of any Scottish holder

attempting to exercise his right. Sir William Forbes
mentions that only one case arose in England, when an
individual of the name of Grigby endeavoured to take the
law out of Messrs Oakes Son, of Bury St Edmunds, in 1801,
for which he was severely reprimanded by Baron Hotham,
before whom he brought his petition.

Throughout the twenty-two years of the Restriction
Act, such was the trust placed in the banks by the Scots
people, that a paper currency based merely upon such
specie as could be collected in the ordinary course of business from the amount circulating in the hands of the public, passed from hand to hand for nearly a quarter of a
century without openly losing in value to an extent that
would have entailed payment of a premium for their
exchange ;* while the notes of the Bank of England, which
alone of all the note issues of the three kingdoms were
legally protected, maintained their value for three years
only, and gradually fell to 18s. 4d. per £1 note in 1810,
16s. 3d. in 1811, and at last to 14s. 2d. in 1813, gold standing at the price of £5. 10s. per ounce, or £1. 12s. 1½d.
above the usual mint price.   It is true that this serious fall
occurred in the years when Britain was engaged in her last
desperate struggle with Napoleon, when the Bank of England was almost *compelled* to produce enormous sums to
satisfy Government demands ; for no mere speculation of
commerce could possibly cause the prodigious increase in
its note issue, which in 1784 stood at   £6,000,000

1790	„		10,909,694
1797	„		8,601,964
1809	„	.	19,641,640
and in 1814	„	.	28,291,832

The comparative quietness in Scotland may therefore
be greatly accounted for by its distance from the centre of
the world's finance, which at that time appeared to be
almost in the throes of dissolution.

The protection afforded to the Bank of England was

---

* But see pages 121 *et seq.* as to effects of depreciation on Scots
paper generally.

one of the causes which led to this depreciation of its notes, though of course the war was the primary cause. Having no dread of payment hanging over them, the bank directors issued this huge quantity of notes with the certain effect of lowering the exchanges, and adding to the drain of bullion for military purposes an equally disastrous drain for commercial necessities.

Thousands, almost millions, of these notes circulated on the Continent during the war; and it was the sight of them in Russia passing from hand to hand like gold, that drew from Napoleon the striking words, " I trembled for the fate of our enterprise." An utterance all the more remarkable, coming as it did soon after the defeat of Austerlitz, when his blatant bulletin to his soldiers proclaimed, that *they had scattered to the winds* the last army " on which the commercial spirit of a despicable nation had placed its expiring hope."

In many instances notes were actually sold for 15s. per £1 note, or a gold sovereign exchanged for a £1 note and four or five shillings in silver, the premium being brought about solely by the large inconvertible note issue, which had become so depreciated that the exchanges fell far below the gold points, and would have caused a serious stoppage in trade had the Berlin decrees not accomplished that already. For years after the bank was quite able to resume payment, the House of Commons stubbornly maintained that there should be no difference between paper and gold, Lord Liverpool, amongst others, asserting to Lord Lauderdale that notes were not depreciated, but that possibly gold had risen in price ! The Government, which lavished millions after millions upon the imbecile powers of the Continent, could scarcely be expected to appreciate the difference between a paper promise to pay a £1 and a piece of gold for the same amount ; and through their inability to distinguish between the cause and the effect, they delayed the resumption of cash payments until many years after the bank declared they were able to meet their notes. Up to 1815 this policy may have been reasonable,

as the pressure of 1810 and 1814 would in all probability
have compelled the bank to stop a second time, if it had
begun to pay gold prior to those dates. But even this is
questionable, for had the bank once begun cash payments,
the prodigious note issue would not have been ventured upon,
and the subsequent depreciation would have been avoided.
But having eased their conscience by declaring their ability,
the bank had no objections to fall in with the views of the
Government, which were so highly profitable to them that
they were enabled to pay dividends of 10 per cent. from
1807 to 1822, a rate which had not been reached since
1708, and which since 1822 we are not aware of having
once been paid.

Similar results to those exhibited by the Bank of
England were shewn by the banks in Dublin. Taking advantage of the public indulgence, Irish bankers issued their
notes to an extent which, so early as 1804, reduced their
value 2s. 2d. per £1, and thus brought the exchange on
London of that year from £105. 10s. of Dublin money per
£100 London, as it had been in 1797, to £118 Dublin for
£100 London money. As with the English exchanges,
the cost of conveying the bullion did not account for the
difference. Between Ireland and London such carriage
would amount to about £2 or £2½ per cent. ; and as the
par of exchange was £108. 6s. 8d. Irish to £100 English
money, there is a clear loss of 7½ per cent., which can only
be accounted for by the depreciation of the Irish bank note.
While this was the case in Dublin, the par of exchange was
scarcely affected in Belfast, where the notes were seldom or
never taken to any excess, and, having therefore a small
circulation, did not affect the exchanges as in Dublin.

Thus in England where the bank was compelled to over-
issue, and in Ireland where no such compulsion existed, the
results of an inconvertible over-issue were the same. In
Scotland the principal banks, acting so far as can be seen with
commendable prudence, restricted their issues to the lowest
commercial wants of the time, yet without impeding the
national growth of commerce. The Bank of Scotland and

British Linen Company, instead of an increase towards 1817, as in England, have a considerable decrease; while the Royal Bank, which was very low in 1816, maintained its issues in after years at nearly the same as at 1810. In 1804, from a desire to restrict advances on discounts slightly and thereby check the note issues, the banks began charging from ten to twenty days additional discount on bills payable in certain towns by way of exchange. The most notable of these, from their English connection, were Berwick and Newcastle, bills on these towns being charged twenty days and 2s. 6d. per cent. extra. By this careful pilotage the Scottish banks were able to come out of the years of restriction with good credit and fair resources, having been carried through the ordeal by the confidence placed in their prudent management.

In view of the quietness and success of their procedure in these years, it has often been asserted that Scotch bank notes did not become depreciated, a statement which ought to be received with some reserve; for, with the market value of gold in London at £4, £4. 5s., or £4. 10s. per ounce, it is difficult to see how—though they may not have become so glaringly depreciated as Bank of England notes—they should not have become depreciated relatively, from the increased prices of commodities and the scarcity of gold. The affairs of the two countries were so intimately bound up with each other, that it seems rather absurd to suppose that while a one pound note of the Bank of England, the source from whence gold came, sold for 15s. in gold, a Scotch note could buy 20s. worth of the same metal. A few points may therefore be indicated for measuring the extent of the depreciation.

First, That gold was scarcely ever asked for Scots bank notes *before* the restriction, and consequently was not so much missed *after* it had begun as in England, where a metallic currency was more prized.

Second, The Scots banks found another method of maintaining the credit of their paper, by reverting to the practice of 1770, and settling their exchanges of notes by bills on

London drawn at ten days date,—a rate from twenty-five to thirty-five days below the natural rate of the commercial exchanges. This was clearly a heavy loss to any particular bank, but as on the whole the amounts given and received by each would be tolerably equal, the loss and gain of such payments partially neutralised each other, though the whole method would be a most powerful deterrent to an over-issue. It was probably this course which led them, about 1804, to charge additional days of discount by way of exchange on certain Scots bills, as has been noticed before, so that the burden might be put finally upon the public who obtained notes for these bills, and thus increased the circulation which the banks had to pay off when it came back through the exchanges.

It was not until 1820 or 1825 that the natural rate fell to twenty days on London, while the ten days rate has only been reached during the past twenty years, when railways so greatly reduced the cost of carriage and thus contracted the bullion points. That even this astute move of the banks failed to prevent a certain depreciation, but only partially neutralised it by giving a correspondingly higher value to another class of their paper, there appears to be some proof, for Sir Henry Parnell—at one time member of Parliament for Dundee—in his " Observations on Paper Money, Banking, &c.," 1826, points out, that " This practice of drawing on London by the banks, for the purpose of paying to each other twice a week the balances of the exchanges of their notes, has kept the value of bank paper in Scotland from ever becoming of *less value* than the *current money* of London. *Whilst that consisted wholly of paper, the Scotch paper fell in value with it ;* and now that it consists of paper convertible into gold, the Scots paper is of equal value with gold, because every banker can obtain gold for the bills he receives in exchanging the notes of another banker, if he chooses to require it. It is in this way that the paper money of Scotland maintains the nature of gold, although no gold exists in the circulation." This obligation under which the banks had come compelled them to look carefully to their operations, since any unnecessary issue of notes entailed a loss of fully 9s. per cent. at settlement of the note balances. The par of exchange between Edinburgh and London being from forty to forty-five days, equal to 11s. or 12s. per hundred (bullion point being reached at £100. 15s.), there was a difference in the exchange favourable to Scotland, so far as the note settlements were concerned, of 8s. 6d. or 9s. per cent. over the exchange required for *ordinary commercial business*,—a sum which would materially aid in *raising* the price of Scots bank notes above that of London paper, and bring it so much nearer the rate for gold. This salutary practice is still maintained by the banks in Scotland, the rate for note or clearing settlements having been reduced to four days, as that for the commercial exchange has been lowered to ten.

Third, While gold was seldom asked for in exchange for notes, there is reason to believe that cash payments were not stopped so entirely in Scotland as they were at the Bank of England. All the Scots banks kept stocks of gold, and it is probable that, notwithstanding the theory that the notes of Scotland turned out the gold, there was more gold in the country than was generally supposed, for the prudent measures of the banks in their exchanges and issues could not fail to attract some of the gold which was displaced by the excessive issues of England. That gold could be got when asked for is certain, for Mr H. Monteith —a Glasgow manufacturer and member of Parliament, when examined as to this period by the Committee of 1826— observes, that being in England two or three times a year, he invariably got either gold or Bank of England notes from the Glasgow banks to pay his way. When asked, " Do you think there being no run on the banks was in part attributable to the Scots having lost their habits of metallic currency, and therefore setting no superior value on gold," he replied, " I do not think that was the sole cause. Knowing the Scotch character as I do, I think that the want of gold currency would not induce a Scotsman to take a bank note he had no confidence in." Thus the demand for gold, though legal, was met because it was so small.

The difference between the two currencies seems to have lain in the fact that the Bank of England were *compelled* to produce funds to carry on the war, by means of its world-wide note issues,—funds which, from their very nature and volume (hundreds of millions being issued below par), must have had a deteriorating effect upon the medium of exchange, whereby they were transferred from the public to the Government, and from the Government to its creditors.*

---

* So much was this the case, that, so late as 1819, the exchange on Paris was down to 23·45—*i.e.*, 1s. 4½d. per £, or £6. 16s. 8d. per cent.—*below* the current par of 25·17½, and £6. 10s. below the low bullion point (bullion points being 25·10 and 25·25), a fact only explainable by the stoppage of gold payments and forced note issue of England ; for whenever cash payments were begun, the rate rose in 1820 to 25·60, or 34s. 2d. per cent. above par, and £8. 10s. 10d. beyond the actual exchange of January 1819. Assuming, therefore, that *ordinary commerce* would have made the exchange of 1819 nearly as much in favour of England as that of 1820, if the former had not been affected by other causes, the difference between the extremes, £8. 10s. 10d., when reduced by 34s. 2d., leaves £6. 16s. 8d. to represent the depreciation of cotemporary British legal tender, bank notes, *as compared with gold*. This is easily proved from the average premium on gold for 1819 being £4. 9s. per cent., or £95. 11s. of gold to £100 bank notes ; the difference between £6. 16s. 8d. and £4. 9s. being explained by the above example exchange, 23·45, being the *lowest* point touched in 1819, while the £4. 9s. is the *average* premium for that year, there being great fluctuation towards its close from the legislation as to resumption of cash payments.

To prove, therefore, that Scottish notes were not depreciated, it would be necessary to shew that the Scottish exchange was *above* that of London, and on a par with those of the Continent, which no one will be hardy enough to affirm,—the London exchange with Scotland, all through the restriction period, remaining practically the same, except so far as the ten days drafts, before referred to, gave an increased value to Scottish paper in the London market.

Chapter X.—1800-1826.

"Weighed in the balances, and found wanting."

THE opening of the nineteenth century in Scotland was followed by the establishment of numbers of joint-stock companies, a sure indication that, notwithstanding the heavy war expenditure, the capital of the country was increasing more quickly than was required for every-day business, and could thus be diverted to other channels of usefulness. The varied mechanical improvements which had been perfected during the previous thirty years, had placed Britain at the head of the manufacturing countries of the world. It is true there was at the precise time under notice severe depression, following upon the obstruction of the war ; but as one opening was closed, the indefatigable capitalists of the country soon found other regions wherein to prosecute their commerce. To meet the requirements of the new departure, let us see what position the banking houses of the period were in, as to power and enterprise.

The system of private banking, with the few well-known exceptions, had been gradually losing power over the commercial population. In proportion as they saw their end approaching, they seem to have endeavoured to increase their influence with the old banks by obtaining a voice in their direction.

Again and again their influence was pointed out to the banks, and several efforts were made to throw them off by limiting their credits and deposits, but without success.

Notwithstanding all that has been said and written against them, these gentlemen appear to have managed the old banks with integrity. Their action during the restriction crisis was so cautious as to excite adverse criticism, but Scotland seems to have been none the worse for their caution and professional skill ; and that they had due sense of obligation to meet current requirements, is shewn by the increase of capital of the two senior banks from £1,000,000 to £1,500,000 sterling. The defective part in the arrangement was the manner of granting accommodation to the public. Instead of coming direct to the old banks, it was rather the rule to approach a private banker, who in turn obtained his support from one of the joint-stock banks, making his profit out of the difference between what he paid to his bank and what he got from his customers. Dissatisfaction arose, and as profits were cut more closely in commercial circles, such a waste of *one profit* in their banking transactions was resented by business men, and especially so by the rising Whig party, who believed the banks to be wholly abandoned to the Tory cause.

The idea of new banking seems first to have arisen in the provinces, from the presence of branches of the Edinburgh banks suggesting the possibility of new ventures being equally profitable. The result was anything but satisfactory. In 1802 the Fife Banking Company began with a capital of £30,000, to wind up in 1826 with a call of £2500 per share on its proprietors. In the same year were started the Renfrewshire Banking Company, a considerable affair, having five or six branches, which failed in 1842, paying only from 7s. 6d. to 9s. 2d. per £ ; the Cupar Bank, which retired from banking in 1811 ; and the miserable Falkirk Union Bank, sequestrated in 1816, paying 9s. 6d. per £. Some of the notes of these banks come in to the banks to this day. With the exception of the Fifeshire Bank, which had forty shareholders, all these were purely private banks with sounding names, none of them having over ten partners.

The Bank of Scotland and the Royal Bank, no doubt

remembering the troubles of 1772, refused to receive new country bank notes, a step in marked contrast to their treatment of Sir William Forbes & Co., whom they had at once received upon equal terms with themselves. These new companies, however, bore a close resemblance to Douglas, Heron, & Co., and would fain have forced their notes upon the country. The result proved the soundness of judgment of the old banks, whether it was dictated by their private bank directors or otherwise.

The sure precursor of the crisis of 1810-15, a new rush of banking houses came into existence about these years. In 1809 and 1810 appeared the Dundee Union Bank, the Glasgow Banking Company, the Glasgow Commercial Bank, and the East Lothian Bank. The last named had a capital of £80,000, and did a large business in Haddington-shire until 1822, when it suddenly stopped, owing to the villainous conduct of its manager, William Borthwick, who disappeared with nearly £30,000 of the company's notes, most of which had been put into circulation. The bank received some aid from Sir William Forbes, who retired their notes, amounting to upwards of £50,000.

Suspecting some of the directors of seeing through his intended mischief, Mr Borthwick prepared a scheme for placing some of these gentlemen into large puncheons, with suitable breathing-room, and thereafter having them quietly shipped from Dundee to be landed out of the way at Dantzig, and confined in the heart of Prussia for a time. At first it was supposed that the scoundrel had betaken himself to America, and an Edinburgh merchant crossed the Atlantic in the endeavour to trace him, but it was afterwards believed he had taken refuge in Norway. The creditors of the bank were paid in full.

In 1810 was laid the foundation of the most important Scottish bank since the date of the British Linen Company, certainly the most important joint-stock *unlimited* bank Scotland had hitherto seen. In that year the Commercial Bank of Scotland began business, with the large nominal capital of £3,000,000, having £450,000 paid up. It at once

£1.1.

[Vignette of Edinburgh Castle.]

No. 23 B 274

ONE

GUINEA

EDINBURGH,

1ST OCTOR. 1818.

Of Scotland.

The Commercial Banking Company of Scotland promise to pay to HUGH AULD, or Bearer, One Pound One Shilling Sterling on demand at their Office here.

By Order of the Committee of Management.

W. Mitchell & Cashier

No. 23 B 274

[*Surrounded by Scroll Work of Thistles, Roses, and Shamrocks.*]

Commercial Bank of Scotland.

Copy Note of Commercial Bank of Scotland, from an Original in the Antiquarian Museum, Edinburgh.

entered upon an energetic establishment of branches, a
work hitherto peculiarly that of the Bank of Scotland and
British Linen Company, but which, from the inevitable
relapse attending all sudden expansions, had somewhat
fallen into the background with both banks.   Giving due
credit to the British Linen Company as the real founder of
a successful branch system, it was left to the Commercial
Bank to give the greatest impulse it had yet received.
The British Linen Company steadily increased the number
of its branches, but it would appear that the Bank of
Scotland closed several between 1810 and 1826.

While these two banks had contented themselves with
sixteen and twenty-seven branches respectively up to 1826,
the new establishment, strong in its splendid capital, large
proprietory, and able management, so gallantly carried on
the structure founded by the British Linen Company, that
by 1826—that is, in sixteen years—it had opened thirty-
one new offices,—four in 1811 (the first being in Dalkeith,
then the great seat of the corn trade in Scotland), three in
1812, four in 1813, three in 1814, eight between 1820 and
1824, and nine in 1825, just before the English panic.

The beneficial influence of one such bank so greatly
exceeded that of the various local houses, that for strength,
solidity, and power for good it well deserved Mr Kerr's
eulogium : "From the outset it appears to have been
designed on a *large-minded* plan, and to have met a decided
want.   The new establishment was very popular, but it was
also very discreet, for while it studied the best interests of
the public, it imitated the wisest provisions of the old
banks' practice." *

No banking method seems to have so direct an influence
in extending circulation of notes upon a thoroughly sound
basis as the branch system, and a glance at the towns in
which the Commercial Bank opened its few first branches
will easily show how the authorised circulation came to be
fixed at so large a sum in 1845.   Dalkeith, where the first

---

* A. W. Kerr's "History of Banking in Scotland."

office was opened, was then the centre of a very wide
district, in which, it is needless to add, there were no
railways.   The whole south country, embracing Earlston,
Melrose, Galashiels, part of Berwickshire, and the fertile
Lothians, sent in its grain *in bulk* to the Thursday market,
which had grown up under the shadow of Dalkeith Castle.
The transactions were very large, and as no bills were
taken or given, cash payments by bank notes became the
invariable rule.   These were taken away by the farmers on
their homeward journey, paid out at the south country fairs
for cattle or for wages, and might not filter their way back
to a bank for several months.   Leith was not so marked in
this respect, as any notes given out there soon came back ;
but Tain and Crieff, the next in order, corresponded closely
to Dalkeith,—the former the *entrepôt* for the rich agriculture of Easter Ross, and the latter for Strathearn and the
surrounding districts of Perthshire.   Thurso and Peterhead
were soon visited, and Glasgow and Banff in 1814.

In three of those towns the rising fishing industry of
Scotland was greatly aided.   Placed geographically at
considerable disadvantage, the scarcity of money or means
of banking had hitherto hampered both curers and fishermen.   A free issue of one pound notes gave ready payment
of all sums between employers and employed; and the
circulation of the bank was in consequence widely and permanently extended, a considerable proportion of the paper
being carried away by the workpeople at the close of the
season to their native glens or townships, there to be either
hoarded for a time, or still further circulated amongst
farmers, shopkeepers, and others, until, after the lapse of
months, they gravitated towards some of the towns where
a branch bank existed, and were there converted into
deposits.   Any quantity of the notes which had been at once
returned to the issuing branch by the fishermen, usually
went to swell the deposits of the office, for gold was seldom
if ever asked for, even the Yarmouth fishers often carrying
home their earnings in Scots bank notes.   The class of
deposits lodged by means of these notes was both profitable

and safe, consisting of a large number of small sums which might remain for years undisturbed, the danger in time of panic being minimised by the extent of the area from which they had been received.

At Wick, in 1825, upwards of 14,000 people were employed in the herring trade, one-half of whom came from other towns, or the Western Highlands, Hebrides, and foreign parts. To keep these in employment required 1068 boats, of which 658 were Scottish, and 410 English, Irish, French, and Dutch. The agent of the Commercial Bank in the town made a report to his head office in 1825, in which he says : " The stranger fishermen almost invariably carry home their earnings in bank notes." The circulation at the season in question is " augmented to a degree totally beyond what a district situated so far north might be supposed to require,—the sums circulated in this period chiefly arise from the payments made by the regular curers to the fishermen and others employed. As a fair mode of calculation, it may be estimated that £140,000 is put in circulation by the payments made to the fishermen, coopers, &c., during the continuance of the season."

Then comes the important paragraph : " The small notes are almost the only medium used in circulation in this district. The reason is obvious, because the smallness of their value throws them into the hands of all classes ; and as the fishers, coopers, and women, and others employed are poor, the acquisition of large notes by them seldom takes place.

" Another matter of experience may be adverted to. It frequently happens that foreign vessels coming here to buy or cure herrings, tender gold in payment ; the fishermen, who are ignorant and illiterate, invariably refuse to take it, no doubt in dread of imposition from bad and counterfeit metal, and always ask for bank notes for their herrings. It even occurred last year, that many of the strangers carried gold with them, which they were obliged to get exchanged for notes, as those having bank notes could purchase herrings at 1s. to 5s. per barrel cheaper than those having gold."

Some of the other offices then opened were equally well adapted to the general convenience and the profit of the bank. Many towns were chosen, in which none of the three large banks had branches,—amongst these Lanark, Kilmarnock, and Paisley had an extensive weaving trade ; Alloa and Campbeltown were engaged in the liquor traffic ; while the iron works of Falkirk, and the ship-building trade of Dumbarton, owe something to the Commercial Bank.

In the same year in which the new bank opened, the Bank of Scotland gave another proof, if any were required, of its adaptability to altered circumstances. A rival bank had to be faced, and a heavy drain for mercantile advances required by the panic of 1810 had set in. By one clever stroke the old bank met both these necessities, by increased rates of interest allowed upon the new *deposit-receipts*,—the convenient, but still unnegotiable, successors of the old "treasurer's bond." The rate allowed was 4 per cent., discounts being raised to 5 per cent., with the immediate result that the drain for advances ceased. The Royal Bank and the British Linen Company followed the same course, which was maintained until 1817, when the rate was again lowered by the Bank of Scotland and Royal Bank. In the following year the British Linen Company also lowered its rate for current accounts ; but the Commercial Bank steadily contrived to pay 4 per cent. on all sums lodged with them, even on current account. Thus throughout the severe pressure of 1815 and 1816, with heavy failures in Glasgow, causing severe loss to the Royal Bank, the rates of interest and discount were steadily maintained at such a level as would reasonably check unwise speculation or issue of notes.

The following figures may be interesting, as shewing the great shrinkage in the Royal Bank's circulation at this period. For every £1000 of its notes in circulation on 1st

January 1810, it had, during the undermentioned years, these sums, namely :—

Year.	Average.	Highest.	Lowest.
	£	£	£
1810	950	1080	873
1811	765	826	727
1812	714	774	662
1813	630	732	488
1814	730	882	554
1815	560	713	394
1816	375	554	267
1817	1023	1436	652
1818	1145	1183	1122
1819	1127	1183	1093
Years, 10	8019		
	801—average for 10 years.		

The circulation of the Bank of Scotland upon the same basis, taking 24th December 1810 as the date of the £1000, was as follows :—

Year.	Average.	Highest.	Lowest.
	£	£	£
1810	1000		
1810	952	1000	928
1811	913	944	873
1812	894	916	883
1813	839	877	811
1814	833	852	808
1815	723	769	629
1816	691	722	672
1817	732	754	680
1818	769	748	817
Years, 10	8348		
	834—average for 10 years.		

For sake of comparison of increase, for the figures give no indication of the separate circulation of the banks, we subjoin those for the British Linen Company, whose £1000 were dated from 5th January 1810 :—

Year.	Average.	Highest.	Lowest.
	£	£	£
1810	1008	1075	889
1811	920	1003	762
1812	1097	1258	913
1813	1303	1410	1103
1814	1337	1389	1289
1815	1104	1217	1072
1816	940	1041	882
1817	918	955	879
1818	1171	1334	972
1819	1148		
Years, 10	10,946		
	1094—average for 10 years.		

There is difficulty in ascertaining what each £1000 of the foregoing tables represented ; but if any reliance can be placed on the assumption that the parts of the different circulations bore somewhat similar proportions to each other in 1810 or 1820 as in 1845, when the three banks had a circulation of £936,000 (of which 73 per cent. were small and 27 per cent. large notes), the following results could be worked out.*

In the year 1810 the representative figures opposite the three banks are :—£950 Royal Bank, £952 Bank of Scotland, and £1008 British Linen Company,—in all £2910. Of this the banks admitted that £381,000 were small notes, while in 1815 they admitted that about 39 per cent. of their circulation were large notes. The £381,000 may thus be roundly taken as three-fifths (60 per cent.) of the whole circulation, the total being, therefore, say £635,000 in 1810, as against £936,000 in 1845. Supposing that the respective

---

* Not an unreasonable assumption, as may be proved from the statistics of the Dundee bank, and the Parliamentary Reports of 1810 and 1826.

circulations increased in the same ratio from 1810 to 1845, the £1000 figure in the tables may stand for £124,000 as the Royal Bank's circulation, £203,000 for that of the Bank of Scotland, and £307,000 for the British Linen Company's. Thus the lowest point reached by the Royal Bank—that is in 1816—would probably be £33,000, and their average for that year £46,000, or a fall of £78,000 (63 per cent.) below the sum of 1810; the lowest average of the Bank of Scotland—also in 1816—would be about £140,000, and their lowest point £127,000; while the smallest with the British Linen Company, in the same period, is about £282,000. These variations correspond very closely with those in Sir William Forbes & Co.'s circulation, which in 1810 stood at £251,000; whereas by 1816 it had fallen to £172,000, and in 1817 to £153,000, rising considerably in 1818 to £200,000, but not touching the high circulation of 1810, which seems to have been abnormally large with all the banks.

An examination of Sir William Forbes & Co.'s circulation about this time will shew that the largest variations were caused by the big notes, whose percentage was increased from 1800 onwards to 1815. The Dundee bank exhibits the same feature, its large note circulation rising from 10 per cent. in 1794 to 31 per cent. in 1800, 19 per cent. in 1810, and 32 per cent. in 1820.

The total circulation of these five banks in 1810 was about £1,089,000, to which the Glasgow and country banks would add three millions, bringing up the large total of £4,000,000. Compared with their exchange power in previous years, this amount is no more than might be expected; for, as has already been observed, the whole paper currency of the country at this time had lost from an eighth to a fifth part of its purchasing power, and must therefore have been increased by these parts to move the same bulk of commodities; so that £4,000,000 notes in 1810 or 1815 bought no more than was done by £3,600,000 or £3,200,000 before stoppage of cash payments.

In 1815, when the crisis culminated, having spread itself

wellnigh over the space of five years, the Scottish circulation amounted to £3,551,496, made up as follows :—

	£5 and upwards.	Below £5.	Total.
1. From banks whose returns distinguish between notes of £5 and upwards and notes below £5, .	£749,093	£1,198,490	£1,947,583
2. From banks who return total circulations only, not distinguishing large notes from small, . . .			£1,603,913
Grand total,		.	£3,551,496
3. Estimated total of small notes, £2,185,498, or 61 per cent.			

Notwithstanding the shrinkage in the following year (1816) from the losses in Glasgow and Leith, the circulation soon resumed and exceeded its former amount, until in 1823 it stood at £3,462,000, of which there were £2,065,000 small notes ; in 1824, at £3,997,688 (£2,296,492 small) ; and in 1825, at the huge sum of £4,683,212 (of which £2,736,491 were small).* By this time the Commercial and British Linen Company Banks had greatly extended their branches in remote but industrious parts of the country, which accounts for a considerable part of the increase.

It is impossible to give any particular statistics as to the Glasgow and provincial note issues beyond those given in connection with the Dundee bank, but it has been ascertained that Sir William Forbes & Co. acted as Edinburgh agents for seven of the largest Scots country banks, and also for Lambton & Company of Newcastle, whose notes had a considerable circulation in Scotland from 1815 to 1826. The seven Scots banks were, the Glasgow Ship Bank, the Greenock Banking Company, the Paisley Union Bank, Hunters & Company of Ayr, the Perth

---

* The depreciation of notes from 1810 onwards, and the high prices of 1823-25, forcibly increased the issues, from the smaller quantity of articles they could be exchanged for.

Banking Company, the Banking Company and the Commercial Banking Company both of Aberdeen, all well-founded respectable banks with considerable business.

The total amounts retired by Sir William Forbes & Co. for these eight banks during a number of years stand as follows, and may give some idea of the extent of their issues :—

1815,	per year	£2,138,000,	per week	£41,000
1821,	,,	1,761,000,	..	33.800
1822,	..	1,528,000,	,.	29,300
1823,	,,	1,421,000,	..	27,400
1824,	,,	1,586,000,	..	30.500
1825,	..	1,674.000,	,.	32,100
1826,	.,	...	,.	28,600

The years from 1815 to 1821 and part of 1822 were abnormally swelled by the notes of the East Lothian Bank ; but deducting £400,000 from the total of 1815, and £300,000 from 1821, still shews a larger turn-over of notes in 1815 than in any succeeding year. Amongst the many causes tending to reduce the notes, it may be worth mentioning that the old worn discs of the silver coinage were entirely replaced in the following year by new coin, which being beautifully struck would give the people a certain regard for them, which must have told in some degree on the "small note" issue, and all the more so when the gold coinage was rectified in 1817.

With the year 1817 a sounder and more hopeful era seemed to have dawned on the country. Distress was still widespread, but the war was stopped, and every ballad-singer in the country was shouting at the street corners the now almost forgotten ditty,—

"Oh, Boney, he's awa from his warrings and fightings,
He is gone to a land that he never can delight ins :
He may sit down and sigh o'er the scenes he has seen a',
And forlorn he may mourn on the Isle of St Helena."

But "the evil that men do lives after them," as the British merchants speedily found. Animated with the hope of a renewal of their former gains by means of the wondrous and varied applications of steam, a forced trade began, and over-production choked the markets. A few facts may enable the reader to grasp the revolution in trade caused by the new steam machinery. In 1782 the returns of the cotton spinners were estimated at £200,000; and in 1803, by a regular progression, they had reached £20,000,000. The imports of cotton in 1772 were 4,764,589 lbs., and in 1818 151,000,000 lbs. Canals and improved roads opened up the country to the trade of the world as at no previous time; while the application of steam machinery to printing, gave ample opportunity to scatter broadcast prospectuses for every kind of venture.

The year 1820 almost swept Ireland clear of banks, or bankers. The neighbouring kingdom escaped for a time, but its turn was coming. In 1821 the Bank of England finally resumed cash payments, while the country banks continued to spring up in all directions. Scotland meanwhile, strong in her powerful banks, gradually lost regard for the city private and small joint-stock provincial banks. As the huge joint-stock banks extended, the smaller offices were slowly but surely compelled to adopt one of two alternatives,—either to submit to the inevitable and accept an honourable absorption by one of the large banks, or go into liquidation. Between 1808 and 1826 no less than fourteen banks had ceased to exist, of which the following issued notes :—

The Dumfries Commercial Bank: failed in 1808, and paid 10s. per £.

Scott, Smith, Stein, & Co. : in 1812, paying 2s. 4¾d. per £.

The Falkirk Union Bank : in 1816, paying 9s. 6d. per £.

The Cupar Bank : retired 1811.

The Glasgow Commercial Bank : retired 1820.

The Galloway Bank : retired 1821.

The Kilmarnock Bank : joined Hunter & Co. of Ayr in 1821.

The East Lothian Bank was compelled to wind up in 1822, owing to Borthwick's evil deeds ; having a good partnership, they paid in full.

John Wardrop & Co. : disappeared in 1823.

The Caithness Bank failed in 1825, its business being taken over by the Commercial Bank. A local antiquary of Wick purchases their notes at a few shillings each, with what intention it is difficult to say ; but it is believed that Mr A. D. Macleay of London still pays *in full* any notes which are presented to him.

The period from 1800 onwards was that in which taxation was first directly levied from banks. In that year of the century the long threatened step was taken which had serious effects on banking profits, a twopenny stamp being required to be impressed on all one pound notes. In 1805 this was raised to threepence, with the troublesome addition that no note was to be considered as properly stamped that had been in circulation for more than three years. In 1808 this vexatious restriction was got rid of, on the ground that notes did not usually last more than three years; but an additional penny was put on to the duty, and a licence of £30 exacted from each bank office that issued notes, with the saving clause that not more than four licences need be taken out in all. In 1815 the climax was reached, when the exigencies of war demanded a stamp duty of fivepence to be printed on the back of each pound note. These taxes, which were levied solely to aid in carrying on the war, have not yet been repealed, although, fortunately, modified under the commutation of 1854.

The effects of these measures were serious to the banks. Their ability to have large stocks ready for use was restricted by the heavy loss thereby incurred. Had this provision been in force fifty years earlier, it would have been decidedly useful in abolishing the fallacy that bank notes in the till were as good as money. On one occasion, at a term about 1824, so low had the ready stocks been allowed to run that one of the banks had no more notes to issue, considerable inconvenience being caused in Edinburgh in consequence. The additional expense incurred unhappily deterred the banks from keeping the engraving and style of their notes abreast of the mechanical skill of the time, a neglect of which the criminal classes quickly took advantage.

The forgers, who had found such ample scope for their energies in the rustic one pound note of the Bank of England, rapidly found imitators across the Border, though happily their efforts produced no such fearful effect as in England. From 1806 to 1825 eighty-six persons were prosecuted in Scotland for crimes connected with this offence, chiefly for uttering forged notes, for, strange to say, no actual forgery was proved against any one; of this number eight were executed, forty-nine transported, three imprisoned, six outlawed, and twenty acquitted, leaving sixty-six criminals.

Although, in comparison with England, Scotland escaped thus lightly, a number of forged notes were put in circulation, the engravings of which were easily made quite as good as on the genuine plates. One banking house alone returned thirty-eight of these notes in little over a year, all to different people in various parts of the country. One fellow entered the shop of a respectable Edinburgh grocer, a Mr Lucas, in June 1817, and asked for a few pence worth of nuts, tendering a guinea note of Sir William Forbes & Co. in payment, for which, after some question, he got his nuts and a one pound note and some small change, going off well pleased. Poor Mr Lucas soon found that the note was forged, but too late, the man in the meantime having disappeared. He was described as a tall well-dressed man. Could it have been the villain Mackoull, the murderer of Begbie?

The banks paid several of these notes, which had got into the hands of other banks' tellers, so that a considerable loss must have been made. In 1826 the efforts made by the Bank of England to improve its notes led to the Scots bankers preparing a memorial for the Treasury, in which, after repeating the various efforts they had made not only for the detection, but chiefly for the prevention of the crime of forgery, they sent specimens of a new style of note produced by "the most complicated machinery," pledging themselves to issue notes of that description and call in all their old notes, if the Government would give them some relief from the duties, by allowing them new stamps in exchange for all the comparatively new one pound notes of the *old issue* they should call in. It was clearly the Government's interest to accede to their prayer, as their own stamp, commonly called the "Congreve," was invariably forged, causing loss to the revenue ; but there is no record that any steps were taken, the banks being left to work out their own remedy, which they afterwards did about 1830 by a finer style of note.   Mr, afterwards Sir, Adam Hay of Sir William Forbes & Co., and Mr Macartney of the Commercial Bank, were the two most prominent parties in forwarding this memorial.

While thus dealing with preventions of forgery, a few horrors will bring our Newgate calendar down to date. In 1802 William Marshall, the cashier's assistant in the Dundee Banking Company, absconded to St Omer with about £35,000 of the bank's property.   It was discovered that he had falsified the books so as to cause the circulation to appear as £13,000 only, whereas he had been issuing notes for his own purposes which raised the circulation to £50,000.   Leaving some assets behind him, the total loss was only about £8000.   Certainly the most daring feat of the time was that already referred to,—the murder in 1806 of Begbie, the British Linen Company's porter, in Tweeddale Close, now the entrance to Messrs Oliver & Boyd's well-known premises.   This story has been so graphically told by Mr Robert Chambers in his " Traditions of Edinburgh," that it is unnecessary to give more than the leading facts.   Begbie had come up from the Leith branch with a remittance of notes, closely followed the whole way by Mackoull, his intending murderer.   On reaching the dark shelter of the close down which the bank then carried on business, the villain rapidly closed on his victim, and, stabbing him to the heart, seized the bag from the grasp of the dying man, and escaped.   He had apparently been able to put the £680 small notes into circulation, but finding the " large " too dangerous material, hid about £3000 of them in a wall in Bellevue grounds, where they were subsequently found.

Five years afterwards the same man, with two accomplices, broke into the Glasgow office of the Paisley Union Bank on a Sunday in July 1811, finding good plunder in a box sent through the previous day from Sir William

Forbes & Co., containing £4000 of retired notes. With this and other £15,000 the three made their way to Edinburgh, and thence by Haddington to London, where the congregation of the wicked absorbed them for a time. Through the agency of a London detective called Boxer, £12,000 of the booty were given up by Mackoull, on condition that the lives of his accomplices should be spared. His efforts were in vain; for though of avail for that particular offence, both ultimately received their due reward, White being hung at Northampton for robbing a mail-coach, and Harry French being transported for burglary. The arch-villain himself returned to Leith in later years, where his audacity betrayed him. He was seized and imprisoned, and, after a bold endeavour to defeat justice by an action against the Paisley Union Bank, was condemned to death. Strange to say, the Government, which had mercilessly executed hundreds of starving wretches for stealing the value of 5s., or having something to do with a forged note, granted Mackoull a reprieve. He died shortly after in Edinburgh jail, exhibiting in his last moments the most distressing anguish and remorse.

Two men, John Brown and James M'Dougal, were executed in Glasgow in 1814 for uttering forged notes. There are also records of three executions in 1817—one at Dumfries, in April of that year, of Robert Morgan, and the other two at Glasgow—for the same crime. The two last referred to—James Macneil and William Mackay—had forged in Belfast (a notorious town for forgeries) some notes of the Greenock bank, which they attempted to pass at the house of John Mackenzie, the ferryman at Govan Ferry Point-House of Kelvin. The last recorded execution took place in Glasgow, September 1821,—an unfortunate woman, Anne Wilson or Moore, who had uttered *one* forged note, being the last victim of these savage laws.

On the evening of Saturday 18th December 1824 a parcel, addressed to the Commercial Bank, was abstracted from the Stirling mail coach, near Kirkliston, containing £275 in notes and £1400 in bills, full particulars of numbers, &c., being sent to all the banks. The last event to record is the robbery, by some London gentry, of the Greenock bank, in 1828, of £28,000 notes, most of which were afterwards recovered.

Turning from these dark pictures of sorrow and guilt, we shall glance briefly at the new banks begun prior to 1825. True to its policy of expansion by branches, the British Linen Company had strengthened its position in 1813 by increasing its capital from £200,000 to £500,000. It is disappointing to observe that the two elder banks violently opposed this reasonable measure,—possibly inspired to do so by their private bank directors, who, prudent enough as to ordinary conduct of business, never seem to have been men of great breadth of sympathy. The first new bank was that of Messrs Maberley, exchange dealers and English merchants. In 1818 they began several branches, and are chiefly noteworthy from having successfully beaten down the exchange on London from forty days to thirty, and subsequently to twenty. A premature attempt to reduce it to ten was profitable neither to themselves nor the other banks whom they tried to circumvent. As the latter refused to lower their rate for drafts, Maberley's operations induced merchants having payments to make in London to draw the amount from their own banks in notes, which were taken to the new house and exchanged for drafts at ten days' date. English commercial travellers in Scotland followed the same practice, and instead of paying their drawings into branches for security, to be advised to Edinburgh less commission, they retained the notes until their arrival at Maberley's, where their pockets were at once lightened in payment of the much desired short draft. By these means Maberley & Co. became possessed of large quantities of notes, for which they demanded payment in London paper at the usual note exchange currency of ten days, thus practically, though at second hand, placing on the other banks the burden of granting drafts to the public at ten days, while they kept the profits. The respective banks in no way relished a procedure that deprived them

of their remittance business, and at the same time reduced
their circulation so summarily ; they accordingly resolved
upon a measure which was so novel, and yet so completely
checked Messrs Maberley, that it deserves some attention.

Their plan was the vulgar one of drowning the miller,
by giving him more than he reckoned or hoped for. The
new bankers when determining to lower rates, had not
reckoned upon an absolute fulfilment of the promise on the
notes of their neighbours ; and their consternation may be
imagined, when on handing across a packet of notes for
usual settlement, bags of *gold* were told out in payment !
Argument and expostulation were alike unavailing ; the
promise upon the notes was to pay gold, and nothing else
would be given.   Shortly Maberley's coffers were full of
unremunerative metal, from which there was no relief save
by expensive carriage to London.   The banks continued
this defence, or conspiracy as it might better be called, until
their disturbers were compelled to curtail their business,
being unable to purchase London paper wherewith to
retire the numerous drafts they had granted. Had Maberley
& Co. possessed more ample means, they could easily have
fought the matter out, by drawing away the enemy's specie ;
but the latter had shrewdly guessed the depth of their
opponents' purse, and there was no course open but retreat.
The mercantile business was sold to Messrs Richards & Co.,
who still carry on the flax-spinning in Maberley Street, Aberdeen ; the banking department seems to have struggled on,
making little headway against the deadweight of opposition from the other banks, until 1832, when the firm failed,
their estates being wound up under English law, heavy
expenses in liquidation reducing the dividend to 4s. 5d.
per £.

It is amusing to read of these proceedings being referred
to with pride, in the evidence given before the Small Note
Commission of 1826, as a proof of the strength and ability
of the Scotch banks to meet their obligations ; the real
object of the measure, the conspiracy against Maberley,
being carefully concealed, either from ignorance or of

design, and boastful prominence given only to the fact
of a Scottish bank having refused to satisfy an interloping
English firm with any currency save *gold*.*

In 1821 the Shetland bank began business, and continued to issue notes until 1827. They failed, according to
Mr Boase, in 1830; while Mr Somers, in his " Scotch Banks
and Systems of Issue," mentions 1842. A dividend of from
5s. to 6s. per £ was paid.

While these ephemeral creations were rising and falling,
the old banks and the new Commercial Bank continued
steadily to spread their branches (the Royal being still the
only exception), until the year 1825 brought new rivals to
the front, one of whom was in after years to take its place
amongst the foremost banks of Scotland. The Aberdeen
Town and County Bank still honourably maintains its
good name as the oldest provincial bank. Beginning with
a capital in £150,000, it now has in capital and guarantee
fund a total sum of £408,000, and a note circulation of
about £200,000, issued from fifty-two offices.

The Arbroath bank, and the second Dundee Commercial
Bank, followed,—the former joining with the Commercial
Bank in 1844; and the latter, after losing its identity in the
Eastern Bank of Scotland in 1838, was swallowed up in
1863 by the Clydesdale Banking Company.

Last, but not least, came the tri-une National Bank of
Scotland, the happy result of amalgamation of three different companies projected in the previous year.

Altogether, these banks added £740,000 of capital to
Scottish banking, backed by strong reserves and large
partnerships. The first and last named have increased the
paper currency of Scotland by nearly £900,000, of which
fully £550,000 are one pound notes, while their total liabilities amount to upwards of £19,000,000.

---

* It was not until December 1862 that speedy railway transit compelled the banks to lower the par of exchange on London from twenty
days to fourteen for drafts, and in the following September from
fourteen to seven; the par for transfers by advice being at the same
time changed from twenty-three to seventeen, and at last to ten, days.

Chapter XI.

Joint-Stock Speculation—The Crisis of 1825, and the Legislation of 1826.

"We are well, our pulse and complexion prove it,—let those who are sick take physic."—*Sir Malachi Malagrowther.*

Gratiano. "Why, this is like the mending of highways in summer,
When the ways are fair enough."—*The Merchant of Venice.*

AMID the circumstances of mechanical development in the early part of the century, it is not surprising that speculation and over-production should have increased as they did. South America and Europe had alike regained their independence, the one from the power of Spain and the other from Napoleon. Enormous foreign loans were negotiated in the London markets, amounting nominally to £52,994,571, although none of them were taken at par, while some were so low as 56 and 30 per cent. So far as the latter were concerned, Scotland was comparatively out of the way of danger, but new companies of every kind came into existence. Besides the banking companies already named, the best known of the offices which then began are The Standard Life Assurance Company and The Shotts Iron Company. In England 624 new companies arose in 1824 and 1825, with a total capital of £372,000,000, of which there was actually advanced £17,605,000, as only 127 were in existence two years later.

As reference is made to the panic which broke out in 1825, and to the subsequent legislation to which it led, when dealing with England, it will be unnecessary to cross the Border as to its effects. In Scotland the distress did not take the form of a crisis, but rather that of prolonged depression lasting over several years. Glasgow naturally suffered most, from its mercantile connection ; but beyond some uneasiness, little actual distress occurred. Three small banks failed,—the Caithness Banking Company, the Stirling Banking Company, and the Fife Banking Company,—all bad failures for the shareholders. Against the three Scots banks, whose debts were paid in full, England presented a list of eighty bank failures.

We now come to the first pointed attack of English statesmen against the banking system of Scotland. The noble lord at the head of the Government—Lord Liverpool—proceeded to remedy the condition of affairs, first, in the southern portion of the kingdom, upon entirely fallacious deductions ; and secondly, of the northern portion, of whose necessities and institutions he was in abyssmal ignorance,—a degree of regard highly flattering to the north, inasmuch as it indicated that England had awakened to the fact of Scotland having acquired an affluence which called for a measure of interference in her affairs. To state the matter as briefly as possible, we must go back to the Act of 1708 (7 Anne, c. 7), which gave a monopoly of joint-stock banking, with note issues, to the Bank of England, no company of more than six members being permitted to act as note-issuing bankers. Unfortunately the idea of banking and note-issuing were inseparably connected in the minds of the financiers of last century, and in consequence it was deemed more profitable to have a note issue and a small number of shareholders, than to adopt the alternative of a large joint-stock deprived of that right. Indeed the latter does not seem ever to have been mooted until after 1822. The small English bankers having failed in large numbers, the loss thereby occasioned necessarily fell to a large extent on the note-holders, because the system of *deposits* was practically unknown save in London, and there were therefore few creditors to satisfy save note-holders. As regards liabilities, the condition of the Bank of Scotland, as shewn by its balance-sheet of 1704, was very similar to that of these Southern bankers, although the assets side of the account shews a very different result. Having small capital and little deposit money, resort was made, as in Scotland, to granting advances by an issue of notes, regardless of ability to retire these when presented. These advances, sanctioned in the most reckless way, worked out their own remedy in times of crisis, by bringing the banks by scores into bankruptcy. English financiers, not distinguishing between the imprudence and insecurity of the advances themselves, and one of the media by which they were given, came to the conclusion that the issue of one pound notes was the cause of the evil. Had they gone further, and enacted that *the entire note issue* of private bankers was radically insecure, they would have been much closer to a proper remedy. This, however, they did not see, or, perhaps seeing, did not dare to propose, their hands being tied by the sacred rights of the Bank of England on the one hand, while on the other they knew what a storm would be raised against that monopoly, if their argument against one pound notes had been carried to its legitimate conclusion, in the abolition of the whole country circulation.

When suitable measures were in course of arrangement for England, it was resolved to deal also with Scotland and Ireland. " Because England had eaten sour grapes, the Scottish teeth were to be set on edge ; "* a measure in which Lord Liverpool was eminently successful, though not in the way he had hoped, for no sooner did the news of his proposals reach Edinburgh, than the whole country *en masse* rose against them, the Scottish lion setting its teeth and erecting its mane in a most unmistakeable manner. Correspondence was carried on in various newspapers ; county meetings took the matter up, from Berwickshire to Caithness, deluging Parliament with petitions and remonstrances ; Sir Walter Scott contributed mightily to the cause by his letters of " Sir Malachi Malagrowther on the Proposed Change of Currency," published in February

---

* Sir Walter Scott's Scriptural allusion to the proposed legislation.

and March of 1826, and addressed to his old friend James Ballantyne, editor of the *Edinburgh Weekly Journal.* They were eventually collected and published in form of a pamphlet, which ran through several editions. So keen was the antipathy of some of the English members of Parliament, that on various occasions Sir Walter's letters were angrily criticised, and declared to be little better than open rebellion.

The ponderous reply of Mr Wilson Croker, Secretary to the Admiralty, was considered by English authorities to be an end of the whole matter, while upon Scotsmen it had absolutely no effect save to call forth various other writers in defence of the one pound and one guinea notes.

Sir Walter Scott had little to say of a really practical nature, but rather indulged in the romancing to which his old-world sympathies made him liable when dealing with the stern facts of history or finance; but few writers could have made so dry a subject gleam with brighter or more humorous interest. His overflowing *repertoire* of tradition, story, and legend was drawn upon with magic effect. The letters teem with allusions and incidents, which entitle them to be reckoned as the foremost classics in the literature of the one pound note ; and, as he himself admits, no sooner was his style recognised under the *nom de plume*, than " the heather was on fire far and wide."

. Sir Malachi's opening sentences disarm resentment. " I am by pedigree a discontented person, so that you may throw this letter into the fire if you have any apprehensions of incurring the displeasure of your superiors. I am, in fact, the lineal descendant of Sir Mungo Malagrowther, and have retained a reasonable proportion of his ill-luck, and, in consequence, of his ill-temper. If therefore I should chance to appear too warm and poignant in my observations, you must impute it to the hasty and peevish humour which I derive from my ancestor. But, at the same time, it often happens that this disposition leads me to speak useful though unpleasant truths, when more prudent men hold their tongues and eat their pudding." Then follows a keen stroke at some of the ill-advised legislative expedients which make up statute law: — "Scotland has been too often subjected to the alterations of any person who chose to found himself a reputation, by bringing in a bill to cure some defect which had never been felt in practice, but which was represented as a frightful bugbear to English statesmen, who, wisely and judiciously tenacious of the legal practice and principles received at home, are proportionally startled at the idea of anything abroad which cannot be brought to assimilate with them."

Both Lord Liverpool and the Chancellor of the Exchequer—Mr Robinson, afterwards Lord Ripon—had admitted, in a letter to the Bank of England, that "the failures which have occurred in England, unaccompanied as they have been by the same occurrences in *Scotland*, tend to prove that there must have been an unsolid and delusive system of banking in one part of Great Britain, *and a solid and substantial one in the other*. In Scotland there are not more than thirty banks, and these banks have *stood firm* amid all the convulsions in the money market in England, and amid all the distresses to which the manufacturing and agricultural interests in Scotland as well as in England have occasionally been subject. Banks of this description must necessarily be conducted upon the *general understood and approved principles of banking*."

When the letter was published, of which the foregoing is an extract, the testimony of "those counsel for the opposite side" was not lost on the legal mind of the Sheriff of Selkirkshire. "No proof can be desired better than the admission of the adversary." Seldom has foeman's armour been pierced by more delicate thrusts than those in which he refers to the parrot cry of "For uniformity's sake" raised by the Government officials, or to the punishing of Scotland for the sins of England. In the first, allusion is made to an ancient though hypochondriac laird, who found it conducive to his own wellbeing to swallow one pill every night. On calling some of his friends together to supper, he invited each and all to take just "one leetle pill," as he

had found them so beneficial for himself. In spite of all
remonstrances and resistance, strong or weak, according to
the character of the guest, every man from the first to the
last was compelled to bolt a pill ; the moral being drawn,
that Scotland would be none the better next morning for
being forced to sacrifice her note issue " for uniformity's
sake." The second illustration cannot be told but in Sir
Malachi's own words :—" I must speak to the justice of this
point, sir. My respected ancestor, Sir Mungo, when he
had the distinguished honour to be *whipping-boy*, or rather
whipped boy, to his Majesty James the Sixth of gracious
memory, was always, in virtue of his office, scourged when
the King deserved flogging. And the same equitable rule
seems to distinguish the conduct of the Government towards
Scotland."

Amongst the many publications issued at this period
may be named " The Life, Adventures, and Serious
Remonstrances of a Scotch Guinea Note," by the author of
" The Letters of a Plain Man." A member of the body of
Writers to the Signet, and evidently well acquainted with
the leading men of the day, he gives an excellent illustration of the uses to which a small note may be put, and
the people in whose hands it may circulate.* The note
struck by Sir Walter was largely imitated, the illustrations
being fairly good, though scarcely equal to those of the
master, indeed many of them were merely adaptations of
those already given by Scott ; but the writer more than
makes up for this lack of literary merit, by a much sounder
and closer argument than Sir Malachi aspired to, of whose
" Squibs " the unknown author of " The Adventures "
speaks somewhat disparagingly on several occasions.

Another of the crowd of writers was " Palœconomicus,"
whose letters, inserted in the *Edinburgh Times* of February
and March 1826, contained more scientific expositions on
the question of the note issues than those of Scott or the
" Plain Man." He points out, that when the commercial

* See pages 180 and 181.

crisis broke out, it at once affected the weakest part,—the English country bankers; and ridicules the idea of suppressing one pound notes alone, when the whole note issue was defective. "It is altogether inadequate, and, as a measure meant to be perfect in itself, is legislation ludicrously *de minimis*; as if, in a fire, one should knowingly snatch up a box of gold, and neglect a box of pearls of equal weight." He concludes as follows:—" On the general question, therefore, it seems to be apparent that the views and the measures of Government are contracted in their scope and erroneous in their object. They have been concocted hastily, without enquiry; and are not suited either to work a present cure, or to exhaust and put to rest for ever the vital question of our currency."

One of the most important petitions was that prepared apparently by some committee of notables, and addressed in the "Vox Populi" to Sir Robert Peel with the other members of the select committee appointed to inquire into the state of the currency. It is an euphoniously worded print of four and a half pages foolscap. After touching generally on the loyalty of Scotland and the soundness of its banks, as witnessed to by Lord Liverpool and his chancellor, it proceeds to give some particulars of the circulation of specie and paper amongst the 831 banks of Great Britain. The annual land rent of Scotland is then discussed, to prove that the note issue did not equal one year's rent, and was scarcely equal to £2 per head of population, being estimated at three and a half million pounds. Some dubious paragraphs follow on land as a medium of exchange and reserve for notes, which remind the reader strongly of Law's writings of a hundred years before, though more carefully expressed. The petitioners reach safer ground when dealing with the utter impossibility of every bank keeping gold sufficient to meet all its liabilities, or any other than a portion of them.

The most important addition to banking literature of the period consists of the reports and evidence of the two committees of the Lords and Commons, appointed by the now alarmed Government, who, having fired their gun and run away, fell upon this expedient to gain some breathing-space. Without an index, huge in size, consisting of nearly 300 foolscap pages, the reports contained a mass of undigested and indigestible matter. One and all the Scotch bankers maintained the perfection of their system, declaring —from ignorance, possibly—the total absence of all "runs for gold," or losses from failing banks, in Scotland up to their own time. The long period which had elapsed since 1797 might excuse them for forgetting the run of that year ; while the report acknowledges, as to the failures, "that there have been only two instances in which the creditors did not ultimately receive the whole amount of the principal and interest of their debt."

It is remarkable that the Commons committee chiefly based their argument for non-interference upon the comprehensive and well-founded principle of Scots law, which while giving creditors ample security for their debts, at the same time conduced to the proportionate safety of the debtor and of commerce in general. The system of public records enables the merchant or banker to be absolutely certain of the security of any heritable property which may be disponed to him for debt, and can inform him of other properties held by his debtor, with the degree of burdens upon each, thereby giving a fair idea of his standing and means. All secret understandings or alienations of property, were utterly valueless until they had ceased to be secret by being recorded in their appropriate registers, open to all who cared to inspect them.

With almost a touch of envy, the committee dilate upon there being no limitation to the number of partners of a banking company in Scotland. The Commercial, National, and Aberdeen Town and Country Banks, with their 2205 partners, might well lead them to ponder the condition of things in their own country, where not more than six partners were allowed for such companies. In 1826 each one of these 2205 was liable, jointly and severally with his co-partners, to the full extent of his fortune, for all the debts of the company in which he had an interest. The difference between the laws of the two nations was still further exemplified, in the ability of creditors in Scotland to adjudge the heritable estate of his debtor as well as to attach the personal, "for payment of personal debts, among which may be classed debts due by bills and promissory notes, and recourse may be had, for the purpose of procuring payment, to each description of property at the same time;" not only so, but death itself did not prevent the creditor from obtaining his legal remedy.

However unwise the original views of the Government may have been, the questions to which their committees applied themselves were not so unreasonable as was at the time supposed. England had just resumed metallic currency for all sums under £5, and it was considered unfair to that country that Scotland should still be allowed to avail herself of her paper currency for similar amounts. An interesting calculation was drawn up on this point in 1826 by an Edinburgh banker, in which an attempt is made to prove, that from wealth and the smaller proportion of population to the square mile in Scotland than in England, the latter ought to be possessed of a currency five times the value of what was suitable for Scotland, and that therefore the five pound note of England only placed her upon an equality with the one pound note of Scotland.

The serious error of reckoning the currency of Scotland at £2,847,000 only, instead of £4,000,000 in round numbers, deranges the author's whole argument and conclusion; but his contention is a reasonable one, and applies even yet when the population of Scotland is only 125 per square mile to the 484 of England. The greater distances at which such centres as Wick, Lerwick, Aberdeen, Berwick, Thurso, Edinburgh, Inverness, Glasgow, and Dumfries are placed from each other, without the gaps between them being filled up, necessitate a currency of such a nature as will cost less for transit than metal, and be more secure against theft from the ease with which it can be concealed in transmission. The natural advantages of Scotland are

not equally distributed over the whole extent of her surface ;
consequently, when capital or material have to be removed
from one part to another, the distances traversed have often
to be much greater than in England, and the charges are therefore proportionally increased. For example, coal is found in all
parts of England, but only in the central lowlands of Scotland to any extent ; the cost of carriage to other parts is
therefore most serious, inasmuch as railways do not profit
by a heavy local traffic as in England, but have to pass
through many miles of absolutely unproductive country,
not getting a single passenger except those going considerable distances.   The geographical features of Scotland thus
make railways more expensive to construct, slower when
constructed, and dearer to the traveller than those of the
south.   It would be difficult, if not impossible, to strike the
exact balance of advantage in the required currencies of
England and Scotland ; but from the foregoing observations,
it may be seen that Scotland is certainly entitled to a
cheaper currency than England, and would incur a serious
loss if her present currency were taken from her,—a loss
which would have been very much more serious in 1826
than now, but which would still shut out all banking
facilities from many parts of the country where they are
most required.

To these questions the committees of the Lords and
Commons do not appear to have given much attention,
although abundant evidence bearing upon them was placed
before them.   Arguing that, on general principles, the rule
which had been adopted for England should also be applied
to the other parts of Great Britain, they considered that the
common burden should be spread over as wide a field as
possible (forgetful, apparently, according to the Edinburgh
banker, of the greater number per square mile to bear the
said burden in England than in Scotland), as " The wider
the field over which a metallic circulation is spread, the
greater will be the security against its disturbance from the
operation of internal and external causes, and the lighter on
any particular part will be the pressure incidental to a

sudden contraction of currency,"—a statement which the branch system of Scotland has proved to be much more true regarding a paper currency, than it was supposed to be of one of metal.

The committee then referred briefly to the claims of Scotland for an exemption from the rule which they had laid down for their general guidance,—such as the existence of one pound notes from the earliest days of Scottish banking ; the concurrent progressive increase in manufactures, agriculture, fisheries, and wealth ; the stability of the banks, and the reliance placed in their notes in all times of panic or distress.   It was admitted that, for twenty years prior to the Restriction Act, the two countries were in *precisely the same position to each other, as they would be in the future*, one pound notes being altogether prohibited in England from 1777 to 1797, without any serious consequences arising from their currency in Scotland.   And, lastly, the evidence led upon the reduction of the number of branches and closing of cash credits was so unanimous, that though the committee did not think the dislocation would be so serious as was anticipated, yet they were "unwilling, without stronger proof of necessity, to incur the risk of deranging, from any cause whatever, a system admirably calculated to encourage the use of capital, to excite and cherish a spirit of useful enterprise, and even to promote the moral habits of the people, by the direct inducements it holds out to the maintenance of a character for industry, integrity, and prudence."

Only two possible dangers were alluded to,—the circulation of Scots one pound notes in England, and the increase in forgery.   As to the former, the directors of the Bank of England, in their evidence, urged no objection to the *status quo*, provided suitable measures were taken to keep the Scottish notes out of England ; while the dread of forgery was dismissed in few sentences, the final verdict being,— " Your committee cannot advise that a law should now be passed prohibiting the future issue in Scotland of notes below five pounds ; " a kind of negative answer, more to be expected from a cautious Scot than from a body of English gentlemen.

The opinion of the Lords was more statesmanlike and concise, and though it is of some length it is thought well to give it verbatim :—" With respect to Scotland, it is to be remarked that, during the period from 1776 to 1797, when no small notes were by law issuable in England, the portion of the currency of Scotland in which payments under £5 were made, continued to consist almost entirely of notes of £1 and £1. 1s., and that no inconvenience is known to have resulted from this difference in the currency of the two countries. This circumstance, among others, tends to prove that uniformity, however desirable, is not indispensably necessary. It is also proved by the evidence, and by the documents, that the banks of Scotland, whether chartered or joint-stock companies or private establishments, have for more than a century exhibited a stability which the committee believe to be unexampled in the history of banking ; that they supported themselves from 1797 to 1812 without any protection from the restriction by which the Bank of England and that of Ireland were relieved from cash payments ; that there was little demand for gold during the late embarrassments in the circulation ; and that in the whole period of their establishment there are not more than two or three instances of bankruptcy. (!) As during the whole of this period a large portion of their issues consisted almost entirely of notes not exceeding £1 and £1. 1s., there is the strongest reason for concluding that, as far as respects the banks of Scotland, the issue of paper of that description has been found compatible with the highest degree of solidity, and that there is not therefore, while they are conducted upon their present system, sufficient grounds for proposing any alteration, with the view of adding to a solidity which has so long been sufficiently established."

And so the question of Scottish currency went to sleep for nineteen years, after the most vigorous awakening it had received since 1765.

The following is a list of the banks of issue in Scotland at the end of 1826, showing the number of partners, and number of branches, if any :—

	Names of Firms or Banks.	Head Office.	No. of Partners.	No. of Branches.
1	Bank of Scotland . .	Edinburgh	Charter	16
2	Royal Bank of Scotland .	„	„	1
3	British Linen Co. . .	„	„	27
4	Aberdeen Banking Co. .	Aberdeen	80	6
5	Aberdeen Town and County Bank . .	„	446	4
6	Arbroath Banking Co. .	Arbroath	112	2
7	Carrick, Brown, & Co., or Ship Bank . . .	Glasgow	3	None
8	Commercial Banking Co. of Scotland . . .	Edinburgh	521	31
9	Commercial Banking Co.	Aberdeen	15	None
10	Dundee Banking Co. .	Dundee	61	None
11	Dundee New Co. . .	„	6	1
12	Dundee Commercial Bk.	„	202	None
13	Dundee Union Bank .	„	85	4
14	Exchange and Deposit Bank	Edinburgh	1	4
15	Greenock Banking Co. .	Greenock	14	3
16	Glasgow Banking Co. .	Glasgow	19	1
17	Hunters & Co. . .	Ayr	8	3
18	Leith Banking Co. . .	Leith	15	4
19	National Bank of Scotland	Edinburgh	1238	8
20	Montrose Bank . .	Montrose	97	2
21	Paisley Banking Co. .	Paisley	6	4
22	Paisley Union Bank .	„	4	3
23	Perth Banking Co. . .	Perth	147	5
24	Perth Union Bank . .	„	69	None
25	Ramsays, Bonars, & Co.	Edinburgh	8	None
26	Renfrewshire Banking Co.	Greenock	6	5
27	Shetland Bank . .	Lerwick	4	None
28	Sir William Forbes & Co.	Edinburgh	7	None
29	Thistle Bank . . .	Glasgow	6	None

Annexed is the circulation of the Scots banks in 1825, taken from the report of the committee, from information supplied by the different banks. Some of them did not distinguish between small notes and large, but the

committee estimated the proportion as indicated by the
figures marked with an asterisk :—

	£5 and upwards.	Under £5.	Total.
Highest Amount	£1,118,896 *827,825	£1,572,828 *1,163,663	£2,691,724 1,991,488
	£1,946,721	£2,736,491	£4,683,212
Lowest Amount	£752,461 *570,990	£1,200,025 *910,623	£1,952,486 1,481,613
	£1,323,451	£2,110,648	£3,434,099

Both amounts shew an increase of about £700,000 over
1824, of which £400,000 was in 20s. notes. It may be
observed that the difference between the highest and the
lowest, £1,240,000, is almost exactly what it is at the present time,—a coincidence indicative of two opposing causes
of elevation and depression. The first may be found in
the excessively high prices of 1825, which, by reducing the
relative value of money, forced an increase of notes to effect
the same work as formerly. This high level, of necessity,
shrank violently when prices collapsed towards the end of
the year, and extended the difference between the extremes.
The other cause, which has tended to decrease the proportional advance of notes since 1825, is the vast increase in
the cheque system, which has only come into existence
since that year, and is as reasonable an advancement on
bank notes, for its own special purpose, as the latter were
on a metallic currency. Each now has its place,—specie,
the reserve basis of all ; notes, the public currency ; and
cheques, the private medium of the innumerable settlements of commerce,—while only two hundred years back
the entire duty was performed by specie alone.

Chapter XII.—1826-1844.

LAST EFFORT OF LOCAL BANKING, AND ITS GRADUAL ABSORP-
TION BY THE NATIONAL BANKS—EXTINCTION OF PRIVATE
BANKING—INCREASE OF BRANCHES—PANIC OF 1837—THE
END OF THE FREE NOTE ISSUE.

> *Macbeth.* "I have lived long enough; my way of life
> Is fallen into the sear, the yellow leaf;
> And that which should accompany old age—
> I must not look to have; but, in their stead,
> Curses not loud, but deep, mouth-honour, breath,
> Which the poor heart would fain deny, but dare not."—SHAKESPEARE.

IT may have been observed by students of the reports
of 1826, that nearly all the Scottish witnesses were
connected more or less directly with the large joint-
stock banks of Edinburgh or Glasgow, local joint-stock
banks or private bankers not having much to say for themselves; for though Mr Kinnear, the well-known banker,
appeared as a witness, it was chiefly as a director of the
old bank.   This fact is not without significance in the light
of subsequent history, for it shews the value which was put
upon the one pound note by the leaders of those institutions, who required its powerful aid to establish branches
throughout the country.

Whether it be that the smaller local banks did not
interest themselves in the matter, being indifferent to the
continuance of small notes, or that they saw only too clearly
the weapon of destruction these notes would prove to be
against local banking when utilised by the large banks to
open branches, it is almost impossible to say; but the fact
is worth remarking, that the chief opposition to the proposed legislation came from Edinburgh and Glasgow, and

the county committees,— provincial bankers, with few exceptions, remaining passive.

In 1828 the small fragment of the intended legislation for Scotland came into force,—the Act 9 Geo. IV., c. 65, prohibiting Scottish or Irish notes under £5 from being issued in England.

For several years after 1826 branches were steadily extended, few being withdrawn compared with the period 1800-15 ; and it is well to bear in mind, that all these branches were begun by means of the small note issue, which alone could make them profitable for the time. *The note* was the *unseen* engineer, mining its way through the country, " hoisting " the unhappy local bankers, by means of its connection with the large and influential establishments who issued it, for joint-stock banks alone would satisfy the people. Signs were not wanting, among the local and private bankers, that an effort must be made to meet the increased requirements of the time, if their powerful antagonists were to be kept at bay. These requirements were not little, for Europe, under the enjoyment of profound peace (only broken by the brief struggle at Navarino), was increasing in wealth with rapid strides. In Britain this was at first tempered by the distress arising amongst the working classes, from the want of labour, and the restrictions laid on the import of corn. The cholera, too, ravaged Scotland somewhat severely in 1832, its influence being alarmingly felt in Edinburgh, not so much from the direct effects of the plague, as from its dreadful havoc in some of the surrounding villages. In consequence of pressure, several small banks failed, and others amalgamated* for mutual strength ; while one, the second

---

* BANKS AMALGAMATED. — The Montrose Bank, began 1814, joined the Dundee Union Bank 1829 (one writer says 1826).

Thomas Kinnear & Sons with Donald Smith & Co. in 1831,—who, as Kinnears, Smith, & Co., failed in 1834, with liabilities over £300,000, of which 11s. per £1 have been paid.

The Commercial Banking Company of Aberdeen joined the National Bank in 1833.

L

private banking house in Scotland, Ramsays, Bonars, & Co., gave up their business to the Clydesdale Bank, who still occupy the site of the old office, in the High Street of Edinburgh, though formerly it entered from the Exchange Square.

Thus in about six years the list of Scottish banks was reduced by thirteen. To take the place of the failures, and to carry on the vastly increased business which rose rapidly from 1833, new banks were originated of a totally different character, being, according to the desire of the time, joint-stock banks, with large capital and proprietary,* and *unlimited liability ;* even the new chartered banks being unable to escape this dangerous security.

The return of prosperity led, as it invariably does, to over-production on speculation ; the railway mania began to make its influence felt, but joint-stock banks were the favourite institution both in England and Scotland. At the time that these English banks (numbering nearly 220

The Thistle Bank joined the Glasgow Union in 1836, after an existence of seventy-five years.

Perth Union Bank joined the National Bank in the same year.

In 1837 Paisley Bank gave up business in favour of British Linen Company ; and the Ship Bank of Glasgow joined with the Glasgow Bank Company under the name of The Glasgow and Ship Bank, the latter joining the Glasgow Union Bank in 1843. In 1838 the Paisley Union Bank joined the Glasgow Union Bank.

BANKS FAILED.—James & Robert Watson, Glasgow ; established 1793, failed 1832, paying 4s. 9d. per £. Did not issue notes.

Maberley & Co., Edinburgh and elsewhere, in 1832.

Kinnears, Smith, & Co., as above, in 1834. Did not issue notes.

Robert Allan & Son, established 1776, stopped 1834. Did not issue notes ; paid 4s. per £.

James Inglis & Co., in 1835.

* THE NEW BANKS were,—The Ayrshire Bank, in 1830; followed by the prosperous Glasgow Union Bank in the same year—capital, £350,000 ; then came the notorious Western Bank in 1832, with its capital of £209,000 ; in 1834 the Central Bank of Scotland was opened at Perth, with £80,000 of capital ; and, lastly, The North of Scotland Bank in Aberdeen, in 1836.

in the years 1835 and 1836) came into play, the foreign exchanges of London were close upon par, indicating that any increase in the currency leading to an appreciation of the value of gold, would inevitably produce a drain of bullion, and an adverse exchange. The high rates of interest in America had already been too attractive to investors, and gold had left the country in considerable quantities, reducing the exchange to par. Totally regardless of these signs, the country bankers extended their note issue from £2,799,000 in December 1835 to £4,258,197 in the same month of the following year. The Bank of England had already considerably raised its rate of discount ; but this increase in the country notes, together with the millions of cheques, bills, and similar documents, floated by the same houses, completely upset all calculations. The exchanges began to fall rapidly, and a renewed export of gold took place from the reserves of the Bank of England. In the heavy losses and banking failures which ensued, Scotland had little share ; the Western Bank not having developed its peculiar style of banking to an extent beyond remediable measures.

Under the guise of a joint-stock, then deemed infallibly safe, it had gained an undeserved credit amongst depositors, and was besides hugely admired by such impecunious individuals as are ever in need of cash or accommodation. Beginning business in 1832, two years sufficed to obliterate the memories of 1826, and revive in full force the delusions of Douglas, Heron, & Co. ; there was the same reckless discounting, with waste of capital, deposits, and note circulation upon a speculative market, and the same supreme indifference to reserves of Government securities or other convertible assets. So early as 1834 their difficulties compelled them to ask the assistance of the Edinburgh banks, who only reluctantly gave the required aid, on condition that it should be utilised in the purchase of Government funds to be retained as reserve. This check had merely a temporary effect, to be forgotten in four years, for the bank was again pulled up in 1838 by the same guardians of the public security. In view of the extended area and amount of their own operations, the Edinburgh banks were resolved greatly to increase their coin and investments in Government funds,—the latter having been somewhat checked for a number of years from 1810, by the action and influence of the Commercial Bank. The Western Bank received this second remonstrance with virtuous indignation, upon which they were told, that after the 21st of July in that year, the other banks would decline to receive their notes. Last century this measure would have been matter simply for gratification to the defaulting bank, as its only effect then would have been to increase the issue,—for in 1772 it was on the directly opposite policy that the Bank of Scotland collected as many of Douglas, Heron, & Co.'s notes as they possibly could, and returned them against them, receiving in exchange short dated bills on London, thus bringing about that bank's collapse more speedily,—but in 1838 the Western Bank could not afford the loss of *prestige*, and was compelled to submit. Notwithstanding this concession, the Bank of Scotland and the other banks deemed it their duty to send a memorial to the President of the Board of Trade, Mr Poulett Thomson, who in consequence of the information supplied, refused to grant the Western Bank the charter they had applied for.

In footnote is given a list of new banks begun in 1838,* of which only the Clydesdale Bank and the Caledonian Bank remain to tell the tale of failures and amalgamations. The following year, 1839, was the black-letter year of Scottish banking history, for in it the City of Glasgow Bank saw the light of day. In 1840 four more banks opened, which have all disappeared. With these the free note issue came to an end. In 1843 another strong bank appeared upon the scene under a new name. In the Union Bank of Scotland were incorporated many of the better-class banks, who had

---

* In this year the Clydesdale Bank, the Caledonian Bank, the Eastern Bank, the Edinburgh and Leith Bank, the Paisley Commercial Bank, and the Southern Bank of Scotland, all began business.

stood the test of time and its vicissitudes for many years. Amongst these were the old Glasgow Ship Bank, begun in the middle of the eighteenth century; the Thistle Bank; the Glasgow Banking Company; Hunters & Co. of Ayr; the Kilmarnock Banking Company; and the Paisley Union Bank. In later years the Perth Banking Company and the Banking Company of Aberdeen were added to the list, two of the strongest and best of the provincial banks of Scotland. The framework of the new bank was composed by the union, in 1838, of the ancient house of John Coutts, Sir William Forbes, & Co. with the vigorous Glasgow Union Bank of the West. In consequence of its numerous branches opened prior to 1844, it was favoured with one of the largest authorised circulations under the settlement of that year; while its subsequent absorption of the two banks before-named, has placed it at the head of the list, with a total authorised circulation of £454,346.

Chapter XIII.—1844-1845.

A Retrospect of the Place and Power of the One Pound Note during the Free Issue—The Act 8 & 9 Vict., c. 38, and its Effects.

"Weel, weel, my Lords, that's the end o' an auld sang."

SO said Lord Seafield, the last High Chancellor of Scotland, when in 1707, with a laugh on his face and sorrow at his heart, he put his seal to the Treaty which was to end the ancient *régime*. Tradition sayeth he had English gold in his pocket, which, if true, would scarcely lighten the load elsewhere. To a lover of his country, who has searched through the story of its banking, with all its evils and varied defects, it is impossible to consider the end of the "auld sang" without experiencing a feeling stronger than regret.

In striking contrast to the temporary legal expediency of some countries, the law of Scotland, upon which its banking and note system were founded, has ever had its base on principles which seem applicable to every age of mankind,—principles which enabled the different creations springing out of them, not merely to meet the necessity of the time which gave them birth, but, partaking of the nature of their parent, to adapt themselves to each new condition which might emerge in the ever-changing stream of life.

It has been seen that at the outset, in 1696, the ancient Scottish law had absolutely nothing in it to limit, much less to prevent, the free issue of bankers' notes, nor did the Scottish judges seek in any way to put obstacles in the way of their negotiability. In England both of these positions were exactly reversed. The only restriction in Scotland—the twenty-one.years' monopoly to the old bank —was owing solely to the influence of the law and practice of England upon the mind of the Englishman who drew up the constitution for the new Scots bank, and had no lasting effect, inasmuch as it dropped out of sight in 1716.

By way of authority, let the reader glance at Macaulay's vivid sketch of the scene upon which the bank note made its debut, and the character of its rivals on the road to fame :—" In the autumn of 1695 it could hardly be said that the country possessed any measure of the value of commodities. It was a mere chance whether what was called a shilling was really tenpence, sixpence, or a groat. . . . Three eminent London goldsmiths were invited to send a hundred pounds each in current silver to be tried by the balance. Three hundred pounds should have weighed about twelve hundred ounces. The actual weight proved to be six hundred and twenty-four ounces. The same test was applied in various parts of the kingdom. The evils produced by this state of the currency were not such as have generally been thought worthy to occupy a place in history. Yet it may well be doubted whether all the misery which had been inflicted on the English nation in a quarter of a century by bad kings, bad ministers, bad parliaments, and bad judges, was equal to the misery caused in a single year by bad crowns and bad shillings. . . . When the great instrument of exchange became thoroughly deranged, all trade, all industry, were smitten as with a palsy. The evil was felt daily and hourly in almost every place and by almost every class,—in the dairy and on the threshing-floor, by the anvil and by the loom, on the billows of the ocean and in the depths of the mine. Nothing could be purchased without a dispute. Over every counter there was wrangling from morning to night. The workman and his employer had a quarrel as regularly as the Saturday came round. On a fair-day or a market-day the clamours, the reproaches, the taunts, the curses were incessant ; and it was well if no booth was overturned, and no head broken. No merchant would contract to deliver goods without making some stipulation about the quality of the coin in which he was to be paid. Even men of business were often bewildered by the confusion into which all pecuniary transactions were thrown. The simple and the careless were pillaged without mercy by extortioners, whose demands grew even more rapidly than the money shrank. . . . The ignorant and helpless peasant was cruelly ground between one class which would give money only by tale, and another which would take it only by weight."

Such, then, being the field on which bank notes were first issued, both in England and in Scotland, it is manifest that their primary duty was to replace a large proportion of this miserable currency. Gold was extremely scarce, and was therefore seldom seen, so that the great bulk of payments was made in the clipped, worn, rudely made, and often spurious, discs which struggled to pass current as silver coin. From such competitors it may readily be imagined that bank notes had little to fear, the small note specially so, for it was the lack of a *small* currency that was most keenly felt by the mass of the population. Merchants could make a shift with bills of exchange for their larger transactions, but the millions of small traders, workmen, farmers, and others were powerless to extricate themselves from the whirlpool of confusion to which their Stuart rulers had abandoned them. When therefore their merits were once understood, the nation turned with thankful eagerness from this rude and wrangling barter in bags of metal to these "*papers*," representing "rights" only, but "rights" which general confidence in the issuers had converted from *jus ad rem* to *res* itself. Their steady equal value, when compared with the varying silver coin, soon led them to be regarded in the same way as money is now defined. They were, *first*, a general standard of value; and, *second*, a general medium of exchange. Of course it is unnecessary to remind the reader, that, being intrinsically worthless reckoned as pieces of paper, their whole basis was one of confidence on the part of the receiver, and of prudence on behalf of the grantors ; but they fairly filled up, indeed they performed better than *anything that then existed*, the functions of money. Uniform in value, portable in size, and though not of great value yet truly representative of great value ; and, thirdly, they were most certainly "something desired or demanded." In these different offices they saved time in calculation, steadied prices, gave a more uniform measure of value, and prevented much expense for carriage of coin to the merchants and people of the early years of the eighteenth century. In a few years their PLACE and POWER were assured. By their agency, in small degree at first, but in greater volume as time went on, one pound notes assisted materially in opening up the resources of the country to civilising influences. Viewed as a power in political economy, which has for its primary object the consideration of the nature of wealth, and of the laws which guide its production, exchange, and distribution, the small paper currency of Scotland could not have been introduced more opportunely than in 1699 or 1704. The different parts of the country were separated from each other by tracts of uninhabited waste, across which it was dangerous to travel, alike from the terrors of robbers as from the inclemency of the seasons. Roads were present merely as tracks worn deeply into the soil by centuries of traffic, along which strings of pack-horses crept from town to town twice or thrice in the year, forming the only general means of conveyance open to the public. To settle a debt of £1200 Scots (equal to £100 sterling when exchange was at par), by forwarding by such means a bag of silver weighing from eighteen to twenty pounds, was clearly as direct a stoppage to trade as any legal enactment could have effected. Nor must it be supposed that the bills of exchange then current amongst merchants could in measure meet the difficulty, for, as John Coutts's cash-book showed, even down to 1740, in the best of credit and widely acquainted as he was, he had yet the greatest diffi-culty in arranging payments and exchange in different towns, *from the total absence of any agency in these places by which it could be undertaken.* A payment of £100, made in small notes, would not weigh a sixtieth part of a bag of silver for that amount, and could be hidden with ease about the person of the traveller; so that any merchant or trader, after his long journey across country to some fair, vastly lessened his labour, risk, and inconvenience, by the new medium of exchange.

From any dangerous part of the country, where silver could not with safety be risked, and on which there was no facility for obtaining a bill of exchange, trade was completely shut out, and *could not* be commenced. Or if by good fortune "exchange" could be bought on the particular place to be visited, the first trouble was, that it had to be *bought* with a price, and not drawn for nothing, as bank notes were; and, secondly, there was the risk of non-payment by the drawee, which compelled the would-be-trader, on arriving at his destination, to cash his draft before he made any purchases, lest at the end of the day he should not be able to obtain the money wherewith to pay for his goods or stock. In this way he was exposed to a third expense, for although compelled to get ready cash, he might not find anything to purchase to his mind, and would thus have the disagreeable alternative of buying that which he did not require, or of *repurchasing* a bill of exchange on the town from whence he came.

It is not to be wondered at that trade was slow to enter the straths of Scotland, having such difficulties to overcome; or that merchants should hesitate ere risking the performance of journeys as profitless as John Gilpin's to the village of Ware. While this was the condition of the trader *before* bank notes were introduced, let us follow him a few years later, with the same slight swelling of clothes in the region of his heart which still betrays the "bundle" of notes in the modern drover. He would probably have a stouter stick long ago than is now needful for a lowland lad, while if he came from the far north it is quite probable a dirk might be found lurking amidst the notes, ready upon the smallest provocation to settle accounts with more summary diligence ; but whether the particular individual be highland or lowland, it is astonishing to see the numbers of "shepherd callants and farmer bodies" from the south, hob-nobbing with so many "shentlemen drovers and crofter craturs" from the north. What has caused this wonderful change? Would it be wrong to suppose that it was at least helped on by the "sma' note;" and that the highland drover had at last found a safe and ready means of selling his shaggy clean-limbed cattle to a lowland farmer in exchange for a portable and concealable kind of money? To the highly strung though somewhat superstitious Celt, everything in the shape of paper and erudition has an awe-inspiring effect ; once give the cautious man a sound belief that the note with its elaborate printing is worth twenty silver shillings, and he will stick to it with more sense but with as much tenacity, as the Polynesian to the chip of wood on which missionary Williams told his wife to "hand the bearer an axe."

If two races so irreconcileable as the Celt and Saxon could find common ground for increased trade by means of the small notes, how much greater must have been their power in the respective parts of the country in which they had found their *place*. Acting the part of local bankers before any existed, they gradually accumulated in the hands of some person or persons far distant from the bank town, who, pondering what to do with this increased and new form of wealth, hears that the new bank, whose notes they have already learnt to respect, will give them £3, or £4, or £5 per cent. per annum for all money lodged with them on deposit. There will be some dubiety, possibly, as to whether the bank does not mean any other money than its notes, which further enlightenment soon settles. The smallness of the bundle in which his wealth is wrapped, enables the new depositor to journey to town with comparative ease. There the "rights," the *jus ad rem*, are presented to the bank, and then comes the ticklish moment. No matter what they are considered outside, *here* they are only a right to the

thing signified, not the thing itself. It is possible that the
cautious capitalist would first ask for gold or silver, and then
pay *that* in as a deposit? Such things have been done in
the nineteenth century, and there is no reason to doubt of
its having been done in the eighteenth.

ERRORS IN THE ISSUE.—Our note having thus returned
to the bank in its travels, brief notice may be taken of
the dangers and abuses of the issue in the early times of
banking, before dealing with their effect on deposits.

Repeated reference has been made to the fallacy that
printed notes were money, even when lying in the bank's
till. Save with William Paterson and a very few other
sensible men, the haziest notions were afloat at the beginning
of the banking era, as to convertibility of paper money. If
gold or silver needed no conversion, why should paper notes
require it? the convenient theory being, that land was the
only true measure of value or medium of exchange,—surely
a more gross form of filthy lucre than the metals usually
burdened with that epithet. As this delusion never got a
footing in Scotland, it is unnecessary to mention it further,
than as shewing the unsound ideas prevalent upon the
paper currency. It also gives an estimate of the difficulty
of the Bank of Scotland in choosing the path of safety in
preference to those in which no regard was paid to the
issuer's liability, when called upon to implement the promise
on his notes. At their first start, judging from their small
capital and infinitesimal metallic reserve, as shewn by their
balance-sheet of 1704, it is evident that the bank were
not free from the current fallacious opinions, as they had
the large sum of £50,847 sterling of notes issued, against
which only £1,600 of silver was in stock, the rest of their
reserve having been drained from them in the run. That
they had profited by the experience gained in 1704 and
1715, is evident from their views expressed in the old
" Account of the bank " previously referred to, the author
of which in 1727 says, " For the quota of credit in a banking
company must be proportioned to the stock of specie in the

nation, learned and understood by long experience, and not extended to a capital stock subscribed for ; which cannot in the least help to support the company's credit, if the specie of the nation decay." Mr Macleod observes on this extract, that "this doctrine contains the refutation of many wild schemes ; and the true plan of regulating a paper currency, is simply to discover how a certain proportion shall be maintained between specie and credit." Precisely the doctrine which Sir Robert Peel afterwards attempted to enforce on the country bankers of England by his Act of 1844. "Let the variations of the foreign exchanges be the rule for the restriction or expansion of your paper circulation," was his watchword ; and had he been able to include not circulation of notes merely in the scope of his remedy, but the vastly greater circulation of credit on advances, his plan would have been as nearly perfect as any measure could have been, which has for its object the regulation of monetary affairs.

It is possible that a somewhat rigid adherence to the rule pointed at by the writer of 1727, combined with natural aversion to expenses of collecting and maintaining a larger stock of specie, were amongst the causes which kept the old bank running in its narrow groove until the foundation of the Royal Bank ; but the extract suffices to shew that it was a current opinion, in 1727, that notes might be issued to the full extent of the subscribed, though uncalled, capital of a bank,—the old bank itself, with its £100,000 capital, of which only one tenth was paid up, affording a striking example.

The most deadly error, and the one that cost most effort to eradicate, was the fallacy that notes were money. Professor Leone Levi, in a recent lecture, remarked that this notion " is quite modern ;" so far, however, as British or Scottish banking is concerned, it is as venerable as the system itself. It was simply a part, almost a corollary, of the whole "inconvertible" doctrines, whether based on land or debt, or upon nothing at all. There is no trace whatever of the Royal Bank being tainted with it, and had subsequent banks acted upon the same rules no more would have been heard of the delusion. Unfortunately a second factor for evil stepped in, when the doubt as to summary diligence upon promissory notes broke down all the old bank's endeavours to inculcate the lesson it had learned upon the Glasgow banks of 1750 and onwards. A third complication arose in the wretched option clause, which continued the mistake in full force until the Act of 1765 remedied both evils, and in a great measure destroyed the fallacy, after an existence of two-thirds of the century. Douglas, Heron, & Co. made one furious attempt to break loose into the old paths, but their speedy collapse in 1772, under the new order of things, was the final blow to the system, which never again raised its head in Scotland in the *same form*.

After Douglas, Heron, & Co. had passed away, there is scarcely any trace of a general over-issue of notes down to the present time. In special cases, such as those of the Western and City of Glasgow banks, the notes helped to keep up the rotten corporations by means of their power in the branches; but the advances granted by these banks were not issued in the form of notes, but of discounts and advances on account, drafts, retirements of London bills, and other forms of credit,—the *notes* having little or no part in the transactions which brought on the ruin of the banks. Large as the circulation of the City of Glasgow Bank was, it was not excessive, compared with that of other banks, in proportion to the number of its branches. The notes and the branches gave a strength to its constitution, which kept it alive long after the centre was hopelessly decayed. To this extent, these strong parts of Scottish banking postponed, and therefore aggravated, the final collapse; but the fact that a national *good* is occasionally put to an evil use, is small argument for its abolition. This was partly the cause of the English dislike to the small note, and was as unreasonable as it would be to abolish the British Parliament because it sometimes deserves Carlyle's epithet of "The Great Palaver."

Mr Tooke, and many other English writers, blame small notes for much of the speculation which led to the crisis of 1825, not seeing that they could have had almost nothing to do with it, being too fully employed as a much-needed currency, supplying the place of gold, of which the previous issues of other notes, and war demands, had denuded the country. The guinea note, whose "Adventures" have been referred to, speaks very sensibly on this point :—" Whatever such fellows as my relations, the hundred and the fifty pounders, may have been about, I have been very little connected with great speculations ; as when thousands and thousands have to be paid, there would be little thrift of either time or trouble in fyking with such insignificant beings as us sma' notes."

THE PLACE AND POWER OF THE NOTE. — Having noticed these burrs and faults that had attached themselves to the skein, the fair thread of the system may be again taken up. The first task of the note was accomplished, and that most successfully. It had established itself as a means of exchange upon so secure a basis, that to this day Scotland has never sought to return to a currency of coin. While England has been torn with her bi-metallic contests, the sure evidence of a scarce currency, Scotland has maintained itself in perfect quietness and ease by the aid of its one pound note.

Theoretically, the first work of a currency is to be a means of *exchange* of WEALTH ; and having shewn how that had been accomplished, the effect of the one pound note upon its *production* and *distribution* can now be followed.

The production of wealth requires the use of land, the employment of labour, and the possession of capital ; and for our purpose the greatest of these is capital. The Bank of Scotland, averse to increase of capital, and yet desirous of equaling the accommodative powers of the Royal Bank, undertook a most original operation when it grafted the deposit system upon the cash credit in 1729. The importance of this step can scarcely be estimated, unless, by some impossible combination of events, Scotland were suddenly to find herself without a bank, and even in such a case the innumerable agencies at work for transferring capital in the nineteenth century would partly make up for the want ; but, for the Scotland of 1729, the new departure effected the *re-construction* of the country. For a time its influence was restricted by the lack of branches, or provincial banks ; but as the latter sprang up from 1750, the prosperous era began, and continued with ever-increasing force, until the foundation of the joint-stock bank branches gave its final impetus.

In this mighty work the one pound note was the original, and, during many years, one of the most important instruments. Let us hear what a Frenchman says of this :—" It is only by the aid of either perverted or ill understood facts that people have been led to suppose that the bank note performs an important part in Scotland. The brilliant success obtained by the institutions of credit in that country rests on a different basis, though wide and solid,—that of the enormous effective capital accumulated by deposits. The illustrious Macaulay was right in saying that her schools and her banks had transformed Scotland. We are quite of the same opinion ; but we make a distinction between *banks*, as active intermediaries between the capital whose formation they encourage and the labour that they nourish, and the *bank note*,—a secondary instrument, that produces but a very slight economy in the circulation, and that is more valuable by its facility of transport and convenience of using, than by the slight saving effected by it in the metallic mechanism of the exchanges."* It is well known how Mr Somers' pen has exposed this misconception. M. Walowski admits the extreme meagreness of literary work from Scottish bankers, and the absence of definite and particular

---

* M. Walowski's " Les Banques d'Ecosse ;" Somers' " Scotch Banks," &c.

information. In his second chapter he acknowledges that he (or rather concealing himself under the plural),—" We often discuss arbitrary imaginings until we lose sight of facts, and then the accumulated results of experience find themselves overlooked." In these two admissions we have the reasons for M. Walowski's singular mistake. Having few facts to trust to, and these chiefly of the present century, he simply looks for the largest item in our accounts, finds it to be "deposits," and proceeds to work out his "arbitrary imaginings" until he loses sight of the few facts he began with. Had he been aware that in one of the years of the present decade, notes were exchanged in Scotland, *between the banks alone*, amounting to £170,000,000, without taking into account either the incalculable value of transactions this sum represented of settlements amongst the *public before they are paid into a bank at all;* or, *second*, the amount of such transactions now paid by cheque or bill, which prior to 1800 were made by notes, he would scarcely have written such a libel upon the note issues of Scotland. Nevertheless his argument is adroit, for by replacing the word "deposits" in his first paragraph with the word "banks" in his second, he succeeds in opposing *bank notes* to *banks*, instead of *bank notes* to *deposits*, and thus endeavours to place his opponents in the position of maintaining that a part is greater than the whole,—that notes are greater than the banks of which they are the instruments.

When the deposit system was inaugurated, cheques, or "draughts" as they were then called, were little known. Payments of accounts were *never* made by cheque,—though of course, for distant creditors, bills of exchange were usually drawn when that could be done with profit, but for ordinary hand-to-hand payments, cheques or draughts *had no existence*. When they were used, it was by direct presentation by the drawer to the bank, who paid the amount in notes and reduced the deposit of the customer. So that in comparison with the present mode of settlement, the *proportion of bank notes* used for payments of accounts was vastly in excess of payments made by mercantile paper, and this fact alone gave them a superior position and importance, which lasted well down into the present century. We have already seen how the first deposit might be made, —a certain quantity of notes accumulating as money in the hands of some individual, who conveyed them to the bank, and exchanged them for a new species of right. As deposits and depositors increased (and let us not forget that by their acceptance as a superior standard of value and medium of exchange to the old silver coinage, the notes had their share in economising the nation's capital from whence these deposits were drawn), the bank found itself in possession of funds, for which it was bound to pay interest, and which, therefore, it must utilise in some way. How was this to be done ? They could not be all laid out in return for discounted mercantile bills, for these are only present in healthy volume where considerable trade is carried on. In Scotland however the trade had largely to be *made*, before it could be *so carried on ;* and to assist in this desirable object, the cash credit system had been invented by the Royal Bank to employ its capital, and afterwards adopted by the Bank of Scotland, to be fertilised by its deposits. By this means another great principle of economics was performed,—the distribution of wealth by means of the bank, whose instruments were their notes, and, of these, chiefly their small notes.

Thus while a measure of *wealth* already existed in the country, we have endeavoured to shew how it was increased, and how that increase was *produced* by means of the *exchangeable* power of the note. It will be seen how much greater production resulted from more equal *distribution.*

The bank thus possessed of sums belonging to all classes of life, who might or might not have connection with, or knowledge of each other, proceeded to lend these out to second parties, who were equally ignorant of the first. Without the bank's intermediary aid, the capital could not have been collected and distributed. So far, then, M. Walowski is right, but we differ from him as to the position accorded to the *means* by which the bank made these distributions. Without their note issues, what had the banks to *give ?* They had absolutely *nothing.* Specie was not to be got in such quantity as to carry on increased trade. The expenses of obtaining it were so prohibitive, that it would have been as utter an impossibility to continue the deposit or cash credit system, if deprived of a paper currency, as for George Stephenson to have run his first train without steam. Let us adapt M. Walowski's words to our illustration :—" The illustrious Macaulay was right in saying that her schools and *railways* had transformed Scotland. We are quite of the same opinion ; but we make a distinction between *engines*, as active intermediaries between the capitals whose formation they encourage, and the *steam*,— a secondary instrument, that is more valuable by its facility of transport and convenience of using, than by the slight saving effected by it in *the cost of locomotion !* "

Specie did *not* exist. If notes had not existed, some other means must have been introduced, or the nation *would have stood still.* Cheques might have been used, and M. Walowski might have appeared triumphant. But what are cheques but paper money? though for special purposes not so convenient as bank notes. Each is good in its place ; but clearly cheques of private parties could never have circulated as money in the nation, and the want of a proper circulating medium would have paralysed trade entirely. The English at various times were compelled to resort to barbarous bits of notched wood, tied up in bundles, styled " Exchequer tallies," otherwise Scottice " nick-sticks ;" does M. Walowski propose that these would have been more suitable? From so shrewd a writer in general, we imagine very different propositions would have come, had he been more intimately acquainted with Scotland, its people, and its banks of the eighteenth century.

When depositors, or the possessor of a cash credit, wished to draw money from the bank, their position was equally the same ; each presented his cheque and obtained notes,—*invariably notes !* unless for an occasional trip to the south. The great proportion of the banks' creditors and debtors were men of the middle classes,—shopkeepers, farmers, and tradesmen of different kinds. The transactions of Scotland's commerce at that time were not large, and payments were principally made in *small* notes ; at least a large proportion of these was used, for their convenience in making up any number of pounds, and their general suitability to the wants of the lower orders. Employers of labour used a good deal of silver, as a workman's wages did not amount to so much long ago as to need a paper pound to pay them, but the usual average of small notes for *town* requirements has remained tolerably steady all along at about 50 or 60 per cent. When branches were opened, and a more widely spread and poorer population had to be met, a considerable increase in the proportion of small notes took place. In Dundee, from its connection with the surrounding agriculture of Forfarshire and its mill population, the proportion of small notes was always very high. In other districts it sometimes reached 80 and 90 per cent.; but the common rate was very much what it still is, 65 to 70 per cent. of the whole circulation.

The manner and time during which these notes circulated, before a proper national exchange system was introduced, is very well related by "A Plain Man," in his "Adventures of a Guinea Note":—"Sir,—I am now nae chicken, for I was born a good many years ago in the Parliament Close of Edinburgh, within the house of Sir William Forbes & Co., on the south side of King Charles and his bell-metal horse. My *debût* in life was by entering into the service of a worthy customer of the house, who drew me out in part of an order on his cash account for £10, and the lad who was sent was bidden 'bring a' sma' notes, for the mistress wants siller for her marketings.' I was then given to the wife, who, with her lass and her basket, took me down to the laigh market, where I was soon exchanged for meat, and then I came to serve a butcher. He gave me for tea and sugar, and a grocer became my master. This man gave me in exchange for a £5 note to a builder, and from him I was transferred in

payment of wages to a working mason. He bought clothes
with me. I then served an opulent clothier, but was soon
paid by him to a writer to the signet, his agent, who put
me into the hands of an advocate, with one or two more, as
a fee 'to revise Condescendence and Answers, and make a
Note of Pleas in Law' according to a new form of process.
Some one of this family was taken ill, and a doctor was
sent for ; there is no rest for the wicked, and I was again
obliged to change my quarters, by being slipped into his
hand on his leaving the sick room. The doctor paid me
away for corn to his horses, and I then took a jaunt to the
country. I was carried to St James' Fair [Kelso] ; from
thence I went to the Falkirk Tryst ; then to Glesterlaw
Market, after which a shopkeeper in Montrose got me, and
a bagman one day coming up to him, scraping and bowing,
and begging 'for money and orders,' I found my way in his
pocket to Glasgow, where I again led a town life. I was
handed from master to man there, and became the
medium of no small comfort to warpers and weavers,
and very many of the numerous people of the West ;
and during all my track I was most eident in the service
of my liege lords, bringing them by my labour, every
year, more than one shilling sterling."

Time after time, as these notes accumulated, from
profits in the hands of different traders, they were as
regularly brought to the bank, to swell the volume of
deposits and increase the capital available for cash credits.
These might in turn be drawn upon, but *always in notes ;*
which, after circulating longer or shorter time, came again
back to the bank, either directly to swell its own deposits,
or from a source that indicated they had added to the
deposits of some other bank.

BRANCHES.—Mention has already been made of the great
increase in deposits obtained from the country branches,
when these were begun about 1760. The progress was
steady, until the Free Trade and Railway period added so
greatly to the responsibilities of the banks in this direction.

In aiding in the establishment of the branch system, the one pound note again displayed its adaptability to the altered circumstances of time and place, and gave its strongest assistance to the profitable distribution of wealth throughout the land. To open branches, maintained by stocks of gold, in remote parts of a country unsupplied with railways or other regular means of conveyance, would not have been profitable to the banks ; and consequently, had they not been enabled to meet this want by means of their notes, the system could not have come into operation. When giving evidence as to the results of the withdrawal of small notes in 1826, Mr Kinnear, director of the Bank of Scotland, states :—" In Scotland the remote parts of the counties in the Highlands and the Islands require a circulating medium almost exclusively in notes of a low denomination. The people employed in the fisheries, in the kelp manufacture, and the purchase of cattle, although the money employed in these in the aggregate amounts to a large sum, require one pound notes for the purposes of the trade. The consequence is, that the one pound note circulation of some of the banks near these districts exceeds the circulation of the notes of £5 and upwards by two and a half to one, while that of the banks in some of the considerable towns is less than the large note circulation by a half."

If the banks had been compelled to keep gold, the pressure would thus have fallen most heavily on those parts of the country whose inhabitants were *least able to bear it;* for the town population would naturally object to pay increased rates of discount, or to receive decreased interest, induced by the necessity of keeping gold at the country branches ; although, as far as the city merchants are concerned, the destruction of the deposits entailed by the loss of branches would cut off from them the source from whence they draw their advances. Should such an event ever occur, it may be one of the first things to lead to the successful establishment of non-issuing banks, upon the same principles as those of London, and which, like the latter, would confine themselves largely to mercantile centres

such as Glasgow or Dundee.   The future new bankers of
Edinburgh will, we think, be found to come out of its legal
profession.   Many of these firms of writers to the signet
have large sums deposited with them by clients, and the
latest departure has been to supply these clients with
regular cheque books, drawn upon the firm, and payable at
their place of business.   There is no reason why banks of
deposit should not arise as safely among lawyers, as banks
of issue did from merchants.

But we are anticipating.   Under the branch system the
old "till money" theory found its right place.   Delusion as
it had proved under the early state of things, just as that
was passing away the new branches were opening, and we
find our old friend corrected of all his errors, and, chastened
by experience, reduced to the "till money" of the existing
banks.   The cheap management obtained by this measure
was seriously affected when the stamp duties came into
play in 1800 and 1808, a loss which probably accounts for
the Bank of Scotland's withdrawal of a number of its
branches subsequent to the former date.   The branches,
however, gradually increased, but their greatest extension
took place *after the burden of these duties had been removed*
from their "till money."

When the stamp duties were commuted in 1854 the
branches numbered about 550, inclusive of 40 of the Western
Bank.   In thirty years, with the number of banks reduced
to one half, branches have increased to 929, equal to 69 per
cent., though the population has only increased by 26 per
cent.   The immense advantage to the banks of the new
settlement, for their branch system, was most obvious.   At
present a bank with over a hundred branches keeps, as a
general amount, from two millions to two and a half millions
of notes *ready* for issue, to maintain a total circulation of
seven or eight hundred thousand pounds.   The amount of
"large" and "small" delivered from the issue department are
not in the same proportion as when in circulation, being, for
such a bank as above about three of large to two of small
notes; so that, of the above two and a half millions, nearly

one million would be small notes, which under the old stamp duty of fivepence on each note would cost the large sum of £20,833. Upon the assumption that these notes would last for *three* years, the annual expense would be equal to £6944. Under the new system, calculated only upon the average circulation of say £700,000, of which 65 per cent. are small notes, *i.e.*, £456,000, the cost at 8s. 4d. per cent. for the latter would be only £1890, a difference saved to the bank of £5054 on small notes alone ; multiplying this by eight (seven large banks, and the circulation of the three small) there is a total economy of £40,432, a great part of which must have been met by the branches, had they been opened, notwithstanding the disadvantages of the old duties.

The annoyance and expense of the Government stamp was not removed until nine years after the period up to which our history has so far been taken, and it seems strange that no effort was made in 1844 to bring the whole question to the notice of Sir Robert Peel, though it is probable that he would have at once refused to grant alleviation of any means which tended to keep down private issues of notes. In the full burden of this weight, over 500 branches had been opened throughout the country ; and though their rates were necessarily higher than they now require to be,—to such an extent as covered the higher expense,—yet they were of the greatest benefit to agriculture and manufactures. Into these it is unnecessary to enter, but it is well again to remember the position of the one pound note in regard to the whole branch system. It was the instrument by which they were at first rendered profitable to the banks, and therefore practicable for the country ; it was the instrument by which the capital of widely separate districts was collected, to be conveyed to the districts where it was required,—only the instrument, but still as necessary, as essential to the whole banking system, as is gunpowder to the science of war.

EXCHANGE OF NOTES.—With the increase of banks

and branches came the exchanges of notes, whereby the circulating medium was economised and prevented from depreciation. Reference has been made to the manner in which these were at first objected to and resisted, until gradually, as more enlightened views prevailed, they were welcomed by all prudent bankers as a benefit in place of an evil. The cheap expansive power of a small paper currency, at such periods as the Scotch half-yearly terms, is one of its greatest advantages; but it is necessary that, when the special purposes for which the increased issue is granted have been served, systematic means should be adopted for removing the superfluous currency. A large sum might come in, in the ordinary course of business, but a system of exchanges spread over the whole country removes it with certainty and rapidity, and constantly maintains the supply of circulation at a fair proportion to the demand for it, rendering local depreciation well-nigh impossible.

SIR ROBERT PEEL'S ACT.—Such were the conditions which Sir Robert Peel undertook to improve and secure by his new measure (8 & 9 Vict., c. 38), entitled "An Act to Regulate the Issue of Bank Notes in Scotland" (21st July 1845).

So far as he wished additional reserves of specie to be kept, it has had little effect, all the banks now deeming it prudent to maintain larger gold reserves than the limits of their authorised circulation require, save at the two half-yearly terms, when the whole currency has to be temporarily enlarged. At these seasons the Act of 1845 needlessly compels banks to bring gold from London, often to be returned without changing bags. The doctrine of averages had so fascinated Sir Robert, as to lead him to adopt the course which produced this unnecessary security. Upon hasty and uncertain data, he fixed the limit of unsecured issue by an arbitrary process, as unjust as it was illogical (clause VI.). Refusing to recognise the possibility of the perfectly natural termly payments being as naturally cleared away by the note exchanges, he insisted that gold should be taken from

London to cover them, and thereby succeeded in partially destroying the very purpose he had most at heart,—the regulation of the foreign exchanges.

The most important enactment was that effected by clause 1, restricting the future power of note issues to the banks possessing that right on 6th May 1844. By one hidden stroke, the establishment of new banks according to Scottish notions was thus rendered impossible, and a monopoly given to the existing offices, which, in view of the fact that these have decreased from nineteen in 1845 to ten in 1885, is cause for some anxiety as to the future currency of the country.

Sir Robert Peel's active and intelligent mind had been cognisant of many of the evils of English banking, some of which he did not dare to touch; but the chief defect, according to his vision in 1844, was the rash use of their rights of issue by the country bankers. These establishments, having no offices in London, took little interest in the peculiar movements of the foreign exchange, with which it was supposed only a London banker had any concern. Under the venerable monopoly the whole burden of maintaining proper gold reserves for the nation fell upon the Bank of England, and consequently, when the foreign exchanges reached the adverse point, the whole drain had to be faced by the bank. Of the many causes affecting the exchanges, few are more important than the state of the paper currency of a country; as it increases beyond the true necessities of commerce into the region of speculation, the effect invariably is, that the competition of various bankers, all promising to pay gold on demand (and yet at a future date), replaces a certain amount of gold and throws it into the market. As the note issues increase, by way of discounts or other advances, the gold decreases; and as the latter is removed from circulation, it accumulates (being after all only an article of commerce) until, from the want of demand, it *falls in value*, and is eagerly purchased and exported by foreign capitalists; but as the prices of other articles are stated in gold, the immediate effect of the decreased price of gold is to give a fictitious value to general prices, so that every one thinks that fortune is within his reach. When these high prices are seen abroad, imports are poured into the country of a value which the exports cannot equal, and the increased indebtedness causes the foreign exchanges to fall rapidly to the bullion point, after which specie has to be exported to meet the nation's debt, thus further reducing the stock and raising its price, according to the urgency of the demand. General prices at once *nominally* fall from the high price of gold, while the glut of foreign imports produces as serious a practical fall. Home manufacturers are at their wits' end to raise money on their huge speculative stocks ; importers are equally distressed for want of gold to pay their foreign creditors ; both classes are equally anxious to sell before another fall occurs, and force their goods upon the market at ruinous prices ; heavy loss, of course, ensues, followed by acute demand for money ; discounts are looked on with suspicion ; all available notes are run in upon the banks, who, having issued beyond their gold or other convertible reserves, are compelled to stop payment, and general panic ensues. The periodic recurrence of these destructive storms had led Sir Robert Peel to fix on the country bankers' rights of issue as the weak point in the banking edifice, and he accordingly prevented any future over-issue, by fixing a strict line beyond which no English country banks could go, prescribing such heavy penalties for excess that the English country issues have in many cases been kept from 10 to 15 per cent. below the authorised limit. The Bank of England was suitably altered to meet the supposed requirements of the new state of things, being divided into the since famous Departments of Banking and Issue.

Turning to Scotland with, we are afraid, somewhat indefinite information before him, the Prime Minister determined to compel the banks there also to do their part in regulating the exchanges. His connection with all the financial parliamentary reports of the century ought to have made him well acquainted with the prudence and skill of northern banking. Over-issue of notes had not been one of its failings for many years, and even if it had, the note exchanges would speedily have remedied the evil. To some extent Scottish banks were specially favoured in comparison with those of the south ; but it is important to notice, that the Scottish people were not secured in any way against possible weakness in the banks by the means adopted under the Act of 1845.

Returns were called for from the various banks of the amount of their notes in circulation, but from the uncertainty as to the Government's intentions, some of these were sent in with the *largest* amount current during the year, while others, in the dread that taxation of the issue was intended, returned the *smallest* amount. Without further inquiry, and with no regard to proportion to other items in the accounts of the banks, these sums were at once fixed as the amounts of the authorised circulation ; but, in view of their sound character, the Scottish banks were not prohibited from further issue, provided they held specie in reserve (clause VI.). The inequality of this method gives rise to some glaring anomalies in the security of different banks,—*e.g.*, the greater the amount of authorised notes outstanding, the less is the sum of specie kept to meet it ; and, conversely, when the danger to the public was lessened by a bank having *a small authorised circulation*, the security was increased by compelling it to keep a larger specie reserve to meet its issue beyond the authorised limit. Sir Robert Peel thus succeeded in producing the ridiculous proposition of,—" The greater the risk, the smaller the security ; and the smaller the risk, the greater the security."

Another defect in his plan arose from the gold required to be kept not being appropriated solely for the payment of notes,—an omission which, in event of a run, gives depositors an equal claim to the gold fund which was intended primarily for the security of note holders; and as the former exceed the latter in extent of obligation by nearly twelve to one, they could compel any bank to stop payment in a single day, leaving the note holders entirely unprotected.

Nor is the position of the banks improved; for whereas, prior to the Act, their gold or silver was always an available asset at any sudden emergency or for everyday necessities, by it they were absolutely locked up, or at least a large portion, and are of no avail as an asset except at the winding-up of the bank.

The monopoly of note-issuing was the bait by which Sir Robert caught the bankers of 1845. Both he and they believed, that so long as Scotland had a paper currency, no other bank could begin business devoid of a note issue with any hope of success. To obtain the necessary deposits to make advances and payments, notes would be required; and if those could not be issued by the bank, they must be obtained from another bank, and *paid for*,—a most serious preliminary expense, for it placed the new bank in the position of having to pay for its till-money, which all issuing banks, *no matter how small their authorised circulation*, would escape. Bank of England notes or gold would incessantly gravitate to London, and would be no cheaper to purchase. To open a branch system would only aggravate the difference between the bank's expenses and those of its issuing rivals, and thus the new institution would find itself blocked at the very outset, from the want of a proper instrument as a medium of exchange. The stop put to the opening of public banks is, in this respect, more than coun-terbalanced by the injustice of the monopoly, of whose pernicious influence we have not yet had time to see the final results. Amalgamation of issues was fortunately permitted (clause IV.) when two banks united, otherwise the consequences of a bad principle might have been sooner felt; but if, in the future, time works its remorseless ravages on the Scottish banks as it has done in the past, it may be found absolutely necessary to sweep away the monopoly entirely, unless the changed circumstances of the country enable it to adopt some currency different from that of the last hundred and ninety years.

As in 1826 considerable discussion took place while negotiations were proceeding, but general interest was not so strongly excited as in that year. The country was much wealthier, and was therefore not under the same necessity of looking at both sides of a penny; but the arguments used were practically the same. Hugh Miller contributed several articles to his paper *The Witness*, which formed the only approach to the famous Malagrowther Letters, of 1826. Sir Archibald Alison entered the lists with his " Free Trade and a Fettered Currency," in which Sir Robert Peel was torn to pieces, to the complete satisfaction of the author. His pamphlet displays the same vigorous, thrashing style of argument adopted in his other works, but his complete confidence in his own perfection combined with his lack of insight to lead him into many glaring errors. The division of the Bank of England into two departments was a puzzle he could not master, the most absurd blunder being made on this question, that £20,000 of gold taken out of the bank really lessened its ability by £40,000. His argument regarding the restricted issues of the Bank of England during the preceding panic is worthy of attention, in connection with the duties of a note issue at such a period. Sir Robert Peel had stated in Parliament that the whole mischief arose through the bank directors giving too large advances in the autumn, when every one saw a storm was brewing; had they curtailed their advances, and called in their resources, the evil might have been averted. Upon this Sir Archibald remarks : " The argument of the right hon. Baronet is, ' We are starving for want of money in May ; if we had begun to starve in October, we should by this time have been all right.' It is rather a singular way, to be sure, to effect a remedy to a summer famine by adding a winter one to it." Here Alison's style is displayed to perfection. If not extreme, he was nothing. To him there was no difference distinguishable between *starvation* and *economy*. Peel was entirely correct. The Bank of England should not have encouraged advances which results proved to be largely speculative, and had they refused these in the autumn, the spring would have found them with resources sufficient to carry them on without the sudden sharp restriction of *all* advances, which created distress, not only among speculators, but also among *bonâ fide* traders. Plethora in autumn, and starvation in spring, might thus have been equalised, so as to spread an economical supply over the entire year.

Since the Act of 1845 came into force, it has become common with writers of recent times to depreciate the usefulness of the one pound note, under the foolish argument that the country was not in need of so cheap a form of currency, or rather that it was so much increased in wealth, as to be able to pay for a dear currency ; surely a most extraordinary argument, and worthy of all condemnation from every thrifty Scot. In these times of the keenest competition, no effort should be spared, or opportunity missed, of *lessening* the cost of production, where that can be done *without grinding the faces of the poor.* The cost of currency is a factor which affects every interest in the country. No trade, profession, or manufacture can plead freedom from its operation, and each is profited to a certain extent by the cheapness and character of the medium through which their transactions are carried on. Nor can it be said that the NATION is unconscious of this, although long familiarity with the small note currency may have blunted the public perception to its real value ; for it can never be said that a currency is not appreciated in Scotland, when, upon certain proof, it is known to be preferred to all others in the settlement of debts amounting annually to *hundreds of millions of pounds.*

NOTE.—On the next page is given a list of the banks existing in Scotland in 1845, nineteen in number, now reduced, by two failures (embracing three banks) and six amalgamations, to ten. For comparison, the authorised circulations of 1845 and 1884 are given, with the average circulation and coin held in 1884 ; shewing that, though the authorised limit has decreased 13.3 per cent., the note issue has increased 89.9, while the banks now existing have exceeded their authorised limit by 120 per cent.

Banks Existing in Scotland at the Banking Settlement of 1845.

Banks.	Authorised Issue.		Average Circulation of 1884.	Coin held 1884.	Proportion of Coin to Circulation in 1884.
	1845.	1884.			Per C.
1 Bank of Scotland	£300,485	£343,418	£867,383	£684,319	78
2 Royal	183,000	216,451	795,812	712,748	89
3 British Linen Company	438,024	438,024	663,567	358,008	54
4 Dundee	33,451	..	...	...	...
5 Perth Banking Co.	38,656	..	...	...	...
6 Aberdeen Bank	88,467	..	...	...	...
7 Commercial	374,880	374,880	800,383	572,431	71
8 National	297,024	297,024	655,855	483,892	73
9 Town and County	70,133	70,133	208,811	172,840	83
10 Union	327,223	454,346	803,425	508,611	75
11 Ayrshire	53,656	...	...	...	...
12 Western	284,282	...	...	...	...
13 Central	42,933	...	...	...	...
14 North of Scotland	154,319	154,319	390,430	285,080	73
15 Clydesdale	104,028	274,321	577,735	386,878	65
16 Caledonian	53,434	53,434	101,600	61,451	60
17 Eastern	33,636	...	...	...	...
18 City of Glasgow	72,921	...	...	...	...
19 Edinburgh and Glasgow	136,657	...	...	...	...
Total	£3,087,209	£2,676,350	£5,865,001	£4,226,258	72

Present authorised Circulation, £2,676,350
Forfeited between 1845 and 1885
— Western Bank, . . .   284,282
Ayrshire Bank, purchased by
the Western, . . .   53,656
City of Glasgow Bank, . .   72,921
                                        —
Total, as at 1845, . £3,087,209

Average amount of Coin held in
1884, ... £4,226,258
Average circulation for
1884, . . . £5,865,001
Deduct authorised
Circulation, 1884 . 2,676,350
                                        3,188,651
Amount of Coin held in 1884
beyond statutory requirement, £1,037,607

Chapter XIV.—1845-1880.

THE WESTERN BANK—THE CITY OF GLASGOW BANK—BANK NOTES EXCLUDED FROM LIMITED LIABILITY.

"Proud and serene the evening sun went down
On many a home, the last for poor and great;
Dying from off the vale, where slept the town
In dull oblivion of impending fate: . . .
At morn, the new-born earthquake's throbbing beat !
Sounds the alarm amid the tottering street."
—THE FALL OF LISBON.

FROM the close of free banking to the present time there are not many incidents to record bearing upon the one pound note, though some of those form the darkest blots on the mercantile fame of Scotland.

Scarcely had the effects of Sir Robert Peel's Act been felt, when an attempt was made by various companies to get to the windward of the note-issuing banks, by opening banks styled exchange companies, which, had they fallen on better times, might have succeeded upon the same conditions as the great joint-stock banks of London. Coming, however, in the full tide of prosperity preceding 1847, they were led by its influence to depart from the prudent principles which have been the rule for the English institutions, and the crises of 1847 and 1848 were fatal to several. A few struggled on for some years, while one is still in existence in Glasgow, though what it does, or how it survives, no man can tell. The year 1847 witnessed the second warning of the Western Bank, and the break-up of Sir Robert Peel's settlement of the Bank of England. The automatic machinery having got clogged, it was found necessary to allow its issue department to give notes to the banking department without receiving gold or securities in

N

return, and upon its becoming known that accommodation could thus be got the demand instantly ceased. Though Scotland remained very free from panic, there must have been some disturbing influences at work, for the prices of the banks' stocks all fell considerably, as the following list may shew :—

	1845	1847
Bank of Scotland, . . , . .	£178,	£169
Royal Bank	170	149
British Linen Company . .	230	200
Commercial Bank . . .	171	161½
National Bank . . .	166	136

Their circulations are also considerably enlarged, compared with those of the sum fixed as the authorized limit two years previously :—

Excess in 1847 beyond 1845, of Bank of Scotland .	. £40,000
,, ,, Royal Bank . . .	22,000
,, ,, British Linen Company	9,000
,, ,, Commercial Bank .	51,000
,, ,, National Bank . (no increase)	
,, ,, Union Bank . . .	24,000
,, ,, Western Bank . .	60,000
,, ,, Clydesdale Bank . .	17,000
,, ,, City of Glasgow Bank .	40,000

These figures may be the measure of the difference between the minimum circulation said to have been returned to Sir Robert Peel in 1845, and the maximum of the same year. The British Linen Company and the National Bank seem to have had the most accurate idea of the purpose for which the returns were required; the increase in the Western Bank of £60,000 is, however, ominous of another cause of increase,—their reckless advances.

When the troubles of 1847 had passed, there came the usual ten years cycle. At first much repentance for past sins, and dread of cholera, kept the country quiet, until the Crimean war, followed by the Chinese war and Indian mutiny, disturbed her repose.

In 1854 a great boon was granted to the banks by the commutation of the oppressive note duties, which necessitated a stamp of the value of fivepence to be printed on all one pound notes, except those of the three senior banks, who had already received relief from some part of the burden. The new system of charging 8s. 4d. per cent. per annum upon the averages of circulation, was so extremely profitable to the banks, that it is difficult to see how a government with a Crimean war debt on its head could think of foregoing the old method.

The failure of the Western Bank in 1857 gave another proof to the world of the truth of King Solomon's sarcasm, —" Though thou shouldest bray a fool in a mortar among wheat with a pestle, yet will not his foolishness depart from him." Time after time had this foolish bank received the poundings of the pestle and the remonstrances of the wheat, amongst which its lot had been cast, with utter disregard and scorn. Excessive over-production prior to 1857 had necessitated large advances to merchants, while bankrupt-cies in the United States had caused uneasiness in England ; but beyond some small bank failures, and stoppages of several mercantile houses, no imminent danger was antici-pated, so that, though the Bank of England's reserves were much reduced, it was hoped that the worst had been passed. This was on the 1st of November, and the excitement was beginning to abate, when it was suddenly and fiercely aggravated by the news of the Western Bank's failure in Glasgow.

Remittances having been cut off from America, the bank's heavy unsecured advances compelled it to seek the assistance of those whose advice it had ever rejected. The Edinburgh banks and the Union Bank, with generous prudence, advanced £510,000, in consols, on 29th October, receiving bills in security for £767,520. 16s. 8d., but on other severe losses coming to light further aid was refused. The bank's liabilities for its note exchange balances had been very heavy. The large excess circulation (a genuine case of over-issue) had been rendered worse than useless to its issuer by the merciless exchanges, through which it was returned to head-quarters in heavy sums. In the year 1855 the balances *against* the bank for exchanges had been £4,109,726, against £125,080 in favour. In 1856 the sums were £3,494,139 against, and £114,213 in favour ; and up to 9th November 1857, the date of stoppage, £3,393,553 *against*, was met by £101,813 *in favour.* Thus in three years the bank had been compelled to find funds in London to meet upwards of *ten million pounds* returned against it by the exchange, a very large portion of which was for notes alone,—one of the best testimonials to the worth of the exchange system it is possible to have.

On the 9th of November the directors found it impossible to meet the debtor balance of that day for £112,974, —those of the three last days being £384,696 in all,—and the bank's doors were at once shut, the news spreading through Glasgow with proverbial speed. The liabilities to the public were £8,911,932, all of which were afterward paid in full from the proceeds of calls upon the unfortunate shareholders.

The circulation on 26th October stood at £515,863, of which £205,740 were large notes and £310,123 small. It fell rapidly to £424,000 on the last day of the month, the chief fall being in the large notes, £69,000 (probably held by merchants), the small notes having only fallen £22,000. On the 4th of November the large rushed up suddenly £160,000, and the small nearly £38,000 ; increasing the circulation to £619,551, for which no doubt term payments were largely responsible. There appears to have been no run of note holders to any extent, though the deposits were being drained away, which would of course increase the note issues for a time, until the paper was paid into other banks as deposits, when the exchanges presented them again to the Western Bank. At its failure the circulation stood at £720,083,—£332,720 large and £387,363 small,— but from this falls to be deducted £112,974, that day's exchange remaining unsettled in the hands of the banks. For two days the circulation remained stationary, as the notes had been refused payment by the other offices, until the frightful panic which ensued compelled them, on the

11th November, from prudential motives, to advertise their readiness to take up all the notes. In these two days a most determined "run" had been made upon two of the banks specially, though it is said all the others suffered in some degree ; but the daily returns of the circulation, shewing as they do the respective amounts of large and small, indicate more a "run" of depositors than of note holders ; for, except in the case of the City of Glasgow Bank, the issues were considerably increased for a few days, even beyond what might be required for the Martinmas payments. This is particularly marked in the issue of the Union Bank, whose circulation £654,000 on the 9th, rose to £812,000 on the 10th, and £934,000 on the 11th November, falling suddenly on the following day to £674,000. The great increase was in the *large* notes, the small only rising a few thousands. The good business of the bank in Glasgow doubtless increased its term responsibilities ; but the evidence of its manager, Mr James Robertson, to the "Select Committee on the Bank Acts of 1858," fortunately enables us to see how and from what class of creditors the bank suffered most. A run for gold on the savings branches of the City of Glasgow Bank, when opened the previous evening, had shewn the Union Bank authorities what might be anticipated next day. "On the Tuesday morning, the 10th, a great number of persons appeared with deposit-receipts demanding gold ; in fact, our own establishment was quite filled with parties within a quarter of an hour of the opening of the doors." The other banks were in a similar position. In the course of the day the error of not receiving the Western Bank notes was felt very strongly, but, notwithstanding the failure of the City of Glasgow Bank, the Edinburgh directors still refused their sanction to the step. The run of depositors continuing, the same evening it was resolved to begin to pay the notes next day. Either on Tuesday night or Wednesday morning the military were asked to be in readiness by the Magistrates, who, fearing a disturbance, ordered their collectors to take any Western Bank notes offered to them in payment of

taxes.   But further precautions were unnecessary, for
whenever the announcement of the bank's decision to take
the notes was made public, the whole " run " so completely
collapsed, that by two o'clock in the afternoon the telling-
room of the Union Bank had scarcely half-a-dozen people
in it, though in the morning it had been crammed with an
excited crowd of nervous depositors.

During the crisis no attention was paid to having the
specie reserve kept against authorised circulation, all comers
being served, in notes if they would accept of them, and in
gold if not.   Upon the Wednesday and Thursday £620,000
of gold (obtained from the Bank of England by presentation of its notes, got by sale of consols) were carted through
the. streets of Glasgow with considerable parade, to be
delivered to the Union Bank, a sight which did much to
inspire the populace with renewed confidence.   At the same
time that the successor of the old Glasgow Ship Bank was
coming through this ordeal in the west, its Edinburgh connection, that of Sir William Forbes, had also to bear a
heavy run for deposits, caused almost entirely by the
Glasgow *fama*.   Both establishments had a narrow escape,
and were only borne through the trial by thoroughly sound
management, both prior to and during the crisis.

While the Union Bank thus stood the test, the City of
Glasgow Bank had succumbed on the second morning of
the " run."   The circulation of this bank is the only one
which exhibits serious decrease, standing at £477,174 on
the 9th November (a little over one-half small notes) ; it
rose, to pay depositors and meet term payments, to
£640,000 on the 10th, of which £381,000 were large and
£258,000 small.   Next day's note exchange could not
be paid, and the circulation rose to £714,000, of which
£450,000 were large notes.   After the stoppage the amount
fell with astonishing rapidity, £553,000 being paid on the
12th, and £88,000 between the 12th and 21st November,
when the circulation stood at £41,000 large to £31,000
small.   On the 14th of the following month, the bank
reopened, and recommenced its career of folly and crime.

Particular details have been given of this " run," not because it had *any connection* with one pound notes, but to shew that one pound notes were in *no* way responsible for it, the whole danger arising from the depositors, who seem to have been thoroughly alarmed ; and as a " run " is usually associated with notes, it may be well to make it clear that that danger had largely passed away, to have its place taken by a much greater. Mr Robertson, of the Union Bank, states :—" The fact is that very few *note holders* came forward ; it was almost entirely *depositors ;* " and again, when asked if *small notes* had caused much inconvenience in the run, his reply is :—" Not the least ; no doubt people exchanged one pound notes for gold, but it was to a very limited extent."

The lesson of 1857 is, that the *one serious danger* to be apprehended by the Scottish banks, for which it is almost impossible for them to make sufficient provision, is a " *run* " *of depositors,*—a danger which the years elapsing since that time have regularly and considerably increased. Four-and-a-half millions of gold are but a small security when deposits amounting to eighty million pounds can be demanded at an hour's notice. Yet while the danger is theoretically great, in its very magnitude may be said to lie the safety of the banks, for in the event of any colossal panic shaking the nation's credit to its centre, the only possible course remaining open would be to adopt that tried and proved in 1797, and refuse all cash payments until credit is restored. Necessity recognises no law, and all questions of the illegality of their action would probably be stayed by warrant of the Privy Council, such as has in the past secured the Bank of England in similar circumstances. The physical impossibility of meeting the demand in gold, would be sufficient warrant of itself for the banks to refuse payment before their whole specie was exhausted ; for, upon the supposition that only twenty millions (one-fourth) of deposits were demanded, it is extremely improbable, in the face of such a panic in Scotland, that English banks would part with so large an amount of gold to satisfy the demands of even one quarter of the Scottish depositors. While a run upon *all* the banks could be met in this way, a run upon *one* might be attended with more serious results, as it could scarcely of itself be entitled to defy depositors in the way indicated.

In short, nearly all the evidence on the subject given to various Parliamentary committees, as well as the experience of the past, goes to prove that it is the demand for gold by *depositors* which brings down a bank, and not that of the note holders. In guaging the position of small notes in connection with the failures of the Western and City of Glasgow banks, it is necessary to keep distinctly in view the two operations which combine to make up banking,—namely, *collection* and *distribution* of funds. If the collection of *deposits* is carried on by a system of branches spread over a wide area of country, clearly it is a banker's interest and duty to minimise the risk and magnify the benefit by spreading his *advances* over an area equally extensive ; and in following out such a principle in both its parts, no instrument has been found more effective than the one pound note. Sir Robert Peel's disciples insist upon the distinction between banking and note - issuing ; but the distinction between collection and distribution of wealth is even more reasonable and obvious. Let us therefore see how the principle was looked upon by Scotland's two *in*famous banks. Being compelled to obtain funds, they naturally collected them in the usual way, in deposits from their branches, in which their note issue performed part of its legitimate work,—and so far all was well, as no blame can possibly be attached to notes in this connection. But how about the other side of the account ? Was the second part of the principle recognised ? or does history not tell of something more than a return to the exploded delusions of last century, when it was deemed easier to lend to a few large firms than to distribute over an entire country ? The failure of the Western and City banks to spread their advances, necessarily harassed them through their circulation ; for notwithstanding the excessive issues, principally

drawn out on the deposit part of their business, the number
of their general country advances was too restricted to
utilise so large a quantity of notes, and they accordingly
went back to the banks to be paid through the exchanges
by continual purchase of exchequer bills, or the more
ruinous short drafts on London so effectual with Douglas,
Heron, & Co. No better proof could be given of the
nature of the Scottish note issue, and of its total want of
connection with the operations of the Flemings and Mac-
donalds who broke the banks, than the fact that in 1858
and 1879 the circulation of the remaining banks was
steadily extended to nearly the amount of the lapsed
issues; shewing that the *currency* had been *nationally*
required, and that if one source of supply was to be cut
off, the banks left standing must increase their circulation
by a corresponding amount. Small notes have therefore
their twofold use, while the two banks employed them
only in one; their abandonment of the other materially
increasing the friction which led to the disasters now so
well remembered.

In the ten years following the failure of the Western
Bank, the country developed its resources, and advanced in
prosperity at a rate hitherto undreamt of; railways, steam-
ships, telegraphic communication, mechanical invention
and scientific research, all combining to provide revenue
and accumulate capital by " leaps and bounds," interrupted
alone by the havoc of the American War of Secession.
Several of the smaller banks amalgamated with the larger
institutions, as their business and existence were threatened
by the branch systems of the latter.

The year of 1866, eventful and disastrous to England
by the failure of Overend, Gurney, & Co., passed by in
perfect tranquility to the Scottish banks. From this year
onwards the latter began to open offices in London, for
which the National Bank had set the example in 1864.
This step naturally led to the keenest discussion amongst
English bankers, rising almost to uproar when the Clydesdale Bank opened several branches in Cumberland. This

was no new step, as the Leith Banking Company had been
registered in Carlisle as an English company, and had
carried on a large business there for some years prior to
1837, yet had never been asked to abandon its issue in
Scotland.   Maberley, also, was an instance of an English
banker opening in Scotland ; not to speak of the competition for deposits caused by the presence of London and
Colonial banks in Edinburgh and elsewhere.   But all these
precedents were completely lost sight of, in consideration
of *the right to issue notes* retained by a Scottish bank
for its offices in Scotland, while opening an office in
London,—a right which had been denied to English provincial banks, from the influence of the Bank of England
monopoly.   Refusing to see the defect in the anomalous
law of England, Mr Goschen and other leaders of finance
pressed the matter so strongly on the Government, that the
latter were fain to get out of the quandary by adopting the
usual course,—adding to their accumulation of verbosity a
large blue-book, the labours of the Select Committee of 1875,
the masterly result of which was, to let well alone.   The
evidence produced by the Scottish bank managers gave
ground for believing that banking profits in Scotland were
not so large as had been generally thought, and that they
stood in favourable contrast to English provincial banks,
the people, in consequence, reaping the benefit.   One
important result of the agitation was to lead to daily
exchanges of notes throughout the kingdom ; some facts
brought out in the evidence having produced a fear, that
the note issues would be interfered with, if greater attention
was not paid to a closer conformity with the Act of 1845.
Under the old method of exchanging only thrice a-week, it
had been found that the secured limit of authorised circulation, plus the specie reserve, was sometimes exceeded
during the week ; and though it was known that the excess
was chiefly in the hands of other banks, awaiting the next
exchange, it was deemed wise to take this weapon out of
the enemy's hand by securing greater economy in the
circulation.   Sir Robert Peel's banking settlement pro-

vided for the average being fixed every four weeks, and if
a limit of circulation was to be fixed at all, it was a reasonable period to fall upon. If the troublesome weekly
returns could have been avoided, and the circulation taken
only on the fourth week, a statement could have been
appended that the *average* for four Saturdays did not
exceed the authorised circulation ; and in this way, without
publishing to Government the fact that possibly one Saturday out of the four was above the authorised limit, the
Government, on their part, would have been assured that
the limit was not excessively strained. This would have
given a degree of elasticity to the circulation, without laying
it open to the charge of being loose or uncontrolled, which
it might easily be, were a longer period fixed than four
weeks. Some currency writers have advocated a yearly
average, a most delusive expedient, which would probably
lead to the starvation of one season, and abundance at
another, to which Sir Archibald Alison refers.

In general, banking obtained a fair share of the prosperity attending the return of trade in 1870, until the
usual run of over-trading brought about the failures of
1875. Severe depression followed, notwithstanding which,
the number of new branches steadily increased, until they
reached, in 1878, the large figure of 950 offices.

Throughout the early part of the year all was quiet, and
nothing of note occurred to shake public confidence, except
some slight rumours about "one of the Scotch banks,"
which appeared in the Glasgow papers, until, on the 1st of
October, Edinburgh and Glasgow and the whole country
woke up to find that the City of Glasgow Bank had
closed its doors. The whole story is exactly a counterpart
of the Western Bank, but of five-fold magnitude ;—the
same character of folly, the same fraudulent efforts to
conceal their condition, the same widespread ruin when
concealment was no longer possible, magnified beyond
comprehension by the length of time over which the
bank's good credit had carried it, when in a state of
insolvency.

The day following the failure, the remaining banks, wisely profiting by the experience of 1857, advertised that all City of Glasgow Bank notes would be taken up at their respective offices. This measure helped to maintain popular confidence, though the blow seems to have come so suddenly that it took several days before the public fully realised the case. Upon investigation of the bank's books, it was found that it had been reserved for its officials to perpetrate the most extraordinary fraud that errant bankers of Scotland had been guilty of.

Their balance-sheets were "doctored" systematically, being first prepared with some measure of truth by the accountant, and then gone over by him, in company with the manager and one of the directors, to be made ready for the public view. To do this they were under the necessity of making false returns of their notes and specie to the Commissioners of Stamps and Taxes, under the Act of 1845.

The gold and silver found to have been in the cashier's hands at the head office amounted to	£231,500
To which fell to be added that held by the tellers	12,156
And at the branches	49,889
Total	£293,545
Their authorised circulation was	72,921
From which their circulation should have been only	£366,466
But the circulation-book showed a total of	604,196
Bringing out an excess of issue beyond prescribed bounds, of	£237,730

When it was found that all expedients to raise cash were failing, the specie reserve was ruthlessly sent to London to meet acceptances, at first to the extent of £60,000 in January of the same year, and afterwards at intervals, until £200,000 of gold had been removed. To cover this, the books, returns, and balance-sheets were falsified in the most audacious manner.

Although the bank was liable to a heavy penalty in respect of the over-issue of notes, the Government, in view of the heavy losses already incurred by the shareholders, mercifully took no steps to enforce their rights, the only notice taken of the matter being in the cold, formal intimation of the facts made to the London and Edinburgh Gazettes in the form of a supplement to the usual monthly notice under the Act of 8 & 9 Vict., c. 38. The bank had failed to send in the return for 28th September, so that the notice for that day appeared with the words "not received" opposite the name of the bank. Next month the following statement was appended to the list of the bank's notes and coin :—

"The above-named Bank, which has had in circulation an amount of notes beyond that authorised in its certificate, has not held the amount of gold and silver coin which it is required to hold during the period to which the return belongs. (Signed) W. H. COUSINS,
Dated, 17th day of Oct. 1878. *Registrar of Bank Returns.*"

The return referred to shews £216,942 of large notes and £400,131 of small,—in all £617,073, or £229,163 beyond its limit. So disappeared the City of Glasgow Bank.

The total loss which the unfortunate shareholders had to make good was nominally £5,190,983. 11s. 3d., but was in reality far greater. The country is still suffering from the tremendous collapse of prices that ensued. Upon a market already extremely depreciated, stocks were forced by the reckless shareholders, many of whom, knowing themselves to be utterly ruined, were regardless what prices their investments produced.

The dreadful suffering caused to the shareholders, under the principle of unlimited liability, led to the passing of an Act, in 1879, which has, and may yet have, still more important interest for note holders. Act 42, 43, Vict., c. 76, the Companies Act (1879), provided for the limitation of unlimited companies on the basis of a certain amount of paid-up capital, backed by a reserve liability, only to be called up in the event of bankruptcy. While this was to be the rule for all ordinary debts, Section VI. continued the provisions of the Companies Act 1862 for the security of debts upon *bank notes*, in respect of which the liability of the shareholders was to remain as unlimited as if they were members of an unlimited company.

One of the original clauses in the bill was specially designed to harass the Scottish banks who had, or wished to have, offices in London, as they were not to be allowed to retain the right of issue in Scotland if they should wish to remain in London and register under the new Act. It was pointed out by the *Standard* that this would unjustly affect the unlimited Scotch banks, as the three old banks, being already limited, would not require to come under the provisions of the Act, and could therefore remain in London without giving up their issue. The London press had little sympathy with their countrymen, wisely seeing the real cause of the evil in the state of their own law. The *Times* advised the Chancellor of the Exchequer to be cautious, and not rouse multitudes of Malachi Malagrowthers, for "the pith of the case lies in the indefensible fact that English provincial banks cannot open branches in the capital without relinquishing their note issue, while Scotch banks labour under no such disability. But anomalies are not to be cured by fresh anomalies; the true course, in such circumstances, is to trust to freedom, and to *throw down* restrictions instead of enacting new." The *Daily Telegraph* characterised Sir Stafford Northcote's device as "not only paltry, but will be to a large extent inoperative," the three senior banks already enjoying "under their charters the particular *limitation* which Sir Stafford designates *reserve*. If the London bankers really feel the rivalry of their Scottish neighbours, and wish to deprive the public of the facilities these active invaders offer, it would be more manly and straightforward to say so openly, and invite the House of Commons to sanction this latest development of guild jealousy and trades-unionism." Language like this from the three most powerful supporters of the Government, naturally made the latter pause, and finally led them to abandon the objectionable part of the bill, to the profound disgust of the justly annoyed English bankers.

For some time no action was taken upon this measure, owing to the varied constitutions of the banks, the three seniors, of course, declining to bring themselves under an Act which had no benefit to bestow other than they already possessed. After ascertaining the hostility of the Treasury to private bills which they had endeavoured to place before Parliament, they withdrew entirely from the controversy; so that the question as to the liability of their shareholders for *notes*, apart from their other obligations, has not been settled, though probably it would be found that, were the much debated point of their limitation judicially decided, no difference would be found to exist between the two classes of creditors. Either the banks would be held wholly limited, or their position would be the same as that of the other unlimited banks prior to 1881.

The latter finding that further co-operation was impossible with their seniors, wisely undertook the matter for themselves, and on the 3d day of April 1882 effected the most important alteration Scottish joint-stock banking has ever witnessed. Notwithstanding the magnitude of the change, so thoroughly was the public mind prepared for it, and so well was it understood, that scarcely a voice was raised, nor a deposit uplifted, the banks resuming their business next day as limited companies as if nothing had happened.

This extraordinary change, so peacefully accomplished, brings down the history of the one pound note to the present time. If Sir Robert Peel's Act failed to secure its convertibility on demand, no legislation could have more effectively secured its *ultimate* payment than that of the Act of 1879,—unless it should ever happen that bank notes are made a *first charge* upon a bank's assets, all other debts, no matter how secured, being ranked in a second place, to be paid out of the funds remaining over after the last note has been paid, or funds set aside for its payment.

Should occasion ever arise to disturb the *status quo*, the banks might take further advantage of the Act by adding to their notes the clause specially allowed to them, printing upon the back a brief statement, as free as possible from parliamentary jargon and suitable to the ordinary intelligence, declaring the perfect surety for their payment, secured by the unlimited responsibility of *each shareholder* for the *whole circulation* of his bank.

Chapter XV.

CONCLUSION OF PART RELATING TO SCOTLAND.

"'Experience teaches,'—so the proverb goes;
The heedless man gives birth to all his woes;
But he who pondereth his past well o'er,
For learning, hath the *world* for his store."—OLD PROVERB.

O F the effects of the Act of 1845, which was expected to work such wonders, it is very difficult to judge, principally from the veto it put upon all new banks of issue, and the consequent impossibility of calculating what *might* have occurred had the Act not been passed. Had that particular clause not been inserted, it is possible, though not probable, that new banks would have sprung up as of old, when some curious, but profitable, questions must have arisen in fixing the amount of their circulation. The issue of these new banks would necessarily have curtailed that of the other establishments, so that in place of the authorised circulation being exceeded, and gold kept in large quantities as now, there might possibly have been a number of banks all *under* their authorised circulation, the more reckless of whom would not require to have kept any gold stock whatever so far as the Act of Parliament was concerned. Apart from these considerations, it cannot be denied that the leading principle in the Act was one which, had its details been more systematically arranged, would have proved, and has proved, of great advantage to the *nation*,— not to the banks alone, but also to the people whom they serve. *Regulation* had been the felt want of the British note issues, from their origin nearly two hundred years ago, —such a guidance, or control, by a central authority of

O

numerous and widely dissimilar interests, as would maintain
the currency at the precise limit of national requirement for
the time being, and yet progress or decrease as years passed
on, and greater or less need of such a currency arose out of
the changed circumstances of the nation's life. A regulation theoretically perfect will never be seen in Great Britain,
unless some general assembly of bankers, under Government sanction, prescribe the limits year by year, from
careful study of the signs of the times, sternly pulling up
the issues when cheap money causes speculative production
to become rampant, and loosening the reins as the demand
ceases.

Scottish bank issues, thanks to the prudence of their
guides, and the splendid system of exchanges, have been
attended with a much greater measure of success than those
of England, and therefore the need of regulation has not
been so greatly felt; still there have been melancholy proofs
that prudence is not an invariable attendant of Scottish
banks, and Scotland may be none the worse for the Government regulations. At the present time, however, there can
be little doubt that the *self-imposed regulation* of the note
exchange exercises a much more constant and beneficent
effect on the Scottish issues than those imposed by law.
The one is continually active, not a day passes without each
bank being *compelled* to recognise its influence, and meet
its requirements in hard cash, or its still more expensive
equivalent,—payment in London at four days after date.
£100,000 paid in Edinburgh in gold *could* be brought
from London at an expense not exceeding £20, while
payment of a similar sum in London involves a direct
payment in Edinburgh of £32. 14s. 9d. for interest. The
system of exchanges would have stopped Murdoch & Co.,
and all the band of over-issuers of last century; it *did* stop
Douglas, Heron, & Co., and its influence in sucking the
little life-blood left in the Western and City of Glasgow
banks has never been fully appreciated. Like the law of
holy writ, it is a continual punishment to evil-doers, and for
the praise of those who do well. Why then has such an

efficient remedy not been made matter for legal enactment throughout Great Britain? In Scotland, at the present time, such a law would simply carry on *compulsorily* that which is already *voluntarily* in force, but its future effects would be great, not only in Scotland but in England. The banks in the latter country should endeavour by every means to enlarge their system of exchanges upon the same footing as in Scotland, not merely at head offices, but in every town where two or more banks exist. Let the great bank itself descend from its throne, and agree to take up its notes when presented at its various branches,—not necessarily in specie, but, as in Scotland, by London payments. By these means contraction of paper currency would take place, which would have no effect in restricting banking facilities, but would only tend to prevent depreciation of the paper, and consequent elevation of prices, which invariably ensues when notes are not regularly taken up.

It is by the aid of the exchanges that the value of the one pound note can best be measured. More than half a million of notes are delivered at the exchanges in Scotland every business day. Once every ten days the whole circulation of Scotland is renewed; nearly £6,000,000 being drawn out, passed from hand to hand, and returned to the banks thirty times every year. Of the sum constantly in circulation one pound notes represent from 65 to 70 per cent. of the whole, and in view of their smaller individual value represent an innumerable number of transactions. Large notes come more rapidly back to the bank, the percentage passing through the exchanges differing at times from the exigencies of the moment. At the terms of Whitsunday and Martinmas they rush out and come flowing back with the strength and suddenness of a Highland spate; but the small notes, though going out also somewhat rapidly, take a much longer time to come back, so that for days after the stream of "large" has subsided to its usual level, the "ones" continue in a steady current of considerable volume, until gradually the circulation falls to its normal limits. In the months of February, March, and

April, when the circulation is usually smallest, the averages of the three kinds of notes passing through the exchange may be taken as follows :—

	Per cent.
£100 notes, . .	. 21
Large (£20, £10, and £5),	. 34·8
	—— 55·8
Small notes, . .	44·2
Total, .	100·0

At the terms, such as from the 10th to the 20th of May, the averages may be approximately taken at,—

	Per cent.
£100 notes, . .	25·6
Large (£20, £10, and £5),	. 36
	—— 61·6
Small notes, . .	38·4
Total, .	100·0

Thus it will be seen that, though one pound notes form more than two-thirds of the circulation, they only form about two-fifths in value of the notes exchanged, indicating apparently that the public must find them proportionally more useful than large notes, and therefore retain them longer in circulation. But in *number* of transactions the small notes have a prodigious advantage over the large ; and from various calculations of the numbers coming through the exchange, it has been estimated that they exceed the latter in *number* in the proportion of 8 or 9 to 1. If this is so in the exchanges, where they are only two-fifths in *value* of the whole, how much greater must be the number of transactions performed by them when in circulation, where they exceed the large by 2 to 1 in *value*, and may be reckoned to exceed them in *number* by about 20 to 1 !

Of the total £170,000,000 of notes passed annually through the exchanges, a *very moderate* calculation would give of that amount £60,000,000 for small notes, while the remaining £110,000,000 of large notes could not probably exceed 5,000,000 in number. In computing these amounts every advantage has been given to the volume of large notes, and correspondingly taken from small notes, so that, if it were possible to obtain official statistics on the subject, it would be found that the small notes represent even a larger proportion of transactions than is shewn by the above statement. It has often been regretted by English financiers that no means could be discovered of tracing the number of transfers effected by the gold coinage ; but in view of the gigantic circulation of the Scottish one pound note, representing as it does only a *small part* of its work, namely, that *between bank and bank*, they have some insight afforded them of the manner in which the precious metals are wasted in England, and economised in Scotland. Even upon the assumption that only one transfer took place outside of the bank,—that the money was drawn out from bank A by customer Lawson to be paid to his creditor Jones, and by creditor Jones paid into his bank B, the three or rather six countings upon hard mahogany tables, jingling into Lawson's pocket, thence into Jones', to be rubbed down upon various hard keys or fustian breeches, must involve a considerable loss when carried on throughout the entire year to the total amount of one hundred million pounds in gold ; but with the Scottish currency shewing no such waste of metal, the most inveterate statistician would have difficulty in calculating the average waste of vegetable fibre or " size " rubbed from a piece of printed paper, which at the first costs only one penny sterling, even when multiplied by four million.

Yet we are told in the face of such testimony that the one pound note is daily losing its hold upon the Scottish people ! Since 1845 the extraordinary increase of branches throughout the country has been one of the causes tending to prevent the proportion of notes from increasing in the same degree as other forms of credit. When one branch existed in a town or village, naturally the exchange of notes would be sluggish, and circulation remained much longer in the hands of the public ; but now, when nearly every township can boast of its two or three banks, the exchanges are brisker, being more convenient, while larger amounts pass through than formerly, so that the same notes go oftener through the banks than in years bygone. It is an incontestible fact that the amount of currency, whether metallic or paper, has *not increased* in the same ratio as the volume of business ; but, on the other hand, we have it on the authority of Professor Leone Levi, that " the proportion of *coin* to the general amount of *currency* is less and less every year,"—a fact which affords evidence of the increased appreciation of paper money, alike from necessity and economy. The Professor adds,—" Paper currency is universally displacing metallic currency ; " while the necessity for the former does not *increase* as it formerly did, as " the system of paying by cheques, and the wonders of the clearing-house, have a powerful influence in lessening the need of bank notes." Lessening the need in proportion to the *increase* of business, does not infer that the amount of bank notes is actually decreasing ; on the contrary, the circulation of Scotland shews that they have been slowly increasing, while the average of one pound notes has maintained itself with surprising regularity at from 60 to 70 per cent. for more than a hundred years. Once very poor, now very rich, Scotland, through all the various gradations, from the one condition to the other, has employed the same proportion of small notes out of its total bank note currency. Notwithstanding all the agencies at work at different times, or in combination,—cheques, bills, bank drafts, bank cheques, post-office orders, postal orders, postage stamps,—nothing seems materially to affect the position of the one pound note, or the proportion of its appreciation by the public.

If anything can be said to have shaken public regard, it will be found in the gold discoveries of California and Australia, for it is only since these were made that the public necessity for small notes is *said* to have decreased. In combination with these extraordinary additions to the world's wealth, came the great changes effected by steam machinery, railways, and free trade. For thirty or forty

years Britain multiplied her capital at an incredible rate,
and so old and humble a servant as the one pound note
seemed to be in danger of neglect by the Alnaschars of
modern finance ; the giant " steam " appeared to be driving
the world into a millennium, until at last the hatmakers, the
bootmakers, the cotton manufacturers, and the button-
makers are only now beginning to realise the alarming fact,
that they can make more hats and boots, and cotton and
buttons, than the world can consume. The change from
hand labour to steam power was so utterly beyond the
power of experience to estimate, that, of necessity, production of wealth advanced, as has been said, by "leaps and
bounds," where formerly men had been contented with a
much smaller and less universal ratio of increase.

If no new invention of British genius gives an additional
and unheard of impetus, and if Continental nations continue
to supply themselves with manufactures in place of import-
ing from this country, it is very probable that in the next
forty years Britain will discover that she cannot continue
the express speed of the past forty,—that a slower and
safer speed must be adopted ; that capital will not increase
as it has done ; that, in fact, the *leap from hand labour to
machinery has been made*, and the country must return to a
rate of progress more suitable to the necessities of its
population. For while the revolution of recent years has
brought in its train unheard of blessings, it has also been
followed by untold misery ; the cheapening of the cost of
production has told as fearfully upon the poor as any of the
old sorrows of the Corn Laws. Mr Bright is correct when
he says that never were articles of common use so cheap ;
but that is only one side of the picture,—they are so cheap
to every one, because the labour which produces them is
likewise cheap. If the working classes are indeed so well
clothed, how has the producer of these clothes been paid ?
A modern writer, who has given considerable attention to
production, answers the question. In London, large firms
" give out coats to be made at sixpence each, and vests at
threepence ; and these low rates are paid to 'sweaters,' who

let out the work at still lower rates, and leave the workman and workwoman to find their own thread. And if the labourer and the labourer's children are going about decked in the 'sweater's' finery, they are—fortunately for themselves unconsciously—wearing a piece of the starved workwoman's shroud."

The dumb misery of the very poor was perfectly well known for years past to London philanthropists, though the gifted author of " The Bitter Cry " has only recently attracted public attention to it. Machinery, which was to find employment for and put a coat on every man's back, has only driven men with its own irresistible force, until the experience of the last seven years is beginning to prove to them that the pace is killing, and that our present dull trade is not necessarily a sign of decay, but simply that the rate of progress, produced primarily by our practical monopoly of the world's trade for fifty years, and latterly by steam, free trade, and other causes, has reached its maximum, and cannot be maintained.

Conjoined with this slackening of the current, and perhaps two of its causes, are the important changes in the position of the precious metals forming our metallic currency. Gold is becoming scarcer year by year, not so much from decreased output from mining, as from increased demand on the Continent and elsewhere. At the same time silver is becoming cheaper and cheaper every day, from exactly the opposite reasons which are tending to make gold dear,—viz., Continental demonetisation, and superabundant supplies from new mines. Within about sixteen years silver has fallen from 5s. to 4s. the ounce, which, with gold steady at £3. 17s. 9d., implies a fall from one-fifteenth the value of gold to one-nineteenth. Should this increase in the demand for gold continue, so as to cause its appreciation, the one pound note will take a new lease of life, for it will become a matter of urgent necessity for all to economise the national and the international stocks of specie in every possible way.

So far as can be seen it is extremely improbable that

Scotland will return, for many years, if ever, to a purely metallic currency, for sums less than £5 ; but as this subject has been a good deal canvassed in past years, it may be well to notice slightly, national effects to which the abolition of the one pound notes would lead. At present the banks have a small note circulation of about four millions, against which £2,866,000 of coin is *nominally* kept,—*i.e.*, £730,000 *beyond what is required by the Act of 1845*. For the past forty years, but especially since the failure of the Western Bank, the other banks have uniformly maintained a gold reserve of such size as leads to the supposition, that it is not held so entirely on account of the note issue as it once was, but is rather held against the entire liabilities of the bank for deposits and otherwise. Sir Robert Peel's Act omitted to provide for any hypothecation of gold against notes ; and as a *note run* is of itself a thing extremely improbable now, it is the duty of bankers to spread the cost of the gold reserve over the whole of the bank's debts, and not load it upon one item, when facts shew that the burden gives no corresponding security to the item so burdened. Mr Fleming, of the Royal Bank, when asked, in the Committee of 1875, by Sir Stafford Northcote, whether the doubling of their authorised issue would lead the Scotch banks to do without so much gold ? replied, " I am not prepared to say that there would be less, because, as I have already stated, I think it is fortunate for Scotland that we have such an amount of gold as £4,000,000 lying to *meet any possible contingencies*. No doubt it lies locked up in a vault, and is untouched from the beginning to the end of the year ; but notwithstanding that, I am not prepared to say that it would be wise to interfere in any shape or form with the existing regulations, which have led gradually to the accumulation of a store of coin, increased from about £400,000 in 1844 to £4,000,000 now ; and I think it for the advantage of Scotland, and for the stability of the Scotch banks, that it should be so."

Here Mr Fleming speaks of " *any possible contingencies*," surely implying that he recognises the gold to be held against any of the liabilities, a view of the matter which receives strong corroboration from the steady increase in the amount of specie held *beyond* the requirement of the Act of 1845 (now £1,037,607); so that in place of the cost of the four millions of gold being placed against the six millions of notes, they should more correctly be spread over the ninety millions of liabilities,—out of which the paper currency would bear its share of one-fifteenth part and the one pound notes their twenty-second part, namely, £177,777, which at £3 per cent. yields £5331 as the true interest expense for gold against small notes, leaving a profit, at the same rate of interest, of £114,669 on the small note circulation of Scotland. From this there falls to be deducted the cost of production, the Government duty, and cost of note licenses, all easily ascertained. One pound notes cost one penny each, and may be said to last for three years at least; 4,000,000 notes at 1d. amount to £16,666, which divided by the three years of the notes' life produce £5555 per annum. Duty at 8s. 4d. per cent. on £4,000,000 is £16,666, and licenses cost annually about £16,000, of which £11,000, or two-thirds, may be placed as against small notes. Thus the three items of charge,—manufacture of the notes, Government duty, and licenses,—amounting to £33,221, when subtracted from £114,669, leave a direct profit upon the one pound note circulation of £81,448,*

---

* Interest at 3 per cent. on small note circulation
 of four millions, ... £120,000
Deduct—1. Interest at 3 per cent. on £177,777
   proportion of gold held nominally
   against small note circulation, £5,331
  2. Manufacture of four millions
   notes at 1d., £16,666 for three
   years, and for one year, . 5,555
  3. Government duty, 8s. 4d. per
   cent. on four millions, . . 16,666
  4. Licenses to Government,—
    say, . . . £16,500
   Less one-third due by
    large notes, . . 5,500
         ———— 11,000
            ———— 38,552
              £81,448

or about 18s. 10d. per cent. on the paid capital of the
banks, and 2s. 4d. per cent. upon £80,000,000 of deposits.
To these figures might be added the indirect advantages
accruing from the ability to conduct business all over the
country, while there would be deducted the sum of the
increased charges incurred by banks with a number of
branches.

While the money advantages of the present system are
seen not to be large, yet sufficiently appreciable to make
a difference in comparison with non-issuing banks, the
expense of keeping gold would be a much more serious
item.   In the first place, the whole labour and expense of
bringing down from London £4,000,000 of specie to replace
their one pound notes would fall upon the banks, who would
have the additional trouble of withdrawing their own notes
and issuing the coin.   This might be spread over years, but
nevertheless would be a costly toil.   To maintain such a
circulation would necessitate the keeping of at least twice
the amount of gold presently held by the banks,—probably
more ; so that, in addition to the actual loss of their own
issues, the banks would have the loss of maintaining an
additional supply of gold as " till money,"—a task formerly
performed by the notes free of all expense, except that of
manufacture ;* while the *nation* would have to face the
absolute loss from wear upon the gold currency,—unless,
as usual, the burden were thrown upon the banks,
who would of course, be compelled to recoup themselves
for this, and the other loss of revenue, by decreasing the
interest on deposits, or raising the rate for discounts.
Depositors would suffer more than discounters, as the
latter *even now* are endeavouring to get facilities in London,
and thereby compel the banks to sink to the London rates.
Depositors thus discouraged by low interest would uplift

---

* The till money presently supplied by notes may be roundly taken
at £13,000,000, small notes being £6,000,000.   At 3 per cent. the latter
sum implies a saving to the banks of £180,000 annually (less £8000
charges for the notes), or 4s. 5d. per cent. on the deposits, and £2 per
cent. on the capital, which a gold till money would entirely sweep away.

their money, seeking its employment in ways that would leave little doubt that the millions of Scotch deposits are more usefully invested in the *banks*, than they would be by *individual depositors;* and thus action and reaction decreasing the banking fund, and its consequent profit, disjointed speculation would take the place of united investment, with little gain either to the banks or the nation.

The question of a national state issue is left for some short consideration under the chapter of "Adaptability to England;" but even of that Scottish banks need have little fear, so long as they continue to exercise the same abilities, of which one of Old England's courteous writers remarks with kindly wit :—"Englishmen and Americans, and natives of all countries, may well admire the wonderful skill, sagacity, and caution with which Scotch bankers have developed and conducted their system. There is no doubt that Scotch bankers are guiding the course of development of the banking system in England, India, the Australian colonies, and elsewhere, with conspicuous success. If we were all Scotchmen, I believe the unlimited issue of one pound notes would be an excellent measure."—("Money," S. Jevons.)

Profiting by the experience of nearly two hundred years, the Scottish banks, and the Scottish people, may long retain their issue of "ONE POUND NOTES REPAYABLE IN GOLD ON DEMAND." The original idea, on which William Paterson insisted through good and evil report in 1696, is the same now, with not one whit of change. The instrument, now purged from many of the evils clinging to it in old days, is as powerful, as useful, as cheap, as safe, when properly controlled, as various in its capacity, as ever it has been. It may be giving it too great place to call it the still living architect of a noble edifice, but we are tempted to think, that if the old pound note of 1723 were to uprear itself as did the one guinea note of the "Plain Man" in 1826, we should hear, in the gentle rustle of its ghostly voice,—" *Si quaeris monumentum circumspice.*"

TABLE SHEWING GROWTH OF NOTE CIRCULATION AND STOCK OF COIN
OF THE SCOTTISH BANKS FROM 1845 TO 1884.

Year.	Circulation.	Coin.	Year.	Circulation.	Coin.
1845	3,087,209	(?)400,000	1874-75	6,032,399	4,274,447
1858-59	4,113,319	2,502,899	1875-76	6,062,397	4,323,420
1859-60	4,219,569	2,552,361	1876-77	6,167,432	4,377,079
1865-66	4,434,962	2,500,926	1877-78	5,976,197	4,220,092
1867-68	4,554,376	2,667,727	1878-79	5,582,921	4,203,422
1868-69	4,718,680	2,797,740	1879-80	5,454,582	3,907,621
1869-70	4,878,120	2,960,903	1880-81	5,543,001	3,902,982
1870-71	5,175,933	3,299,703	1881-82	5,640,747	3,929,518
1872-73	5,597,006	3,786,032	1882-83	5,854,565	4,194,312
1873-74	5,857,871	4,067,981	1883-84	5,865,001	4,226,258

The only breaks in the steady line of advance are, the sudden increase of 1872-73-74, the result of commercial inflation, and the temporary decrease of 1878-79, caused by the lapse of the circulation of the City of Glasgow Bank.

AVERAGE OF LARGE AND SMALL NOTES.

Year.	Large.	Small	Total.
	Per cent.	Per cent.	
1815	39	61	100
1825	42	58	100
1845	27	73	100
1855	36	64	100
1865	37	63	100
1870	39	61	100
1875	34	66	100
1884	31·8	68·2	100
1885	31	69	100

The rise in "small" since 1870 is wholly caused by an increase in their amount of nearly £1,000,000, while the "large" have been comparatively stationary. 1845-1885.—History seems here to repeat itself in the want of gold causing universal depression and throwing large notes out of the race.

INCREASE OF DEPOSITS, BRANCHES, AND COIN KEPT BEYOND REQUIREMENT OF ACT OF 1845.

Year.	Deposits.	Branches.	Coin.
1819	...	97	
1830	...	145	Average for 5 years ending Dec. 1869 . £837,851
1845	£33,192,105	382	Average for 5 years ending Dec. 1874 . 899,133
1855	43,270,612	480	Average for year ending Dec. 1874 . . 952,313
1865	56,185,061	654	Average for year ending Dec. 1884 . . 1,037,607
1874	78,405,261	884	
1884	83,293,743	929	

LIST OF SCOTTISH BANKS, WITH AUTHORISED AND PRESENT CIRCULATION,
AS FROM MESSRS OLIVER & BOYD'S ALMANAC FOR 1885.

Name of Bank.	Authorised Circulation.	Circulation, 1884.
Bank of Scotland	£343,418	£867,383
Royal Bank of Scotland . . .	216,451	795,812
British Linen Company Bank .	438,024	663,567
Commercial Bank of Scotland, Lim.	374,880	800,383
National Bank of Scotland, Limited	297,024	655,855
Union Bank of Scotland, Limited .	454,341	803,425
Clydesdale Bank, Limited . .	274,323	577,735
Town and County Bank, Limited .	70,13	208,811
North of Scotland Bank, Limited .	154,319	390,430
Caledonian Banking Co., Limited .	53,434	101,600
	£2,676,350	£5,865,001

Of the actual circulation, large notes were £1,865,000, and small notes £4,000,001.

CIRCULATION	1883. 15 Dec.	1884. 12 Jan.	9 Feb.	8 March.	5 April.	3 May.	31 May.	28 June.	26 July.	23 Aug.	20 Sept.	18 Oct.	15 Nov.	1884. 13 Dec.
6,600,000														
6,400,000														
6,200,000														
6,000,000														
5,800,000														
5,600,000														
5,400,000														
5,200,000														
5,000,000														
4,800,000														
4,600,000														
4,400,000														
4,200,000														
4,000,000														
3,800,000														
3,600,000														
3,400,000														
3,200,000														
3,000,000														
2,800,000														
2,600,000														
2,400,000														
2,000,000														
1,800,000														
1,600,000														

Percentage of Large and Small Notes in Scotland, 1884.

Large Notes.

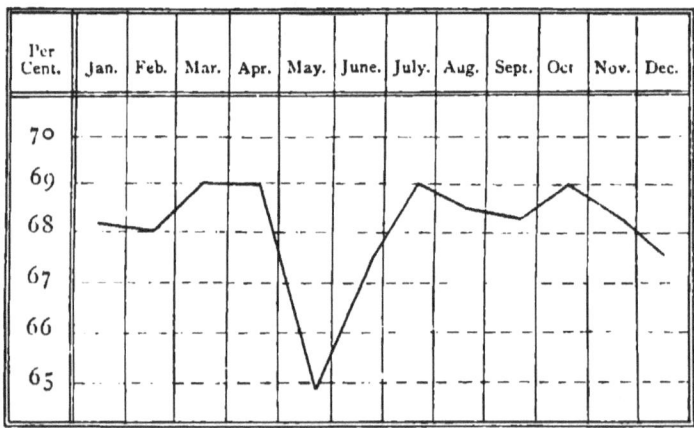

Small Notes.

Note.—For the suggestion of this and the preceding table, the Author is indebted to Mr Galletly of the British Linen Company Bank, Edinburgh.

Chapter XVI.

LAW AFFECTING THE ISSUE AND CIRCULATION OF THE ONE
POUND NOTE, AND RULES OF THE EXCHANGES FOR EFFECT-
ING PAYMENT.

"Law is the command of a Sovereign, containing a common rule of
life for his subjects."—ERSKINE.

1. UNTIL the introduction of the Feudal system, the
Roman law which recognised no difference
in the subjects composing the estate of a
deceased person, had been the rule for the nations of
Europe.

2. With the establishment of feus, whereby the holder
was bound to furnish service to his superior, a new element
and a new law came into existence. From the same desire
to perpetuate a certain line in possession of an individual
estate, which centuries afterwards led to the Entail Acts,
the right of the more permanent or feudal part of the
"*hæreditas*" was confined wholly to one of any number of
individuals who might be in the same degree of consan-
guinity to the deceased ; the other, and more perishable
portion, being left to the next of kin. Thus the ancient
hæreditas was divided into heritable and moveable.

3. Mr Erskine, in his opening chapter on this subject,
states that the doctrine of moveable rights depends chiefly
on the nature of obligations, *i.e.*, "a legal tie by which one
is bound to pay or perform something to another."

4. Under this head are included bills of exchange or
promissory notes, which are simply obligations by writ

founded upon debt, and according to the rule of law, "Debts (*nomina debitorum*) when due by bill, promissory note, or account are moveable." Thus there is a regular *catena*,—first, rights in general, of which moveable rights are one great division; in these in turn are embraced obligations by writ, a large part of which is made up of bills of exchange and promissory notes, the last named covering notes of a banker and "the one pound note."

5. A Scots bank note exhibits in a peculiarly simple way the distinction between obligation and contract drawn by Professor Moir:—"Obligations are distinguished from contracts in this, that the former are unilateral, the latter mutual. There must, no doubt, be always two parties concerned, the one who becomes bound and the other in whose favour the obligation is undertaken; but the latter is under no counter obligation, *e.g.*, where a party promises to pay or perform something to another. In a contract, on the other hand, *e.g.*, of sale, while the one party becomes bound to deliver, the other comes under the counter obligation of paying the price." In the case of a bank note the sole obligation is on the part of the grantor to pay whenever payment is demanded; so that from the superior security presently afforded to the holder of a Scots bank note, over that given by a mercantile bill, arising out of the greater financial stability of the debtor in the one case than in the other, the holder of a note knows, or need know, almost nothing of the duties and responsibilities attaching to the holder of even so simple an obligation as a bill. *Ex facie*, in neither case is there any obligation due to the issuer; but the note holder has absolutely no care as to endorsations or sexennial prescription, and has practically none as to the writ itself, the sufficiency of the stamp, presentation when due, notice of dishonour, liability for a note once held, or necessity for recourse to prior holders; while, if he loses his note, though he has no remedy against the onerous holder, he is recouped should he himself be the onerous holder of a found or stolen note, by the loser having no recourse against him. At the present

time in Scotland we can happily consider the grantor's
duty to pay as the beginning and ending of the whole
matter, but it will of course be necessary to mention briefly
the various perils which may arise in the event of non-
payment or other contingencies.

6. The Act passed by Sir Robert Peel in 1845—8 & 9
Vict., c. 38—defines the term "bank notes" as follows :—
"The term 'bank notes' used in this Act shall extend and
apply to all bills or notes for the payment of money to the
bearer on demand other than bills and notes of the Governor and Company of the Bank of England." As the above
definition, and also those in the Acts applicable to England
and Ireland, failed to prevent some parties from attempting
to evade its provisions, it was further enacted by Act 17
& 18 Vict., c. 83 (1854), that it was expedient to stop such
evasions in future by defining "What shall be deemed to
be bank notes;" and "that all bills, drafts, or notes
(other than notes of the Bank of England) which shall
be issued by any banker, or the agent of any banker, for
the payment of money to the bearer on demand, and all
bills, drafts, or notes so issued which shall entitle, or be
intended to entitle, the bearer or holder thereof, without
endorsement or without any further endorsement than
may be thereon at the time of issuing thereof, to the
payment of any sum of money on demand, whether the
same shall be expressed or not, in whatever form, or by
whomsoever such bills, drafts, or notes shall be drawn or
made, shall be deemed to be bank notes of the banker
by whom, or by whose agent, the same shall be issued,
within the meaning of the three several Acts,"—for England, Scotland, and Ireland,—"and within all the clauses,
provisions, and regulations thereof respectively."

7. The liberty to issue bank notes in Scotland is permitted to the five Edinburgh banks, the two Glasgow
banks, and the three northern banks, and to no other
or future companies or bankers, these ten being the survivors of the nineteen banks of issue existing in 1844 and
1845 to whom the Bank Acts of these years granted a

monopoly of issue, in respect of their being bankers law-
fully issuing notes on the 6th day of May 1844, and thence
up to the 1st of May 1845.

8. The Bank of Scotland, the Royal Bank, and the
British Linen Company had received special rights to issue
small and other notes upon unstamped paper, on accounting
for the duties to the Commissioners of Stamps and Taxes
(Acts 39, c. 107 ; 48, c. 149; and 55, c. 184, of Geo. III.).

9. The lawful issue of bank notes implied that at least
two requirements of the State regarding them had been
complied with,—first, that the banker had been duly licensed
so to issue ; and, second, that the notes were either stamped
according to Act of Parliament, or that arrangement had
been made for issuing them on unstamped paper.

10. The first restriction of a banker's right to issue notes
by requiring a license for the exercise of what had previously been a right at common law, was instituted in 1808
as a war tax. Subsequently, by Acts 55 Geo. III., c. 184
(1815), and 7 Geo. IV., c. 67 (1826), it was provided that
not more than four licenses were required for any number
of offices in Scotland. By the Act of 1844, 7 & 8 Vict.,
c. 32, s. 22, the law was changed, to the effect that each
office opened after 6th May in that year for the circulation
of notes required a separate license, though two covered
three or more branches in one town,—all offices in existence
prior to that date remaining secured as before by the four
licenses. The amount for each license is £30, which has to
be renewed annually, as changes in the partners of the
bank are only covered by the license to the 10th of
October in each year. Any banker issuing notes in contravention of the statute (now 33 & 34 Vict., c. 97, s. 47—
Stamp Act 1870) is liable to a penalty of £50 for each note
so issued, while any one knowingly accepting such a note
forfeits the sum of £20 for each offence.

11. Prior to 1800 no taxation was levied upon one
pound notes, but in that year (under Act 39 Geo. III., c. 107)
a duty of twopence upon each note was imposed to meet
the war expenditure. In 1805 the duty was raised to three-

pence, and no note was allowed to circulate for a longer period than three years without being restamped. In 1808 the vexatious restriction as to time was abolished, but the duty was raised to the following rates (Act 48 Geo. III., c. 149):—

						s.	d.
Not exceeding £1	1 .	.	.	.	.	0	4
Exceeding	1	1 but not exceeding £2	2	.		0	8
,,	2	2 ,,	5	5	.	1	0
,,	5	5 ,,	20	0	.	1	6
,,	20	0 ,,	30	0	.	3	0
,,	30	0 ,,	50	0	.	4	6
.,	50	0 ,,	100	0	.	7	6

These rates remained in force until 1815, when Act 55 Geo. III., c. 184, again raised the duties to the scale at which they now nominally stand, although fortunately robbed of their sting by the commutation of 1854:—

						s.	d.
Not exceeding £1	1 .	.	.	.	.	0	5
Exceeding	1	1 but not exceeding £2	2	.		0	10
,,	2	2 ,,	5	5	.	1	3
,,	5	5 ,,	10	0	.	1	9
,,	10	0 .,	20	0	.	2	0
,,	20	0 ,,	30	0	.	3	0
.,	30	0 .,	50	0	.	5	0
,,	50	0 ,,	100	0	.	8	6

A higher rate being fixed than upon ordinary bills of exchange, on account of the power to *re-issue ;* for, as it has been said by Lord Ellenborough, a bill "is negotiable *ad infinitum* until it has been paid or discharged,"—a bank note possessing the further advantage of being re-issued any number of times. Any notes stamped under the scale of 1808 were allowed to be re-issued upon being stamped with the additional duty. Prior to 1815 the stamp was impressed upon the face of the note, but after that date it was printed in red ink upon the back, a somewhat rough design being employed similar to those still to be seen in the stamps upon patent medicines. Though supposed to form a protection against forgery, it was soon forged without difficulty.*

---

* The stamp was called the " Congreve," from its inventor.

12. By 3 & 4 Wm. IV. all banks of issue were required to send in returns of the quarterly average of their notes in circulation, calculated upon the sum in the hands of the public at the end of each week, the returns to be made upon the 1st of January, April, July, and October of each year.

13. Notwithstanding repeated efforts to obtain such a settlement of the duties as would put a stop to the trouble and expense of sending to London to have a number of notes stamped, only to be useless for some time in the banks' tills before issue to the public, the Government declined to move, until 1853, when a deputation of Scots bankers had an interview with the Lords of the Treasury, who promised to look into the matter with a view to a change. After some negotiation the Government intimated that they were willing to compound, if some mutually equitable principle could be agreed upon. A common basis having been arranged, an Act was passed in August of that year, 16 & 17 Vict., c. 63, stating that as it was advisable to grant to the other banks in Scotland the same right of issuing notes upon unstamped paper enjoyed by the Bank of Scotland, the Royal Bank, and the British Linen Company, and also to arrange some method of compounding with all the banks in Scotland and elsewhere for the stamp duties upon their notes, therefore power should be given to the Commissioners of Stamps and Taxes, or any three of them, to make such arrangement with "all or any of the banks for a composition," "on such terms, and with such security for the payment of the same," as the Commissioners might see fit. In the following December a commutation was finally sanctioned, whereby the banks have since been charged 8s. 4d. annually upon every £100, or part of that sum, of their notes circulating in the hands of the public. Certain of the bank directors were required to give their bond to the Crown for several thousand pounds, as security for due payment of the compositions.

14. Payment of the duty is made half-yearly at the rate of 4s. 2d. per centum, or part thereof, and is calculated by means of the returns sent in to the Commissioners of

Stamps and Taxes under the Act of 1845. A notice is sent to the bank at the beginning of each year by the Inland Revenue in Edinburgh, stating the dates up to which returns are to be made (a notice, by the way, which has to be carefully checked by the bank authorities, as on one occasion lately the Revenue Board tried to prove that there were fifty-three weeks in the year). The accounts by the banks have to be handed in to the Comptroller of Stamps and Taxes in Edinburgh, and the duty paid, within fourteen days after the 1st of January and the 1st of July in each year, bearing an affidavit by officers of the banks that it is a true and just account, to the best of their knowledge and belief, of the amount or value of all unstamped promissory notes in circulation on Saturday in every week, from the date of Saturday following the last entry in the previous half-year's return, to the same day in the last week of the half-year current, together with the average amount of such notes so in circulation, the twenty-six weekly amounts being added up and divided by the number of Saturdays (usually twenty-six), the quotient being the average upon which duty is paid for the half-year; the account is then signed and sworn to before a justice of the peace.

15. A question arose during the first half-year of the new arrangement as to whether the old stamped notes could be re-issued without being counted as part of the circulation, but the difficulty was soon got over by the Inland Revenue allowing the banks' claims to exemption from further stamp duty in this respect.

16. In addition to the penalty for issuing notes without a license, any one not a banker issuing notes payable to bearer for any sum less than £5 incurs a farther fine of £20 for every such note so issued.

17. The issue of notes with printed dates was prohibited by 55 Geo. IV., c. 184, but is now sanctioned by 23 & 24 Vict., c. iii., s. 19.

18. Returns are required to be made to the Commissioners of Stamps and Taxes, London, under the Act of

1845. The first of these is made weekly of the amount of notes in circulation upon Saturday, accompanied by a statement of the total sum of gold and coin,—first, for each day of the week in the principal office or place of issue ; and second, the whole amount held by the bank in Scotland for Saturday only. Second, every fourth Saturday the following items are added to the above return :—(*a.*) The amount of notes, first, of £5 and upwards, and second, below that sum (now, of course, all £1 notes) ; (*b.*) Amount of the authorised circulation ; (*c.*) Average amount of notes in circulation during the four weeks, distinguishing those for £1 from higher denominations ; (*d.*) Average amount of coin at head office during the four weeks, distinguishing between gold and silver, each average being obtained by dividing the sum of the four weeks by the number of weeks. The penalty for neglect or refusal to make these returns, or for any false return, is £100 for each offence.

19. CIRCULATION.—When the issue of the notes is in excess of the amount sanctioned in the bank's certificate, gold coin must be held against such excess to an equal amount, of which it is allowed that one-fourth may be silver coin.

20. The Commissioners may at any time demand an inspection of the banks' circulation books, or other relative books or papers ; they may also require to see the gold and silver coin held in reserve. Any person having the custody of such books, paper, or coin refusing to satisfy the demands of the Commissioners, is liable to a penalty of £100 for each offence. The inspection referred to in this clause has never been put in force.

21. If it be found that any bank has exceeded the amount of its authorised circulation without having the excess covered by possession of an equivalent amount of coin, such bank shall forfeit a sum equal to the excess.

22. Scotch bank notes are not allowed to be issued in England. No bank notes are legal tender in Scotland, Bank of England notes being specially excluded by statute of 1845, while Scots notes are only counted as cash if received

as such. The question of legal tender was decided regarding Scots notes so far back as 1756 in Watson v. Chalmers. Mr John Watson, an Edinburgh writer to the signet, having been offered Glasgow bank notes in payment of a bill by Mr Chalmers, a Leith merchant, declined to accept them, and sued Chalmers for recovery of the bill. Chalmers pled tender of payment by bank notes. The court held that bank notes did not form a legal tender, and that all contracts to pay money must be understood to mean payment in standard coin of the realm, unless otherwise stipulated. It has been held in England, that a creditor taking country bank notes when he might have had gold, thereby lost all recourse against cautioners.

23. To lose sight of bank notes in the character of bills of exchange, is also to forget their other rights, such as recovery by summary diligence ; so that while the popular idea of notes being cash, is correct so far as usage and precedent has made it so, it is well to keep in mind the distinction between the two. So long as gold is the only legal tender for large amounts, notes cannot be correctly termed cash unless they are accepted as such. On the other hand, a bank note has so much of the attributes of cash as to lose its identity when circulated or commixed with other notes or coin ; and " whenever money or cash is used in law, in its popular sense it includes bank notes,—a bequest of cash includes bank notes, and in construing certain old Annuity Acts the Courts attached the same meaning to the words " (Thomson's " Bills of Exchange," p. 122). This was decided in the case of Crawford v. Royal Bank, in February 1749, mentioned in " Morison's Dictionary." " Hew Crawford, clerk to the signet, sent a £20 Old Bank note by post, *noted the number*, and *wrote his name upon it*. It was lost, and the note at last appeared in hands of the New Bank. Crawford raised a process of multiple-poinding in name of the Old Bank. The judges were unanimous on two points,—first, that money is not subject to any *vitium reale*, and that it cannot be vindicated from the *bonâ fide* possessor, however clear the proof of the theft may

be ; second, that bank notes serving the purpose of money must be entitled to the same privileges; and, therefore, that Mr Crawford had no claim to the note in question."

24. By Act 19 & 20 Vict., c. 56, s. 32, bank notes may be poinded by the sheriff for Crown debts ; and under the Fraudulent Debtors Act (Scotland) 1879, 43 & 44 Vict., c. 34, s. 12, the sheriff has power, upon cause shewn, to grant warrant to take possession of *bank notes*, money, &c., open lockfast places, &c., &c. ; but it is understood that they cannot be poinded for any other debt, nor are payments in notes reducible under the preference clauses of the Bankruptcy Acts.

25. When notes are accepted in payment of a debt, recourse can be maintained by taking the debtor's endorsation upon the back of the notes and duly presenting them for payment. Such endorsement is effective even in the hands of third parties, if undue delay has not taken place in presentation, and the usual requirements as to intimation of dishonour have been complied with.

26. In absence of endorsation the holder has no recourse against a prior holder, except when, at the time of its reception, the bank upon which the note is drawn has failed ; and, second, when the bank has failed before the note could be presented, and due presentation and intimation of not payment have been made in both cases ; or, third, when the fact of the bank's failure was known to the prior holder, who will be liable to refund on account of his fraud. A merchant may stop goods *in transitu* for which he has been paid in notes of a bank which has failed. A curious case as to the liability of a prior holder was decided in 1852. Timmins obtained payment of a debt in notes from Gibbons, and paid the sum into another bank, receiving in exchange their deposit-receipt. Immediately thereafter, the bank on whom the notes were drawn failed, and the bank holding the notes called upon Mr Timmins to pay. He did so, and sued Gibbons for recovery under the deposit-receipt. Held that recourse had been lost, and that he could not recover under the deposit-receipt.

27. When a mutilated note is presented the Scots banks pay a sum in proportion to the part so presented, though sometimes in case of notes partially destroyed by fire or otherwise full payment is made upon an affidavit being sworn to by the party in possession. The Bank of England pay full value for a half note after the lapse of a few months, on receiving a suitable guarantee.

28. FORGERY.—The ancient punishment for this crime was death, usually commuted to transportation to the plantations. If the forger returned to Scotland, whipping in the pillory was periodically administered, until he was again carried beyond the seas. Under Act 45 Geo. III., c. 89, s. 6, applicable to Great Britain, various terms of imprisonment were enacted for imitating the paper or watermark, or for engraving the plates or uttering " bank notes," or being in the possession of a forged note knowing the same to be a forgery, or of materials for the special purpose of so forging, or for being art and part in any of these offences, while sentence of death was permissible.

29. Subsequently, about 1800, when a Government duty stamp was first printed on the notes, the forger of such notes was also compelled to forge the stamp, an act which seems to have withdrawn from the Courts the power of awarding any sentence short of death. Soon afterwards the draconic code. of Geo. III. came into full play, and multitudes of forgers were hanged without mercy, a punishment which seems to have had no effect in diminishing the number of criminal attempts.

30. Although the Act before referred to was passed specially to protect Scotland as well as England, by extending to the former the provisions of certain Acts passed previously for England alone, yet its effect was disputed by the judges of the Court of Session in the case of Thomas Gray, charged in 1814 with possessing two Bank of England notes and two Bank of Scotland notes, all forgeries, for the sum of £2 each. " By the narrowest majority, they found that the Act of Parliament libelled, extended to notes issued by the Bank of Scotland, as well

as to notes of the Bank of England." Gray was accordingly convicted, and suffered fourteen years' transportation
in terms of the statute. Bank of Scotland notes had thus
the unexpected privilege of being reckoned legally to be
the only *bank notes* issued in Scotland in 1814.

31. An Act had been passed—41 Geo. IV., c. 57—pro-
tecting the notes of country banks.

32. The punishment of death was abolished as to
special forgeries by the Acts 11 Geo. IV., 1 Wm. IV., c.
66, and 2 & 3 Wm. IV., c. 123, and was finally quashed by
the Act 7 Wm. IV., and 1 Vic., c. 84. Since that date the
punishment has come gradually down from transportation
for life to imprisonment or penal servitude.

33. Not only the leaders in the crime, but all aiders and
abettors, are punishable to the extent of their knowledge.
The artist who engraves the plate, or the workman who
prints the notes, are alike guilty, unless employed merely in
trade, and in complete ignorance of criminal intention,
—according to the maxim, " The act does not make a
criminal, unless there be criminal intention." But if they
know what they are about, or are to receive any part of the
profits, " they are forgers in a one and complex under-
taking " (Hume's Commentaries). It would seem that
were the workman in knowledge of the intention, and stops
his work, confessing his purpose before any evil results have
arisen, his crime will be overlooked, as a distinction has
always been drawn between preparation, or *conatus*, and
perpetrated crime ; although any one relying upon such a
doctrine in regard to forgery of notes, is treading on dangerous ground, for the Acts make each conscious wilful step in
the process a crime punishable as enacted.

34. The custody of forged notes after detection is a
disputed point. Prior to 1818 the Bank of England had
always retained any such notes. At the end of that year
a Mr Ransom, an engraver, paid a one pound note to a Mr
Mitchener, which, on presentation at the bank, was declared
to be a forgery and retained. Mitchener fell back on
Ransom, who refused to pay unless he got the note from

the Bank of England. To meet his wishes an inspector was sent from the bank,—a Mr Fish,—who at Ransom's request handed him the note for inspection, which that individual at once put in his pocket and refused to give up. This was more than the bank could brook, and in Fish's name they had Ransom lodged in jail on the charge of being possessed of a forged bank note. As no one appeared from the Bank of England to prove that the note was a forgery, the jury found him not guilty, whereupon he sued Mr Fish and obtained £100 damages for wrongous imprisonment. Since then the bank has merely stamped the word " forged " in several places upon the notes and returned them to the presenters, a practice which has been generally followed by the Scots banks.

35. Summary diligence is competent upon bank notes under Act 5 Geo. III., c. 49, of 1765, and has already been referred to. The only difference in procedure worthy of note is that effected by the Act 1 & 2 Vict., c. 114, whereby the debtor is not now put to the horn as formerly ; but, on the protest being recorded, an extract is issued, which contains a warrant to charge the debtor on the notes to make payment within six days. Should settlement not be arranged within that time, poinding may follow. Any number of notes of the same tenor may be included under one protest. Payment can only be legally demanded at the place where it is promised upon the note. This invaluable diligence does not appear to have been once required during the present century for the recovery of sums in bank notes, and in consequence of so little being heard of the process, the remedy has almost been lost sight of by the general public.

36. For the greater security of the public against unsafe note issues, it was enacted by the Companies Act 1879, 42 & 43 Vict., c. 76, s. 6 (after repeating a similar clause from the Act of 1862), that no member of a limited banking company registered under that Act would be entitled to limitation in respect of the note issue of such bank ; but that all the members should continue liable,

jointly and severally, for the whole amount of the notes, in the same manner as if they were members of an unlimited company. The last paragraph of the clause allows any limited bank of issue " to make a statement on its notes to the effect, that the limited liability does not extend to its notes, and that the members of the company continue liable in respect of its notes in the same manner as if it had been registered as an unlimited company."

37. Under Act 12 Geo. III., c. 72, s. 39,—made perpetual by 23 Geo. III., c. 18, s. 55,—bank notes are specially excluded from the operation of the sexennial prescription upon bills or other promissory notes which was then intro- duced. Mr Thomson, in his " Bills of Exchange," thinks that " there is no reason for believing that they are exempt from the long negative prescription of forty years, as the words of the Acts include them in the same way as other obligations."—(Acts 1469, c. 29, and 1474, c. 55, of Scottish Parliament.)

NOTE EXCHANGES.

The first exchange in Great Britain, upon the system of the modern clearing-house, was begun in Edinburgh about 1752. For many years during the infancy of the system settlements were invariably demanded in gold, in order to compel the unwilling country banks to retire their surplus notes at regular intervals. No great progress was made until the Act of 1765 gave the banks the right to summary diligence on their neighbours' notes. From early times the final settlement appears to have been effected by drafts on London at ten days date, though about 1810 or 1815 there seems to have been some method of temporary settlement by a stock of Bank of Scotland £100 notes, which, if correct, must have proved highly profitable to the old bank. As amounts became larger from the increased volume of notes, exchequer bills were utilized ; and on this basis an agree- ment was come to in February 1846, by ten of the chief banks of Scotland, the prominent features of which were,— two exchanges to be held each week, upon Thursdays in the Bank of Scotland and on Saturdays in the Royal Bank, the settlements being made on Thursday and Monday by means of exchequer bills of £1000 each; £100 notes of the three old banks, or of the Bank of England, being employed (with gold) to make up fractional parts of £1000. Arrangements were made for compelling banks with whom exchequer bills accumulated, to sell to banks who had run short. The bills were recorded in a special book, kept in the Bank of Scotland, and being marked "Edinburgh Exchequer Bills," were not to be used for any other purpose. Exchanges of notes were also begun in the provinces.

This agreement was continued until 1864, when it was arranged to pay the balances by bills on London drawn at a few days after sight; and in February 1876 the following rules were formulated, which, with a few alterations instituted by the revised rules of March 1880, are still observed in the exchange :—

Instead of exchanges only twice a week a meeting is held daily, except Monday, at 10 A.M., a second exchange being held on Saturday afternoon at 1.30. When Monday is a holiday no exchange takes place on Tuesday. When Saturday is a holiday an exchange is held on Friday afternoon. In case of holidays the general settlement is held next day.

At least two clerks from each bank are supposed to attend at the hour stated, in the exchange room in St Andrew Square, and fifteen minutes afterwards the doors are shut, no more notes being allowed into the exchange ; any dilatory bank must retire the notes handed to it, although too late to give any in return.

Each bank has a separate compartment ; one clerk remains in this to receive notes, while his companion hands the packets to the clerks of the other banks. It is prohibited to place the notes in any compartment unless a clerk is there to receive them, nor is any clerk allowed to enter the box of another bank, as the doors should be locked.

Until all the notes received by each bank have been found correct no clerk may leave the room, and at least one clerk from each bank must remain until all the notes handed by him to other banks have been checked. Notes handed in by different banks are not to be mixed until all are checked ; and should any dispute arise, the bank which is found to have broken the rules in this clause shall be considered to be in the wrong, unless other proof be forthcoming. A competent staff is required from each bank.

The Edinburgh exchange is divided into two departments, namely, the exchange for notes, and the clearing-house for vouchers.

The settlements of the note exchange are made by debiting or crediting the clearing-house department, daily, for the balances arising. These sums are carried forward in the clearing-house, and continued until a settling-day wipes all out.

The final settlements are now made upon Monday and Thursday at 2 P.M. So far as the note exchange is concerned these settlements embrace, first, that of Monday,—the notes collected on Thursday, Friday, and large notes of Saturday ; second, that on Thursday covers the small notes of Saturday, and the notes of Monday, Tuesday, and Wednesday. The amounts in the note exchange proper at Edinburgh, are small when compared with those of the adjoining clearing-house ; but it must be borne in remembrance that the volume of transactions in the latter is enormously swelled by the exchange vouchers, sent to their head offices by nine hundred branches throughout the country, in settlement of their *provincial note exchanges.* The Glasgow exchange alone adds a very large sum to the Edinburgh clearing-house, where it appears only in the shape of vouchers. The remarkable proportion maintained among the different circulations also tends to equalise matters considerably, so that while the amounts passing through may be large, the balances arising are not necessarily so.

Some idea may be had of the extent of these transactions

from the fact before mentioned, that each year notes are delivered in the different exchanges of Scotland amounting to the respectable sum of from £170,000,000 to £175,000,000 sterling.

The note exchanges being thus incorporated with the clearing-house are worked out as follows :—Odd shillings and pence are cleared off in cash, leaving only pounds to be dealt with. The bank having the largest debtor balance pays to the bank having the largest creditor balance; should any remain over, the debtor bank pays it to the second largest creditor bank, who receives the remainder of its amount from the second largest debtor bank ; if the latter happens to have a small balance, and is therefore unable to pay the second creditor bank in full, the third debtor bank is fallen back upon, and so on in regularly diminishing order until all are paid. Sometimes when only two banks are at credit the settlement is easily worked out ; at other times it gets mixed up, and new hands lose their heads completely. Two illustrations are given of the mode of working,—the first simple, the second more complex, though to the regular exchange clerk both are alike easy. The form on the following page is a copy of that used in the clearing-house.

The payments were made for some years by bill on London, but since the banks all opened branches there, instructions are sent to them to pay to the London office or correspondent of the creditor bank, four days after date, the sum required for the exchange. In event of the fourth day occurring on a holiday, payment is usually delayed until the next business day.

Interest is allowed upon the daily exchanges at the rate of £2 per cent. for each day, two days having to be counted for on a Saturday ; and upon the two general settlements it is at the rate of £3 per cent. for the four days during which final payments is postponed.

Example of Clearing=House Settlement at Edinburgh.

No. I.

EDINBURGH CLEARING-HOUSE.

...... *day of* .... *18*..

In favour.	Banks.	Against.	Payments.	To whom Paid.
£		£	£	
24,575	Bank of Scotland	...	...	...
...	Royal Bank .	29,975	29,975	To National
...	British Linen Co.	35,012	35,012	To National
...	Commercial .	5,128	5,128	...
98,684	National . .	...	...	...
...	Union . . .	29,863	29,863	To National
...	Clydesdale . .	23,281	{ 3,834	To National
			{ 19,447	To Bank of Scotland
123,259		123,259	123,259	

Largest Creditor, National . . £98,684
1st Largest Debtor, B. L. Co.. £35,012
2nd Largest Debtor, Royal . 29,975
3rd Largest Debtor, Union . 29,863

                             94,850

Still due . . 3,834 to National Bank.
4th Largest Debtor, Clydesdale . . 23,281

Still due . . 19,447 by Clydesdale, who pays to Bank of Scot.
5th Largest Debtor, Commercial . . 5,128 pays to Bank of Scotland.

£24,575 to clear the account.

NO. II.

		EDINBURGH CLEARING HOUSE.		
		.... *day of* .... *18..*		

In favour.	Banks.	Against.	Payments.	To whom Paid.
£		£	£	
...	Bank of Scotland	70,482	{ 63,489	To National
			6,993	To Commercial
31,477	Royal Bank	...	...	...
...	British Linen Co.	65,293	{ 36,298	To Commercial
			28,995	To Royal
43,291	Commercial	...	...	...
63,489	National	...	...	...
25,291	Union	...	...	...
...	Clydesdale	27,773	{ 2,482	To Royal
			25,291	To Union
163,548		163,548	163,548	

```
1st Debtor Bank, Bank of Scotland £70,482
1st Creditor Bank, National    .    .  63,489
                                     ————
        Leaving    .    .    .    .   6,993   over from Bank of Scotland.
2nd Creditor Bank, Commercial   .    43,291
                                     ————
        Leaving    .    .    .    .  36,298   still due to Commercial.
2nd Debtor Bank, British Linen Co.   65,293
                                     ————
        Leaving    .    .    .    .  28,995   over from British Linen Co.
3rd Creditor Bank, Royal    .    .   31,477
                                     ————
        Leaving    .    .    .    .   2,482   still due to Royal.
3rd Debtor Bank, Clydesdale    .     27,773
                                     ————
        Leaving    .    .    .    .  25,291   over from Clydesdale,
Which pays 4th Creditor, Union   .   25,291   and clears account.
                                     ════
```

Q

The Bank of Scotland and the Royal Bank carry through the settlement upon alternate months, but neither of them incurs any responsibility in this capacity.

Should any bank fail to effect the payment in London within the proper time, and be unable to give a "prompt and satisfactory explanation of the cause," it is liable to be excluded from the exchange-room and clearing-house.

COUNTRY EXCHANGES.—Exchanges for notes have long been established in various provincial towns, and are now regularly held, wherever there are two or more banks, every business day except Monday, with a final exchange on Saturday afternoon.

A rule of the Edinburgh clearing-house says, that "all exchangeable notes received at these agencies must be exchanged there, and must on no pretext be forwarded to meet the exchanges in Edinburgh or at the other agencies."

When the balances of these country exchanges are below £100, they are debited and credited by local vouchers to accounts kept in the current account ledgers of the branches. These are brought into next day's exchange, and carried on until they amount to over £100, or until Saturday afternoon, in which cases the balances are cleared off by exchange vouchers on Edinburgh.

In order to reduce the circulation as much as possible, in view of the Act of 1845, the subscribing banks bind themselves to bring into the exchange all exchangeable notes they have in their possession, and not to issue notes of another bank without sanction first asked and obtained.

The banks in the exchange and clearing-house are as follows :—

The Bank of Scotland, who retire the notes of the Caledonian Bank.

The Royal Bank, who retire the notes of the Town and County Bank, Aberdeen.

The British Linen Company Bank.

The Commercial Bank of Scotland Limited, who retire the notes of the North of Scotland Bank.

The National Bank of Scotland Limited.

The Union Bank of Scotland Limited.

The Clydesdale Bank Limited.

Chapter XVII.

THE MATERIAL AND PREPARATION OF THE BIT OF PAPER.

"Pregnant with thousands flits the *scrap* unseen,
And silent sells a king or buys a queen."—POPE.

THE two chief requisites of a one pound bank note are, that it should be of such strength as to stand the tear and wear to which it may be subjected, and to be so contrived as to present the fewest points of attack to the "infamous forger."

The Bank of Scotland had not been in existence over five or six years, when they found it necessary to adopt some means whereby imitation of their notes would be made more difficult, and detection of fraud correspondingly more easy.

It is difficult to decide whether it is more humbling or gratifying to Scotsmen to know that the superior educational advantages of their country enabled the idea of forgery of bank notes to arise first in Scotland ; although it is more probable that the novelty and poor workmanship of the Scotch notes were the principal attractions in the early part of the eighteenth century. England was not troubled in this respect until the very end of the century, when her national bank began to issue small notes of very poor execution.

Schoolmasters and engravers were the first forgers, from which a lesson may be learned by those who care to read. The early notes both of the Bank of Scotland and the Royal Bank, even after they had invented "special checks against forgery," were of brittle paper, bald and simple in design, and roughly engraved in comparison with those of the nineteenth century.* The printing and the watermark were the only really good features in them,—the former being generally cleanly done, the ink retaining its black colour notwithstanding the lapse of years ; and the latter produced by the venerable wire process, specimens of which are extant on various MSS. dating back to the thirteenth century. At the time the Bank of Scotland began, paper-making was in its infancy in Scotland, the first company starting on the Water of Leith in the same year that the bank opened, so that possibly the paper for our first notes came from France or Holland.

MANUFACTURE OF PAPER.—At all times bank notes were made, as they still are, from new linen rags, which ought to be of good quality, as the better the material so much the tougher and lighter is the note.

From the small size of the notes, and the necessity for having paper exhibiting the deckle edges, most of the bank note paper is produced by modifications of the old "handmade" process. The rags are cut, sorted, dusted, washed, bleached, and comminuted by rotary motion in various cylinders fitted with knives and beaters, in which they are placed, with due proportion of water and strong caustic alkali, to reduce the material to the pure vegetable fibre, until the liquid pulp is poured out upon the wire frames which first convert it into something like paper. These are composed of a network of very fine wire stretched on frames of the same size as the paper to be made (the huge endless-web machines being wholly inapplicable). Into this rectangular network of wire are sewed the designs of the watermark, usually in wire or brass work of various breadth or thickness. The Bank of England's watermark is now produced from brass dies, which ensure that every repetition of the mark, to almost any number, shall be

---

* Specimens of these may be seen in the Antiquarian Museum, Edinburgh.

absolutely identical, a degree of accuracy which it would be impossible to acquire with the wire process in such a complicated mark as that upon their notes. To complete a mould for such a note as that of the Bank of England formerly required over one thousand wires and sixty-eight thousand twists, and "the same repetition when the stout wires are introduced to support the under surface. Therefore, with backing, laying, large waves, figures, letters, and borders, before a pair of moulds are completed there are some hundred of thousands of stitches." To produce perfect similarity by such a method is clearly impossible, as for such as the Bank of England four or five new moulds were needed each year. Much of our Scotch bank note paper is, however, still made by this process, although now simplified and improved.

The mark upon the notes of the Bank of England and some other banks is produced by an invention of Messrs Brewer, Smith, & Co., for which they received a medal at the Great Exhibition of 1851.

The required pattern is engraved on steel-faced dies, which are afterwards hardened by being heated in leather-charcoal and then plunged into cold water. To prevent any change from the dies wearing out, they can be impressed upon soft steel plates which in turn can be hardened, and so the original mark may be multiplied almost *ad infinitum.* The die, once made, is used by a stamping machine to give its impress to soft plates of sheet brass, which thus become embossed, "and are filed at the back to the requisite proportions to allow the moisture of the pulp of the paper to pass through the apertures. The different pieces of brass, when struck, filed, and put together, form the mould for the manufacture of the paper, and are so arranged that each mould 'is designed for two pairs of notes." *

When one mould wears out, a new one is struck, mathe-

---

* Journals of Society of Arts ; Article by Alfred Smee, F.R.S. ; Extracted from Mr E. Wilson's " How to Detect Forged Bank Notes."

matically the same as the old, the only care required being in the filing of the raised parts of the back.

The peculiarities of a genuine watermark lie chiefly in the different shades produced by the varying thicknesses of the paper. When the note is wetted, these appear more distinct in a good note. In a spurious watermark produced by mere pressure, such as many of the old forged notes bore, damping destroys the mark altogether, as it swells the fibre of the paper, the pressed part in consequence becoming of the same thickness as the other. A pressed or rolled mark is always smooth and greasy, compared with that on a genuine note. There are also the tests of *reflected* and *transmitted lights*. In a transmitted light, obtained by holding the note between the eye and the sun, the thicker parts of the paper appear dark ; while under a light reflected down upon the paper, these dark parts appear lighter, as they have more white pulp in their thickness than the other parts. A pressed or photographed watermark exhibits none of these characteristics, and may therefore be easily detected, although by photography it is surprising how the *appearance* of the mark seems to be worked into the very texture of the paper. But even photography will not stand both tests of examination by *transmission* or *reflection* of light ; in one light or another failure is certain, and the fraud may be detected. A new method of imitating watermarks has recently been perfected by an Edinburgh gentleman, which completely defies the water test, but may be detected by heat or other chemical means. As it has fortunately been kept private so far, there is no necessity for giving further publicity to so dangerous an invention, except by saying, that as the process does not affect the thickness of the paper, the spurious watermark may be distinguished from the true, by its being perfectly uniform in surface both to sight and touch.

Each piece of paper is made the size of two notes, and is cut down the middle before printing. After the pulp has settled upon these moulds before described, the superfluous moisture escapes through the interstices of the wire or brass work, leaving only the fibre in a damp and partially coagulated condition ; this is carefully removed, and passed through felt rollers and heated steel cylinders to dry, smooth, and harden it to the required texture. In this condition a Bank of England £5 note weighs about 18½ grains, and a Scotch £1 note from 20 to 25 grains, according to the bank,—some being lighter than others.

When this process is completed the paper is again slightly moistened, and about one grain of " size " is added to each note, the material used being any substance with sufficient gelatinous properties, such as skin, parchment, fish bones, sheep's feet, &c., into which is mixed a small quantity of alum to harden it. The superfluous " size " having been removed by pressure, the paper is again taken to the drying room, after which it is counted and packed in reams ready for delivery. Messrs Portal, of Laverstoke, supply the Bank of England with nearly fourteen thousand reams annually, while a good deal of Scotch paper is made by Messrs Stacey, Wise, & Co., of Northampton,—the old-world trade of the Water of Leith manufacturers, who made all the old Scotch notes, having entirely left them. The production of the paper may thus be seen to be no easy task, and of itself is a considerable safeguard against criminal effort. Mr Granville Sharp, in the Gilbert Prize Essay, suggests that to secure uniformity, which is a good part of the battle, it would be advisable for a number of bankers in a given district, or even in an entire country, to combine, so as to have the same watermark upon all their notes. This could be done in a general way with advantage, as no bank need lose its identity, the general design being the same, while the name of each bank could be added to their respective notes. Mr Sharp's idea would certainly lead to a considerable saving in expense. The paper, when ready for printing, is as carefully guarded and counted as if it were cash, being usually placed under the charge of the bank's cashier until required.

ENGRAVING AND PRINTING.—The engraving of the old one pound notes was the part in which the mechanical skill of the time was furthest behind. The designs were made up of a quantity of flourishing, more or less elaborate, down the one side, by way of a check mark, the remainder being taken up with the words and figures of the promise. Last century, printing gave little or no encouragement to engravers, hence they were few, their work was dear, and often not very good. This kept the banks from expending money upon an elaborate design, and simplified the work of the forger immensely. The workmanship of the Royal Bank note of 1750 for £12 Scots, shewn opposite, may be taken as a very good note for the period ; but careful examination will reveal many weak points, such as in the flourish down the side, where, instead of being smoothly and perfectly rounded, so that no break could be seen in the continuity of the curves, a magnifying glass will shew simply a number of straight lines changing their direction as they are joined end to end ; nor are the letters much better in the scrip part, some are higher than others, while uniform thickness is not maintained throughout. Considerable advance must have been made by 1826, as a forged guinea note of Sir William Forbes, James Hunter, & Co., of that date, shews a style of engraving as superior to the Royal Bank note of 1753 as that was to the Bank of Scotland note of 1723 ; and yet to an engraver of modern times the forgery of 1826 is thoroughly 'prentice work, the fivepenny Government stamp upon the back is rude in execution, and is presumed to be a forgery also, unless the perpetrator was more daring than skilful.

Under the humane influence of Sir Samuel Romilly, Sir James Mackintosh, and others, the public feeling began to revolt at the number of hangings for forgery ; and both bankers and judges were compelled to find some means of proving that " prevention is better than cure," and that to remove temptation from the criminal classes was as much the duty of every citizen as it was for them to award punishment for the perpetration of crime.

So far as Scotland is concerned, soon after 1830, a

£12 Scots Nº 73

The Royal Bank of SCOTLAND is hereby obliged to pay to [signature] Secretary or the Bearer on demand, Twenty Shillings Sterling. Edinburgh the ninth day of February one thousand Seven hundred & Fifty years.

By Order of the Court of Directors:

better style of engraving was adopted, the National Bank upon this occasion setting the example. The large book trade of Edinburgh gave ample employment to such high-class engravers as the Messrs W. & A. K. Johnston and Mr A. H. Lizars, who speedily raised the Scots bank note to a high standard of excellence.

Prior to 1837 copper plates were used, and from their softness, caused much trouble and expense in their renewal. At that time, however, the reproduction of designs by mill and die was brought to this country by Messrs Perkins & Heath, the predecessors of the now famous house of Perkins, Bacon, & Co. The founder of the firm, Mr Jacob Perkins, was born in Massachusetts, and came to England to push his splendid inventions.

The first engraving by this process is upon soft steel, which on completion is hardened. This plate is not used for printing, but as a die from which many impressions are taken upon soft steel plates afterwards hardened. In this way the absolute identity of every plate with its predecessor is ensured, and year after year may elapse without the slightest difference becoming observable. In addition to very fine powers of engraving vignettes, Mr Perkins adapted the old rose-engine for turning patterns upon the backs of watches, to the profession of which he soon became the head, and it is by aid of this engine—a purely mechanical operation—that some of the finest parts of our notes are produced.

The vast saving of labour and time effected by these means is almost incredible. Taking an extract regarding the firm's work upon the postage stamps, and supposing that the new modes had never been invented :—" It took Mr Heath a fortnight's hard work to engrave, on the original steel die, the profile which is the progenitor of all the rest" (that of Queen Victoria). " Since the introduction of cheap postage, Messrs Perkins, Bacon, & Petch have transferred the matrix upon one hundred and forty-two plates, each having two hundred and forty heads upon it. In other words, the number of single heads given off from steel to steel has been thirty-four thousand and eighty. Every one of these, but for the transferring process, must have been engraved laboriously by hand, at the expense of a fortnight's time." To keep up such an amount of engraving would have required one hundred and ten first-class workmen to be constantly employed ; and as these sentences were based upon the figures of 1850, it may be imagined what will be the economy now. The inventor of such a system is more honourably entitled to the rank of public benefactor than many of those who get the name.

The one point aimed at in engraving was, of course, "*inimitability.*" To secure this, not only was *quantity* of work needed, but superior *quality* of art, as also *variety* of work. For all those purposes the engine machinery can be turned to endless advantage. Being accomplished by a peculiar lathe, the process is almost impossible of imitation by a forger, owing to the great difficulty of bringing the parts of the machine to the same positions at which they stood in the maker's lathe ; manual imitation is almost futile, from the time needed for the task. The elaboration on the Scots notes of "one pound," written nearly two thousand times in each, is chiefly produced by mechanical means, the "stump engraver" being employed for this purpose.

A further improvement in Messrs Perkins, Bacon, & Co.'s method of transferring to steel, is to have the original plate made up of a number of separate dies, which can be put together when required, and render it all the more difficult to obtain an impression without combination amongst the employees. Thus from beginning to end, provided the plates are not allowed to get into wrong hands, the work requires that those perfecting it must be artists of no mean ability and skill,—men who could receive so handsome an income as the reward of their honest labours, that the probability of their giving time and attention to that which can only ensure their destruction, is made as remote as it can well be.

The introduction of photography brought a new foe to

the front, and put banks and forgers once more upon the *qui vive*.

Up to the middle of the present century all notes had been printed in black,—a colour perfectly suitable for photographic purposes. Various methods were introduced with a view to secure the note against this danger ; amongst these the most important is printing with coloured inks, and adding some ornamental device upon the back of the note, so that when printing in the sun these back designs come through, appear upon the front, and thus foil the forger's plan. Photographic imitations of the watermark have already been referred to ; and we now quote from Mr A. Claudet's letter to the *Times*, about 1850 (mentioned by Mr Sharp), regarding the effects upon different colours :—" In photography, red, orange, yellow, and green produce black ; while blue, indigo, and violet produce white. Now, from these different properties of the various colours, it is evident that a bank note, with its printing, emblems, devices, writing, &c., printed in variegated colours, would offer the greatest difficulties to the perpetration of the fraud ; for the lightest colours to the eye would produce the darkest effect in the copy, whilst the darkest colours, such as blue, indigo, and violet, would be hardly represented at all, or but very slightly. It is indeed fortunate that photography, while offering to the forger the temptation to exercise his dangerous skill, at the same time teaches us the means to render his attempts abortive. The Bank of England, and bankers in general, instead of issuing notes in their present dull state of black and white, have only to transform them into the most elegant and ornamental coloured designs, and they will frustrate all attempts of the forger." Exactly what the Bank of England has not done, with the result that it is almost the only bank to which forgers still pay their attentions.

The idea of coloured paper was abandoned ; a white ground being chosen, and coloured inks employed in printing.

In the well known case of the Greatrix forgeries of the

Union Bank notes, about 1865, the imitations were produced by photographing the black ink, there being no
colour upon the notes. Two gentlemen (?) appeared in
Dalkeith at the shop of a worthy draper, now departed,
and tendered a Union Bank note in payment of some
purchases. A shrewd shopman, not caring for their looks,
went out into the High Street, and discovered that his
customers had bestowed similar favours on some of his
neighbours. The police were called in, and the gentlemen
were removed to the Edinburgh prison, after a considerable
number of forged Union Bank notes had been found in
their possession. But these were only the utterers ; the
artist himself was wanted, a Glasgow photographer named
Greatrix, who had fled to America. Thither he was
followed by a British detective, now Captain M'Call, chief
constable of Glasgow, accompanied by one of the bank's
officials, who traced him to New York and there lost him.
Quite equal to the occasion, the official spiders spun their
web, advertising in the New York papers "A first-class
photographer wanted," with the result that in a few hours
the fly walked into their parlour, whence he was transported
to Scotland, to receive in the Edinburgh Justiciary Court
sentence of penal servitude for fourteen years.

As in all things the forces of positive and negative,
good and evil, are ever opposing each other, the one
obtaining a temporary ascendancy only to be overthrown
by some application of the other, so in the manufacture of
notes and documents of value, just as a way was beginning
to be seen through the mass of different plans against
photographic forgery, bankers were again plunged into
dubiety by Messrs Glynn & Appel's introduction of their
anastatic process of printing. Immediately struck with the
opening thus created for fraudulent purposes, this ingenious
firm a few years afterwards secured their scheme from the
evil-minded · by another process equally ingenious. To
produce a copy of any print by anastatic printing, the
subject is damped with a weak solution of nitric acid, which
has the effect of attacking only the paper, the printed

portions being completely protected by the greasy nature
of the ink. The print is then laid flat upon a zinc plate,
out of which the nitrous paper eats a surface all over,
except on the portions opposite the printed parts of the
paper, upon which no acid lies. The paper is removed, and
common printer's ink is now rolled over the plate, which, of
course, is only received upon such parts as can assimilate
it, namely, the oily parts transferred from the printing.
Phosphorous acid in solution is poured over the plate, cor-
roding still deeper the unprotected parts of the zinc, and
producing a surface on these parts to which printer's ink
does not attach itself. "The process is now complete,
and from such a prepared zinc plate any number of
impressions may be struck off." As in photography, all
the finest efforts of engravers and engine-turners were
rendered useless, the smallest lines and the most delicate
work being perfectly copied ; while the process had this
advantage over photography, that any combination of
colours could be printed. Messrs Glynn & Appel's defence
consisted in printing the notes upon paper into which some
phosphate of copper is introduced when in a state of pulp,
along with a small quantity of oily non-drying soap. On
the would-be forger wetting a note printed on such paper,
the usual nitric acid solution coming in contact with the
zinc plate firmly cements the note to the plate by a thin
film of metallic copper, which is deposited by the contact of
the salts of the copper with the zinc. So firm is the adhesion,
that the note must be destroyed before it can be removed
from the zinc,—a very profitable beginning of crime for the
banker who issued it. The oily soap used in the manufacture of the paper prevents any attempt to remove the
note by chemical means, while destruction of the soap is in
turn accompanied by the disappearance of all the printing
on the note, leaving a white bit of note paper devoid of any
promise to pay.

Messrs Perkins, Bacon, & Co. can secure notes, by their
patent "facing" process of printing in transparent coloured
ink, against both anastatic and photographic forgery ; but,

apart from that patent, the anastatic process is no longer dreaded by engravers.

The necessity which was forced upon the banks at an early period of having each note identical with every other, was the means of taking the note business largely away from Scotland to London, as such perfection of manufacture could only be obtained through Messrs Perkins & Co.'s patent process, which no other maker dared to use during the continuance of the patent. Other manufacturers could only ensure that from 40,000 to 50,000 notes would be identical, one plate giving off that number of impressions before being worn out, after which a new plate had to be engraved,—a task in itself, not only expensive, but extremely difficult of execution, as the most accomplished workman cannot produce two steel plates perfectly similar. The lapse of their patent, and subsequent inventions, have quite upset the well-merited monopoly of the London firm, as any engravers can now attain to the same identity in their notes. The first of the two principal discoveries which have realised this change, consists of printing from electrotypes. In this process the original plate may be either of steel or copper, usually the former. From the original, casts are taken in stucco or plaster of Paris, which, when hardened, are placed in a bath of distilled water of about 100 degrees Farenheit, in which are dissolved proportions of carbonate of copper, hyposulphite of soda, and carbonate of soda. The action of a current of electricity from a thermo-electric battery, also of about 100 degrees, when passed through the water, precipitates the chemicals so as to give a coating of copper to the casts, which, thus armour-plated, may be used for printing. Bank of England notes are produced from electrotypes at the rate of about 50,000 daily, to replace an equivalent number withdrawn from circulation in the same time.

The second invention to secure identity, is to engrave an original steel plate, which, when hardened, is kept solely to impress its image upon plates of copper. These could be at once used for printing, as in days bygone, were it not that the softness of the metal compared with steel would necessitate frequent renewal. To obviate this, the copper surface is coated with a layer of steel, so fine as not to interfere with the most delicate lines, yet so hard as to give a much longer life to the plate ; when the steel wears out, it can be renewed without the least injury to the copper bed of the engraving.

Before printing, all paper ought to be damped, as where this is omitted, the printing is sure to be defective and unequal. In the Bank of England this is accomplished by placing a number of reams in a chamber, from which the air is pumped out, water being pumped into its place, with the result that in an incredibly short time the solid mass of paper is thoroughly damped ; on being removed, superfluous moisture is driven off by pressure. It is usual with other makers to adhere to the old method of dipping the paper in water by a few sheets at one time, and afterwards pressing it to the condition required for printing.

Scottish notes are printed from steel plates, or copper plates steel-faced, at a rate of 1000 per day for one plate, and when completed their approximate weight is as follows :—

1. Bank of Scotland . 23 grains	6. Union Bank . . 23 grains
2. Royal Bank . . 23 „	7. Town & County Bk. 24 „
3. Brit. Lin. Co. Bank 22 „	8. N. of Scotland Bk. 24 „
4. Commercial Bank 21 „	9. Clydesdale Bank . 27 „
5. National Bank . 22 „	10. Caledonian Bank . 21 „

A Bank of England £5 note weighing 19½ grains.

From the difficulty of pouring exactly the same quantity of pulp into each frame, and also of straining off superfluous water in the manufacture of handmade paper, varying thicknesses occur in different notes of the same issue ; indeed, of two notes cut from the same piece, one might be heavy and the other light, as the pulp may have been shaken more to one end of the frame than to the other, so that the above figures will not apply to every clean note, while to " dirties " or " colliers," as they are called, they are no guide whatever.

Quite a romance might be made of tales that could be told by the Scotch notes, as to the places in which they have sojourned. One dirty Royal Bank note, which had evidently circulated in a greasy population, weighed 27 grains ; while another note of the same bank weighed only 21 grains. One dirty Commercial Bank note weighed $19\frac{3}{4}$ grains, and a still dirtier one was 23 grains. Apparently " evil communications corrupt good manners " as much amongst bank notes as with bankers. If a note on its first issue gets into the hands of a butcher or grocer, a film of grease or saccharine matter is put on it, which not only does not leave it for a long time, but attracts to it dust sufficient to add materially to its weight. The power of such a note to convey disease is worthy of the consideration of the medical faculty. Differences in the materials of the " size " seem to cause a loss of weight sooner in some notes than in others.

The notes of the Bank of Scotland,* the British Linen Company, the Commercial, the National, the Union, and the Town and County banks are all printed by Messrs Perkins, Bacon, & Co., of Fleet Street, London. It is in the marvellous clearness and minuteness of the engine graving that the work of the London firm may readily be distinguished from that of other manufacturers. The broad band at the side of the Bank of Scotland note, upon which is engraved the figure of King William, and the oval medallions bearing the denomination on some of the others, approach more closely to nature's works than almost any kind of artistic effort ; the more they are magnified the more perfect they appear. The celebrated Lizars, in one of his designs for the Bank of Scotland notes, produced work quite equal to this, while in general appearance, his note was

---

* The bank's old note is here alluded to, the new note having been issued since these pages were written. This latest production in note manufacture has been somewhat unfavourably criticised, but this is scarcely the place to point out its merits or demerits. The bank would, however, be well advised to withdraw it, and employ entirely different methods in all stages of manufacture.

superior, both for elegance and security, to any other Scottish note, and only required to be printed in colours to make it the safest, as it would undoubtedly be the most beautiful note in Scotland. The Royal Bank, the North of Scotland, and the Caledonian Bank notes are engraved by Messrs W. & A. K. Johnston, of Edinburgh, and are beautiful specimens of engraving, the vignettes being carefully done, but little attempt is made to secure the note by intricate engine work. The Clydesdale Bank note is engraved by Messrs E. Bacon & Son, of London, and is not beautiful, the three vignettes appear dull and black against the white paper, while the red ink engine work gives it a staring appearance anything but æsthetic. The peculiarity of the two styles of notes is, that Messrs Perkins, Bacon, & Co. "consider the engine-turned parts of the plate a more effectual protection against forgery than the vignettes ; but," they add, "it is very desirable to combine as many kinds of security as possible ;" while the absence of engine-work from other makers' designs, as a predominating feature, is on account of their considering the *vignette parts* the better security, as requiring greater artistic skill for successful imitation, an opinion in which they are supported by many engravers.

On the other hand, nearly all manufacturers and gravers are agreed in looking upon the *general effect* of notes as an important element in their security. The more minute and intricate the design, the more difficult it certainly is to produce a good copy by engraving; but just in proportion to its intricacy is it easy to imitate the *general effect*, for of the mass of the public, few remember distinctly the peculiar pattern of minute engine work, although many recognise the leading outlines and general appearance, especially where a well known view heads the plate, such as the King's College at Old Aberdeen in the North of Scotland note. Following this up, the notes designed by Messrs Johnston are less delicate and intricate, but more pronounced in their line work, than those of Messrs Perkins, Bacon, & Co. ; at the same time it has to be admitted, that the extreme intricacy of the London firm's designs must

R

prove a very powerful deterrent to forgers, who in these days of educational progress would be more bold than prudent to pass *engraved* forgeries of slovenly workmanship. It is not, however, to the engraver's profession that note-makers need now look with suspicion, for the time has undoubtedly come when delicate engraving, once considered the primary security against forgery, must be relegated to a second rank, or at least must share an equality with the discoveries of chemistry. Photography and photographic printing have completely superseded engraving as a means of imitation, unless guarded against by special features in the *original* to be copied. Any one possessed of photographic apparatus, and with no other aid than the light of day, can reproduce in a negative the most intricate engraving it is possible to cut; this negative can then be placed on chemically-prepared paper coated with gelatine (a process common to all photographers), and upon exposure the action of the light renders the gelatine insoluble in water upon those parts alone which require to be printed; after a time the glass negative is removed, and a charge of printing ink is rolled over the surface of the paper, which is then soaked in water until the moisture swells and detaches the soluble parts of the gelatinous coating, which float off, leaving those portions that have been fixed by the light; the workman has only to transfer this to a lithographic stone, carefully prepare his colours, and begin to print off forged notes so perfectly identical with the genuine article, so far as printing is concerned, as to defy the most careful scrutiny.

Fortunately such work can only be accomplished when the original note is printed in black, or such colours as appear dark in a photograph. To provide against this is the aim of all note manufacturers; and, so far as is at present known, those notes are safest which are printed in blue tints with a back plate, and protected by red or brown initial or amount scrolls upon the front. The latter is a special safeguard, as where such a note is placed opposite the camera, only the brown ink is photographed, the remaining blue part making no appearance, while probably the back plate would shine through to add to the confusion.

The cost of small notes, including paper, is about 1d. per note ; those of the British Linen Co. have been calculated by Mr Mackay, the bank's accountant, at 1·043d., and their large notes at 1·135d. The other banks may somewhat vary from this, but of course only fractionally, the greater or less size of some designs and the amount of ink used making a slight difference upon the total. They are usually estimated for per thousand. When the printing is dried, the notes are numbered by the new numbering machine, after which they are packed flat in lots of one thousand each, and delivered to the bank to be signed. When given out to the tellers they are usually tied in bundles of £500, made up of twenty-five packages of twenty each, folded in two for security.

From the severe handling they receive, small notes are removed from circulation every three or four years, as at the end of that period they become so dirty and greasy that on being paid they are not re-issued. The abolition of the Government stamp on the back of the notes on the commutation of the duties, has enabled the banks to maintain a much cleaner issue than formerly, when each note burnt implied a loss of at least 6d. The number of notes now burnt is enormous, almost the entire circulation having to be removed and replaced in a few years, although a number remain in circulation for a much longer period, especially in the northern parts of the kingdom. The English people are very fond of reviling the filthy Scots bank notes,—an imputation which is no longer applicable, except to those which happen to cross the Border. It may be observed by any one in the course of bank work, that the notes received in retirements *from English bankers* are invariably dirtier and more disreputable than any other notes. This does not apply merely to notes received from Yarmouth and similar places, where the fishing population convey a good many notes, but to all parts of the country ;

not only are they dirty, but they are *all* dirty, a clean note coming back from England being quite a *rara avis*, —a fact which can only be accounted for, by supposing that the English are so fond of them that they do not readily part with them.

Each note has its own little bit of history to tell. In addition to the date of foundation on the Bank of Scotland notes, the beautifully graved medal, representing the Great Seal of Scotland as in 1695, exhibits on the obverse side the motto " *Deo favente*," with an equestrian figure of William of Orange standir · on heathy ground, from which a view of Edinburgh is given with its castle rock, set against the Forth covered with shipping, and backed by the hills of Fifeshire. The view is either taken from Blackford or Corstorphine Hill. On the reverse King William is designed *Second of Scotiæ, Angliæ, Franciæ, et Hiberniæ,*—the English title of King William the *Third* receiving no recognition from the only bank created by a Scottish Parliament. From amid the royal arms the face of George I. looks out from the Royal Bank notes, with the words " Established 1727, Geo. I° Reg." around his head. The British Linen Company also bears the royal arms, by virtue of its " Incorporated by Royal charter 1746;" while upon the right, Britannia is meekly seated with a spear in her left hand, and a twig in her right, representing either the olive branch of peace, or the stalk of flax which indicates the bank's origin. Along the top of the Commercial note is beautifully engraved the elegant sculpture which adorns the facade of their head office in Edinburgh. Peace in the centre is attended by Justice, Plenty, and some other figures, while Literature, Mechanics, Mathematics, and Invention are engaged at the corners in various pursuits. Scotland's patron, Saint Andrew, stands between the branches of his cross in the National Bank note, upon a pedestal surrounded by a very fine trophy of the British arms. The Union Bank note revives the old Edinburgh and Glasgow memories of Sir Wm. Forbes & Co. and the Glasgow Union Bank, by its figures of Justice and Commerce at the top supporting the combined arms of Edinburgh—the Constable's Tower—with the Glasgow tree, bell, fish and bird ; while at the foot are the statues of King Charles II. in Parliament Square and the more noble King William in the Trongate. The Town and County Bank exhibits its office in Aberdeen, with a distant view of the city from above the railway bridge across the Dee. The Clydesdale has the Broomielaw, Dumbarton Castle, and the grand old Cathedral, accompanied by six somewhat aimless damsels, all drawn in very cloudy weather. On the North of Scotland note is a beautiful cut of King's College in Old Aberdeen, still more finely drawn in the large notes of the bank, the dark shadows on the heavy buttresses seeming to throw the building to one side in the small notes, a bias which is redeemed by the noble crown dominating the picture. Last of all, Scotland's youngest bank exhibits its headquarters in a fine view of the town of Inverness, as seen from the River Ness below the suspension bridge,—an engraving which is scarcely shewn to advantage on a paper that, although very tough, soon becomes like tracing paper, having rather a black appearance. Upon the corners of the note are figures of a shepherdess with her dog and sheaf of corn, while opposite a brawny Highlander, with a badly swollen leg, sits beside a hind which his two dogs have just pulled down.

The Union and the North of Scotland bank notes have the advantage of a back plate,—the former being in the shape of an elegant ornamental design into which their name is woven ; while the latter gives its name, date of establishment, and relative Acts of Parliament upon a chaste circle containing the arms. The British Linen Company has a very indistinct watermark ;* while the Town and County and the Caledonian Banking Company have none that is visible. The other banks have their own name, of which the Bank

---

* Since the above remarks were written the British Linen Bank have produced a note with a peculiarly distinct watermark.

of Scotland is the largest, and the Commercial Bank (from
the lighter colour of the printing) the most distinct.

The notes of the Bank of Scotland, National Bank, and
North of Scotland Bank, are printed in black, with the
denomination in large letters in indian red; the Royal
Bank, the British Linen Company, and the Union Bank,
are in blue and indian red; the Commercial is also blue
and bright red; the Town and County in black and
green; the Clydesdale and the Caledonian are black and
bright red. In printing the second colours, little care is
taken by any of the printers to have the "register" so
adjusted that each note shall receive its colour precisely
upon the same spot as its predecessors; an examination of
a few of the notes will exhibit such startling differences in
the position of the red colours, as would lead to the supposition of their having been done by design, rather than
through carelessness. The Union Bank alone meets public
convenience by being payable at two places, Edinburgh
and Glasgow; and the Clydesdale has no deckle edge, all
four sides being cut. Such are a few of the features of the
Scots bank notes, which have filled, and daily fill, so
important a part in the everyday life of the nation. They
are evidences of the power of "faith," for surely no other
power could transmute pieces of printed paper into rights
whereby Scotland can adopt the motto of its first bank,—
" *Tanto Uberior.*"

Chapter XVIII.

"Gold, gold, gold, gold !
Heavy to get, and light to hold;
Price of many a crime untold ;
    How widely thy agencies vary :
To save, to ruin, to curse, to bless !
As even thy minted coins express—
Now stamped with the image of good Queen Bess,
    And now with a bloody Mary."—HOOD.

"HERE stands Theory, a scroll in her hand full of deep and mysterious combinations of figures, the least failure in any one of which may alter the result entirely, and which you must take on trust, for who is capable to go through and check them? There lies before you a Practical System, successful for upwards of a century. The one allures you with promises, the other appeals to the miracles already wrought on your behalf. The one shews you provinces, the wealth of which has been tripled under her management ; the other, a problem which has never been practically solved. Here you have a pamphlet, there a fishing town ; here the long continued prosperity of a nation, and there the opinion of a professor of economics, that in such circumstances she ought not, by true principles, to have prospered at all."

In these sentences the glowing pen of Walter Scott throws into vivid contrast the dangers of setting up new landmarks and institutions, based upon theories which have never been tested in practice. For this reason almost no attempt is made in the succeeding pages to prove the applicability of the small note to English institutions, upon other grounds than those which have already stood the trial of a long and varied experience. So far as possible, precedents will be taken from English banking history ; but as these will be chiefly of a *negative* character, there is no sound reason, should occasion require, why the rich mine of Scottish finance should not be permitted to add its quota of *positive* argument. For our purpose, Englishmen are fortunate in not requiring to base opinions upon any theory whatever, as in the hardly earned experience of nearly a hundred years, they have a fund of information from which such conclusions may be drawn as will enable them to decide :—

I. Whether this small note really was the dangerous thing it was represented to be ?

II. What were the different circumstances in their country as compared with Scotland, which caused it to be so represented, and finally abolished ?

III. Whether these circumstances have been in any way altered since 1826 ? and,

IV. What are the probabilities of success now, were the Acts of 1826 and 1845 to be partially repealed, so far as they relate to one pound notes in England ?

In order satisfactorily to answer these questions, it is necessary to go to the very origin of English banking in 1696, when the great Bank was founded. At that time it may be said of the various financial schemers, that if Scotland was scourged with whips, England was chastised with scorpions. Lowndes, Chamberlain, Law, Mackworth, Brisco, and, a little later, the South Sea Company, flourished in one happy family about this time. Fortunately there were not wanting men who could lay bare the delusions gendered by these individuals. Had it not been for the restraining influences of Sir Isaac Newton, John Locke, and William Paterson, or Montague, the evils perpetrated would have been vastly more serious, though perhaps in their very greatness might have been found their cure ; for had Chamberlain and Law been enabled fully to carry out their theories, without let or hindrance, the inevitable catastrophe would have cleared away, not only the particular evils of the moment, but others which in less aggravated form have come down to our own time, and which still, by their strength and influence, bar the road of the one pound note.

Chief amongst these was the monopoly, granted by the Government of the day to the Bank of England in 1697, as a joint-stock bank of issue,—a privilege which it had no right to sell. The severe pressure upon King William's Government, arising from distress of war, internal disaffection, and the renewal of the debased silver coinage, made them only too ready to transfer a national privilege to a private use, in order that they might be supplied in exchange with the " last louis d'or" which was to carry the day against Le Grand Monarque. By this Act, 8 & 9 William III., c. 20, sec. 5, it was enacted, that during the existence of the Bank of England no corporation, society, or company, of the nature of a bank, should be erected or permitted in England by Act of Parliament. As this left the way clear for private joint-stocks, it was at once taken advantage of by the promoters of the " Money Bank," whose subsequent history gave only too good reason for the additional monopoly given to the Bank of England by Act 7 Anne, c. 7 (1708), of which the famous clause 61 was as follows :—

" During the continuance of the Corporation of the Governor and Company of the Bank of England, it shall not be lawful for any body politic or corporate whatsoever, created or to be created (other than the said Governor and Company of the Bank of England), or for any other parties whatsoever, united or to be united, in covenants or partnership, exceeding the number of six persons, in that part of Great Britain called England, to borrow, owe, or take up any sum or sums of money on their bills, notes payable on demand, or at any less time than six months from the borrowing thereof."

This clause, originally aimed for a mere temporary purpose at such concerns as the Money Bank (otherwise the " Mine Adventurers of England "), *was not repealed when the necessity for its existence passed away*, and still exercises its pernicious influence on English banking.

William Paterson's shrewd sense had seen, as early as 1696, that the Bank of England would not suffice even for

London, much less for all England ; and after the resigna-
tion of his seat in the directorate, he endeavoured, in several
instances, to establish joint-stock banks of issue in the
metropolis, but his efforts do not appear to have met with
success.   They were doubtless founded upon premises
much too practical and sound to have attraction for the
company jobbers of his time.   A fair exhibition of the
public estimate of his character was given, when the London
stockbrokers *burned* his " Wednesday Club Dialogues " in
front of the Exchange about 1700.

Great as had been the bank's services to the Government, in enabling it to carry the war to a successful termination, the price paid was a heavy one, and has entailed an
amount of suffering and loss of treasure without parallel in
British history.   By its ready subservience to the rulers of
politics, it has been the means of carrying on wars which
should never have been entered upon, adding mountains of
debt to debt, until the culminating point was reached at
Waterloo.   In its frantic race with the South Sea Company, the bank was fortunately beaten by the latter, whose
proposals were accepted by Government.   Had the result
been otherwise, writers might have recorded the bursting of
the " Bank Bubble " instead of that of the " South Sea."

While thus absorbing to itself so great and powerful
privileges, the absorption necessarily left other members of
the banking profession proportionally weak, from the depri-
vation of their natural rights.   The history of English
private banking up to this period had been most honourable.   Checked for a time by Charles II.'s seizure of the
exchequer, it was beginning to revive under the new
dynasty, and would soon have developed itself into larger
copartneries more suitable to the time, had the fatal Act of
1708 not suddenly and absolutely stopped its growth, and
distorted the whole future of banking in England.

The entire episode—the temporary purpose of the law,
gradually and conveniently lost sight of by the legislature,
who should have left the market to clear itself, which time
would inevitably have done—is only one of the innumer-

able instances of similar, though fortunately less disastrous, interferences with temporary troubles.   What a contrast is presented in Mr Somers's description of contemporary law in Scotland :—" Banking in Scotland was happy in its exemption from the impecuniosity of Governments, and in its freedom from the weakening effects of the monopoly, and exclusive privilege by which Governments, deeply indebted to their bankers, *have pretended to give compensation*, in public rights, for liabilities which they were unable or unwilling to discharge."

In the reasons for the English legislation, the chief consideration which strikes a modern reader, is the extreme value set upon the power to issue bank notes.   From the custom of the goldsmiths, the issue of paper credit had come to be looked upon as *banking*, and the possibility of carrying on the profession without such an issue was for many years not dreamed of, much less discussed as impossible.   Indeed, notwithstanding the daily evidence given to the Bank of England, by the London private bankers, after 1780, the great bank does not seem to have realised the ability of a company of any importance to begin banking, until the establishment of the London and Westminster Bank in 1834.   Thus in England, as in Scotland, the note issue was looked upon as a primary piece of a banker's business.

In view of the importance attached to it, it is amazing that the Legislature of 1708 did not see the dangers attending the lack of reserve security for the notes of these small bankers, whom they were now making *the only means of a national note issue*, as for many years the notes of the Bank of England were little known out of London, while for nearly sixty years more they did not form a common currency, except in the south or midlands, within a hundred miles of London.   This was one of the reasons which led to the sixty-five mile radius being fixed in 1826, as up to that time, from want of branches, Bank of England notes had no general circulation out of London save in Lancashire. Looking at the matter from a theoretical point, the private issues were on a safer footing than those of the bank, inasmuch as the partners of the former were liable to their last shilling of personal estate * for the whole debts of the firm, while the shareholders of the latter were liable only for the amount of their shares. But here, as in many other cases, that which was scientifically weaker in principle, had all the vast practical power which the *prestige* and credit of the nation could give ; and in the panics of the then coming century, when the Bank of England stopped payment, it was invariably floated again upon some new method, while the unfortunate country or private note issues had no such favour shewn them, being mercilessly cleared out of existence.

At the beginning of the note issues, England suffered from the same fallacy as affected Scotland, but it required a much longer and more severe experience to teach the southern kingdom, that notes in a till were not money. Professor Leone Levi, as has been already referred to, asserts that the same error still exists, in the permission given to the Bank of England to issue notes to the extent of £15,000,000 without gold. One of the few sensible writers of 1692 (supposed to have been Paterson), in a " Brief Account " of the intended Bank of England, strongly deprecates the unlimited issue of paper upon an insufficient backing of gold, boldly asserting, " that all money or credit, not having an intrinsic value to answer the contents or denomination thereof, is false and counterfeit, and the loss must fall one where or other. All credit not founded on the universal species of gold and silver is impracticable, and can never subsist either safely or long ; . . . at least till some other species of credit be found out, and chosen by the trading part of mankind over and above, or in lieu thereof."

At a somewhat later date, and subsequent to the first

---

* It was not until many years afterwards (about 1810) that the heritable property of a bankrupt could be attached in England ; and even then, from the want of public records, it was extremely difficult to find out that any such estate existed, or to what extent it was mortgaged.

stoppage of the bank,* Paterson himself had indicated the dangerous example the bank was giving to other bankers, in not retaining sufficient gold to meet its notes, which had become excessively depreciated :—" The discredit of the coin being clipped or worn, and the discredit of the bank's notes, in consequence of the refusal of payments in good coin, on demand, *are the same thing ;* to be safe, they must pay the amount of their notes *in coin on demand, whatever it may cost them.* . . . If the necessity of reforming paper money be clear, can any one doubt of the manner of it ? Was it not a legal security, confirmed by a settled course of payment upon demand when due, that converted paper into money ? Can anything but a return to the first settled course of ready payments restore its value ? " These words might have been written for 1800 instead of 1700, so perfectly do they describe the delusions of both periods, and point out the only remedy for each.

In its desire to extend its note issues, the bank lost a golden opportunity for doing so, by adopting too high a denomination for its notes ; none were below £20, and this, at any time too high a sum for current use, was preposterously so in 1696, when the state of the coinage caused the most serious distress to all ranks of life, from London to Aberdeen. The stoppage of both countries' first banks was owing *primarily* to the same cause,—the state of the metallic currency ; the want of experience in the banks laying them equally open to attack. As in Scotland, so in London, small change could scarcely be got ; and an issue of one pound notes would have been no little benefit to England, as it afterwards proved to Scotland. In addition to the heavy discount of 20 per cent. charged on the bank's

---

* The bank, when consenting to carry out the new coinage schemes of the Government, omitted to notice that the same notes they had given out in exchange for old worn silver, would require to be paid when sent in against them in new coin, worth one-third more than the old. The immediate result was a rush of its enemies with bank notes, to serve their double purpose of ruining the bank and filling their own pockets ;—in consequence the bank stopped.

notes, during its stoppage, the holders of £20 notes had to
submit to other deductions for the mere privilege of getting
them changed, apart altogether from the question of confidence in the bank.   The results of the attack by the London
bankers proved that the common people of the metropolis
had no sympathy with them, but had confidence in the
new bank ; and had the directors availed themselves at
once of the *need* and the *confidence*, their small notes might
have got into the hands of a class wholly out of touch with
the private bankers, who, thus deprived of their principal
means of attack,—purchasing the bank's notes in large
quantities,—could scarcely have forced the bank into failure.

The course of banking in England during the first half
of last century, appears to have run in the same confined
channels as in Scotland.   The joint-stock mania had been
almost entirely demolished, both north and south of the
Tweed, by the bursting of the South Sea Bubble in 1720 ;
the only banking concern of any consequence opened for
nearly twenty years being the Royal Bank of Scotland,
whose proprietors had preserved their talent intact with
wonderful prudence, until a suitable opportunity presented
itself for laying it out to usury in 1727.

In England, where the monopoly barred the way, a very
few private country bankers began business, both they and
the London houses issuing notes for various sums ; but,
precisely as in Scotland, it was not until after the extinction of the Jacobite hopes in 1745-6, that these bankers
increased to any great extent.   In 1793 Mr Burke stated to
the House of Commons, that when he came to London in
1750 there were not twelve country banks in the whole of
England ; and allowing for possible error, from want of
those statistics always so distasteful to an orator and an
Irishman, his estimate cannot have been far wrong, as the
universal alarm caused by Prince Charles's invasion must
have swept away numbers of country bankers, if they had
existed, for the bank itself had to resort to measures to
sustain its credit, from which even Murdoch & Co. might
have taken a lesson.

From the middle of the century the evil of the bank's monopoly began to come into play with greater force ; hitherto it had existed, though its influence had not been felt, from various causes ruling even in Scotland where no such monopoly obtained.   One distinguishing feature of Scottish private banking, compared with English, seems to have been that, *as a rule* (there were many exceptions, doubtless), the rank in social status of the northern banker was higher than that of the southern, and consequently from his better education he was more able to understand and adopt correct banking principles.   In both cases these principles were notoriously neglected by many ; but even after their failure, the Scottish bankers were found to be possessed of more ample funds than those of England, and consequently the *public* loss was so much less than in the south.

From 1750 private banking went on at a great rate, with few serious checks, until 1772 ; and it was doubtless the country issues of small notes, as much as consideration for public convenience on account of bad coinage, which at last forced the bank to issue notes of ten pounds and fifteen pounds in 1759, for these country bankers were perfectly free from all restrictions, and issued notes for sums below one pound in the same way as was done in Scotland, and probably from the same causes.   In Yorkshire thousands of sixpenny notes circulated from want of small change.

Before adversely criticising the large issue of notes below one pound in the course of last century, the culpable negligence of Government, in failing to provide any other, must ever be kept in view.   It would be well nigh impossible to estimate the distress caused by a deficient metallic currency, had the very " small note " issue not supplied its place. So gross was the neglect, that in 1780 an attempt was made to place the coinage under charge of the Bank of England, as no remonstrances had any effect with Government.   In 1798 one firm took the law into their own hands by sending bullion to the Mint, where it was coined under payment of the dues.   On this becoming

known, the imbecile authorities *melted it down*, on the
ground that no coinage was lawful until a proclamation
had been made. In 1717 £46,000 of copper were coined,
and a small quantity of guineas and half-guineas came out
in 1737. From this time on to 1787 almost no silver was
coined, save £5791 in 1762. In 1787 £55,459 of shillings
and sixpences were put out, and at once passed to the
melting-pot, being much too fine to be allowed to pass
current by the bullion merchants. So things went on past
1803-4 (when some Spanish dollars were stamped with the
king's head) to 1816, when the first true renewal of the
coinage was made which had taken place since 1696. Gold
coins had been issued regularly from 1760, but in such
small quantity as scarcely affected the prevailing scarcity.
These facts may afford some evidence of the convenience
of the small note issues of England, weak as their issuers
may have been, and also of the acute distress after 1775
and 1777, when all notes below five pound were summarily
declared illegal. The British public may well set off the
present philosophic distinctions of its rulers, as to *all*
currency being a prerogative of the Crown, against the
shameful neglect of last century, and invite Sir Robert
Peel's school to give finance and currency the same boasted
freedom they gave to trade.

We now draw near the region of those mercantile
storms which periodically swept the private bankers into
bankruptcy. The effects of 1772 in Scotland have already
been named ; 525 bankruptcies took place in England
during that memorable year, the greatest losses being
incurred by some of the leading London bankers, who still
issued notes. The latter fact is not mentioned as having
any connection with the over-trading which led to the
failures ; events subsequent to 1826 prove, beyond a doubt,
that bank notes have no more effect in producing a crisis
than can be as easily accomplished if they did not exist.
The reckless advances leading to the failures of 1772 were
totally apart from the question of the note issues, except
that these might be used to furnish ready cash for discounts,

instead of the *deposits*, which did not then form a part of English banking. The absence of deposits, or some similar fund, such as a large capital, was the chief reason for the *prevalence* and *continuance* of the till-money fallacy in England. A large capital was impossible in the great majority of cases, from the limited number and condition of the partners; and then, in the absence of deposits, the only ready fund—if fund it may be called—consisted of the printed promises lying in their tills, which, when issued, they had neither the means nor the intention of paying

All this came out of the Act of 1708, and its withering restrictions. To give a *privilege* to one company, a *right* was withheld from all others, *except those who could not use it with public safety.* Logic, commonsense, and public right, were alike thrown overboard in the storms of debt and war through which the Governments were carried by the herculean exertions of the great bank. It would have paid England well had her Government left banking *free*, and raised taxation sufficient to have paid the bank a dividend of 10 per cent. for many years, in lieu of their monopoly. But this could not be; it would have been "unpopular;" it might have been correct and righteous! "True," said the Government, "we admit it; but we prefer to cheat the country without their knowing it, to compelling them to stand and deliver in such an unpopular manner."

The testimony of Parnell, Macleod, and other writers, concurs in fixing the seven years prior to 1793 as those in which the bank's monopoly sowed the bitter seed which in that year brought forth such terrible fruit. In these years, in which the three old Scottish banks were deepening their foundations and spreading themselves over the country, let us see how England was endeavouring to accommodate the extraordinary prosperity and advancement of the period. It was the time of invention; canal making, spinning, weaving, and mechanical improvement were making a new England, and the one dead drag upon the wheels was the banking system. What was required, was not a number of deposit banks alone, or note issuing banks alone, but joint-stock banks of deposit and issue, upon some such plan as the Scottish banks,—banks who could provide a currency to supply the deficiencies of the debased coinage, and thus carry on successfully, yet with such prudence as ruled elsewhere, the various enterprises of the day.

The Bank of England *gave no real currency;* her smallest note was of ten pounds, only payable in London, and gold was *extremely scarce.* Of what use, then, could a ten pound note be in the far west or north of the kingdom, or even in the midlands, where the canals were opening up the land to commerce? Yorkshire and Lancashire were beginning to raise their heads, with their host of weaving and spinning looms, yet they had not a single bank of any size, such as those huge joint-stocks which now carry on their business. Writing upon this period, Mr Macleod, with his usual vigour, remarks, that " as England required a currency, and as it could not have a good one, it had a bad one. Multitudes of miserable shopkeepers in the country, grocers, tailors, drapers, started up like mushrooms and turned bankers, and issued their notes, inundating the country with their miserable rags."

Another writer, Mr Chalmers, quoted by Sir Henry Parnell, points out the dangers of such an irruption :— " The vast business of the country *created these banks,* and *these banks created by their facilities vast business.* They tried various projects to force a greater number of their notes into circulation than the business of the nation demanded. They destroyed, by their own imprudence, the credit of their own notes, which must ever depend on the near proportion of the demand to the supply. The whole number of country bankers in England was unknown, their *capitals* and *characters* were unknown ; their imprudence only was known." In this universal increase the Bank of England was not behind ; it enlarged its note issues from £6,000,000 in 1779 to £9,160,479 in 1782, an increase of 3,000,000, in which there were no one pound notes,—none less than ten pounds.

In 1793, with the Bank of England circulation at

£11,420,000, war was declared against France, and instantly the whole fabric fell to the ground. From Newcastle to London, and all over England, only a few banks stood firm. One hundred banks suspended payment, and nearly four hundred of the remainder were severely shaken. Of the failures, seven were in Northumberland, twelve in Yorkshire, five in Lancashire, seven in Lincoln, four in Northampton, six in Sussex, four in Somerset, and others in different counties. To meet the outstanding notes and other liabilities of these hundred banks, the law of England deemed six hundred partners amply sufficient ; or rather the law of England cared nothing for the whole matter, so long as they could get their funds out of the Bank of England, by bolstering it up in its unjust privileges. Judging from later evidence, there would not actually be so many partners, as, in 1826, out of the nine hundred private country banks only twenty-five had six, and all the others had a smaller number ! For our subject, Nemesis could scarcely have chosen a more fitting time for closing on her victims than the year 1793. Entirely misled as to the cause of the failures of 1772, and irritated by the amount of small notes, Government had prohibited notes below 20s. in 1775, and two years later the embargo was raised to cover all under £5 ; so that *the total absence of small notes from 1777 to 1797*, is one of the strongest and most convincing proofs banking history can afford, that one pound notes are *not more conducive* to speculation, panic, and failure, *than any other form of paper credit.* Yet to this fact, as to the whole teachings of experience of nearly a century and a half, Lord Liverpool deliberately shut his eyes, and complacently saw no lesson for English legislators,—another instance of the blind leading the blind, to fall into the ditch of future panics.

But there are other points worthy of notice in 1793. First, there was no real necessity for the panic ; second, it was aggravated by the controlling power of the Bank of England, badly applied ; and, lastly, in its latter phase the distress would have been lessened by a small note issue.

A popular dread seized the people, who, hearing of a large
failure in London, which would probably affect other houses
in the provinces, lost all confidence in their bankers, and
ran for gold,—not only on country banks, but on those in
London, who by this time had largely ceased to issue notes,
and relied chiefly on their large capital to do business with.
These, pressed in their turn, from their limited partnerships
did not, or could not, keep sufficient reserves, and went to
the bank, who, seeing rocks ahead, *refused all discounts and
accommodation*, with utmost stringency. Merchants and
bankers, who were perfectly good for their engagements
could they but have realised their securities, or got advances
against them, were compelled to close in large numbers,
and the panic increased in intensity as it gradually rolled
beyond the banks to the various mercantile classes. With
the lower classes, supplied only with the *inconvertible large
notes of failed banks*, and merchants in a similar if not a
worse position, the boon of an issue of one pound notes, of
any safe bank, against securities lodged, would have been
inestimable. There would certainly have been a risk in
issuing against securities merely, unless gold were kept in
stock, but both the risk and the reasons against such a
course would be reduced to their minimum in a time of such
national necessity. As it was, Government was forced to
give one kind of currency, in the shape of promised accommodation ; and whenever this became public, the whole panic
instantly ceased.

From 1793 to 1797 the extreme scarcity of a good
currency became more and more serious every year.
London bankers had entirely given up their note issues,
while those of the country bankers, not having recovered
from the blow of the former year, were cut down by one-
half, probably as much by want of public confidence, as a
salutary fear on the part of the issuers. The disgust at
their paper currency which was then instilled into the
English nation, began to shew itself in an increased
partiality for a gold currency, which they have not yet
lost. Unhappily no one seems to have touched or observed

the source of the evil ; for while country bankers were blamed and their notes banned, and the Bank of England was accused of various wickednesses, no voice was raised against the vicious laws which, deep down and out of sight, turned the whole ship about whithersoever they listed.   At no period of her history had England so urgently needed a good paper currency, based upon specie, though even paper money was then in a highly dangerous condition from the continued dread of invasion ; for, as it has been remarked by Mr Macleod, no paper money, however secured, has ever been known to stand the shock of war.   Let the dread of war or invasion enter a country, and instantly paper money is expelled from circulation, being returned to the banks, and gold demanded in exchange.   If found to be inconvertible, it becomes depreciated to a greater or less degree, according to the circumstances of each case. Plunged into her foolish struggle with the French republic by Pitt, England was using up her gold currency with alarming rapidity.   It had been slightly increased when the country note circulation subsided, but as the Bank of England could not possibly replace the whole amount, greatly as they added to their own circulation of large notes (as a currency practically useless), repeated demands were made on them by merchants for guineas, of which a considerable stock was held.   Along with this mercantile drain for internal use, came the war drain for foreign require-ments.   The *bank itself* now began to feel in full force the dubious pleasure of being the only bank worthy of the name, the privilege which had hitherto given it a full and unen-cumbered power began now to let it measure its responsi-bility.   Instead of being supported by other institutions as substantial as itself, it found its movements hampered, and its very existence endangered, by the despairing clutch of country bankers, London merchants, and an impoverished Government, who all clung to it as to the one strong man in a sinking vessel.   In 1794 the bank endeavoured to meet the public necessity by issuing £5 notes, which it did for the first time, and that in the face of an adverse exchange ;

but, notwithstanding this, a *smaller currency* was wanted, and the drain of gold went steadily on. As Napoleon, in his splendid victories in Italy, swept the enemies of France from his path, the country bankers, gloomily looking forward to impending dissolution, were eagerly collecting every ounce of gold they could get, a measure which had no other effect than to increase the demand from the bank, until in December 1796 the bullion sank to £2,508,000.

The state of affairs led a number of bankers and merchants to pass the following resolution at a meeting held in the London Tavern :—" 1st, That it is the opinion of this meeting, that there has existed for a considerable time past, and does exist at present, an alarming scarcity of money in the city of London ; 2d, That this scarcity proceeds chiefly, if not entirely, from an increase in the commerce of the country, and from the great diminution of mercantile discounts which the Bank of England has thought proper to introduce in the conduct of the establishment during the last three months." Here, again, is evidence of the effects of the law of 1708. If Scotland gave business for four or five large banks, and a number of lesser but yet strong houses, how was it possible for the one institution in London, harassed by constant Government demands, to answer the need of such a commerce as that of England ? Her position was doubly aggravated from the retiral of the London bankers from note issuing. These gentlemen, doubtless, saw the danger to such houses as theirs of an issue, and, objecting to keep the reserves necessary to minimise the dangers, had stopped their notes entirely, at the very time they were most required ; and now, looking like children to the great bank which the law had placed over them, they met together to complain because it would not, or could not, grant the accommodation they stood in need of.

At this point it would be unfair to found any argument on the contemporary condition of banking in England. The dread of invasion was terrible, and the national mind was so unhinged by alarm, that the strongest species of

banking could not have been blamed for succumbing to
the frantic demands made on it. Public confidence, always
in a precarious state as regards banking in England, was
now completely gone, many of the banks closing their
doors from mere dread of a run, before there was any
immediate necessity for their doing so. It is unnecessary
to detail the further events which at last compelled the
Bank of England, for the second time in its history, to
come to a complete stoppage of payment. The balance-
sheet published in 1797 shews the notes outstanding to
have been £8,640,000, and in the previous February
£10,909,694, an amount which could only be in the hands
of about 800,000 people at the outside, supposing no one
to hold more than *one note ;* so that, in all probability, out
of the whole population of England, then about ten millions, not over 100,000 individuals would be possessed of
a circulating medium in the shape of Bank of England
notes.

In the inquiry made by the House of Commons immediately after the suspension, the universal testimony of
Bank of England directors, country bankers, London
merchants, and others, proved that *one large bank was
totally inadequate to the wants* of the country, whether as
grantors of accommodation, or issuers of currency, metallic
or paper ; that even before the war this had been the case,
but that since the renewed oppressive demands of Pitt, the
bank had been utterly unable to meet the drains of the
two classes of its customers,—namely those of commerce on
the one hand, and those of an impoverished Government
on the other. To satisfy the imperious requests of the
Minister, the vastly more urgent claims of commerce were
ruthlessly put aside ; and to furnish gold for war, discount
and paper money were denied for purposes of peace. The
bank directors protested that their hands were tied by the
huge advances already given to Government. Had these
been repaid, accommodation could have been given to the
public, but not otherwise. The merchants and private
bankers as strongly maintained, what few denied, that it

was owing to the bank's excessive contraction of its note issue that public credit was shaken, and an universal demand was raised for *guineas.* Now this assertion should bear some examination. Public returns shew, that whenever the bank—the only safe banking institution—began to issue £5 notes, they were so eagerly taken advantage of, that the circulation went up from ten millions in August 1794 to thirteen millions in February 1795, shewing that not only an *increased circulation* was required (no matter where it came from, so long as it was safe), but that *notes of a smaller denomination* were seriously wanted. Yet much as a safe £5 note was appreciated, it was practically *useless* for ordinary daily buying and selling,—the purchase of food and other articles for individuals or families, and the paying of wages to the nation's artificers. Instead of meeting this demand, most unhappily, within six months of the increase, and before any other step had been taken to lower the amount of their notes, the bank was compelled to cut down its issues with a considerable severity, in order to meet the monstrous demands of the Government, until, in February 1797, that is, in two years only, the bank's circulation had shrunk—partly from its own will, and partly by external pressure for gold—from thirteen millions to eight millions, a decrease of 39 per cent. Serious as this must have appeared to the merchants and others, to whose evidence reference has been made, the area *primarily* affected was small, being confined chiefly to London ; and from the large denomination of the notes, only a very small proportion of the inhabitants could be possessed of them, —but that small proportion was largely made up of London bankers, many of whom acted as agents for the country banks, and through them the *secondary* effects of the restricted circulation were felt If bank notes were not to be got by the London firms, clearly they would be compelled to look sharply after any advances they, as agents, might be asked to give to their country employers. In this way inconvenience was spread all over the country. The bankers there, discovering the difficulty of their London agents to meet their drafts, of course restricted their issues in turn, lest they should be returned against them in such quantity as would necessitate the granting of bills on London in payment. Throughout the provinces the most intense annoyance was manifested,—growing all the more acute, as the people realised their powerlessness to help themselves. Silver was debased, and was nearly as unreliable as in 1696 ; gold could only be got with the greatest difficulty ; and between these and the £5 note was a great gulf fixed, across which the insane Government declined to erect even a *pons asinorum.* How the lower middle classes endured the evil so long is still a mystery ; but it was fortunate that the bank was at last compelled to stop, before the misery had reached greater dimensions, as Pitt now saw the necessity for doing something to remedy the distress, of which he himself had been a principal cause.

His prime remedy was, as every one knows, " The Restriction Act." Bank of England notes were declared to be legal tender, and the bank was to pay no more gold except in a few specially defined cases. But while the fountain of gold was thus sealed up, *no provision was made* for securing the country bankers, who were liable to meet their notes *in gold,* on pain of legal " distress," unless they were paid within three days after the demand. The greatest benefit, however, was yet to come. Passed chiefly as a sop to Cerberus, the Act of 1797, cap. 28, permitted the issue of notes below £5, both to the bank and to all country bankers. *In this time of national emergency, the one pound note carried the country through its difficulties.* The demand for gold stopped whenever these notes were issued, and in consequence of the exchanges turning in favour, specie came pouring into the country. The London merchants were not to be put off merely with permission and good intentions ; so they met again in the London Tavern, and passed resolutions to the effect, that it was absolutely essential that the bank should greatly increase its discounts and accommodation, in order that a larger currency might be obtained for circulation amongst the public. These resolutions were passed in face of the facts that the bank's circulation had never been higher than in their own time, and that it had been doubled within twelve years. The scarcity which was caused was not merely by the necessities of increased trade, but by the stocks of the bank's notes being locked up as *till money* by many London and country banks who had timidly given up their issues. The prime cause of the evil was still the noxious monopoly, —everywhere the monopoly, which, like a great mist, hung over the land, from Berwick to Beechy Head, hiding the sun, preventing natural growths, yet fostering those parasitic invertebræ, who can but cling to something mightier and stronger than themselves.

The Government was, of course, primarily at fault for permitting the system, but the bank itself is not less blameworthy for its arrogance of the rights of others. When the country lost all confidence in the currency of its private bankers, for whose weakness the monopoly was solely responsible, the latter again came in to prevent the establishment of joint-stock banks, such as those of Scotland, whose branches could have filled the vacuum. Left without a provincial currency, England's bank refused to help the country whose money maintained it, and whose rights it had absorbed ; it would neither open branches, nor allow any other joint-stock bank to come into existence for that purpose ; and, lastly, it only got into direct touch with the working people of England when it was compelled to put forth an issue of one pound notes. How it did so, and with what want of precaution, will be shortly noticed.

To follow the bank's career through the mazes of the long years of restriction would serve little purpose ; their action has been severely criticised, and can only be justified on the ground of national emergency, if it is to be justified at all. Freed from the necessity of paying gold, the directors fully met the wishes of their former critics, and issued an enormous circulation, which soon became and remained depreciated, though, according to the happy ideas of the time, their depreciation was wholly ascribed to

the high price of gold. Never throughout its career had
the old many - sided delusion of till money seen such
glorious days. For nearly a quarter of a century it reigned
supreme at the centre of the world's finance. Its myrmi-
dons were engraved, printed, and scattered broadcast over
the land in return for good or bad bills of exchange, which
had their origin in veritable goods and gear. This was the
time of high dividends for the bank, for, in spite of forgeries,
their profits were great. Parliament resolved that cash
payments should still be postponed ; and the bank directors, after one assertion of their ability to meet their obligations, gave no further opposition to a system which so
prodigiously increased their gains.

The country bankers, though not protected by legislation, seem to have been as little pressed as those in Scotland, and accordingly took advantage of the immunity from
demand to extend their issues as far as possible, until the
rise in prices, from the lowering of that of paper money,
brought about the inevitable rush of imports, fall in the
exchanges, and demand for gold for exportation. Cause and
effect were utterly lost sight of, and the only remedy proposed was an increased paper circulation, with the certain
result of its further depreciation far below what could be
explained by the difference in the bullion points. As
the exchange fell, the price of gold rose above the mint price,
or its supposed value in bank notes, until, in 1814, it touched
£5. 4s. per ounce.

In 1779 we have seen the bank's circulation (all
   large notes) was £6,000,000
In February 1793, also large notes, it stood at . 11,428,000
For the first six months of 1799 it was . . 13,000,000
   ,,   ,,   1804 ,, . . . 17,000,000
   ,,   ,,   1810 ,, . . . 20,000,000

In the last-named year the bank directors maintained
the impossibility of an over-issue of their notes, a notion
pronounced to be most dangerous by the celebrated Bullion
Committee of that year, who saw the real cause of the high
price of gold in the unlimited issue of intrinsically worthless
printed paper, issued without any provision for its absorp-

tion or retirement. Parliament refused to listen to reason, and having supported the directors in their false views, a further increase at once took place in the notes, with the intention of helping commerce, and thereby raising the exchanges.

From January to July 1811, the circulation was . £23,471,000
        ,,   ,,   1813,   ,,   . 23,939,000
        ,,   ,,   1815,   ,,   . 27,155,000
From July to December 1817,   ,,   . 29,210,035

In 1819 the true remedy was proposed, and cash payments were gradually resumed from 1820 ; the true balance between gold and paper being restored by a reduction of the latter by nearly ten million pounds, seven-tenths of which was made up of one pound notes, the steadiest and most truly useful part of the whole circulation.

The country bankers all this time were no wiser in their generation than their betters, and appear to have had their full share in the universal over-issue, with this difference in the result, that they got all the blame of the over-trading and speculation when subsequent committees of Parliament inquired into the affairs of the market. They evidently found the non-cash-payment plan to pay, for between 1800 and 1813 they increased in number from four hundred to nine hundred and twenty-two, scattered all over England. Some houses employed and paid persons to travel round the fairs and markets, taking up notes of rival banks in exchange for those of the banks who employed them ; they were called "money changers," and received substantial commissions for their work. One pound notes were specially easy to change in this way, and when the absurdity was made public, as usual in England, or rather in London, these notes were re-declared to be the cause of all the rise in rents and prices which afflicted the nation.

Throughout the whole period from 1797 to 1820, whatever responsibility may rest upon the *large notes* for their share in the speculations of the over-issue, it is certain that the country would have come to a dead-lock had it not been for the *one pound note as a small currency.* In 1817, of the total circulation of £27,000,000, one pound notes, as may be seen from the following details, amounted to 28·5 per cent. of the whole; and excluding £1000 notes and bank post bills, were 35 per cent.

CIRCULATION OF 1817.

£1 notes .	£7,773,710
5 ,, .	3,120,130
10 ,, .	3,637,670
20 ,, .	1,822,340
30 ,, .	667,860
50 ,, .	1,824,000
100 ,, .	1,406,620
200 ,, .	643,390
300 ,, .	611,820
500 ,, .	570,400
1000 ,, .	3,702,190
Bank post bills	1,389,260
	£27,169,390

Their use as a currency, and their total absence from those fluctuations so often ascribed to them, is absolutely proved by the returns to the House of Lords' committee of 1819. For the three previous years one pound Bank of England notes were upon an average £7,546,701, and large notes £19,837,841. The extremes were as follows :—

Small notes, highest, August 1817,	.	£8,035,340
,, lowest, April 1719,	.	7,168,960
Large notes, highest, July 15, 1817,	.	23,507,020
,, lowest, March 15, 1819,	.	17,222,310
Small notes, highest above average,	.	£488,639
,, lowest below average,	.	377,741
Large notes, highest above average,	.	£3,669,179
,, lowest below average,	.	2,615,531

Difference between extremes,—Small, £866,380 ; Large, £6,284,710.

During all the panics of 1810 and 1815, with their preceding overtrading, a few hundred thousand pounds covered the fluctuations of the one pound note, the principal variations being in the large notes. In 1817 the bank intimated that all one and two pound notes dated prior to January 1815 would be paid in gold ; but the public knew when they had got a good medium of exchange, and only availed themselves of the offer to the extent of about one million. Mr Francis, in his history of the bank, ascribes this to their circulating amongst the working classes, to whom they were a great boon ; and adroitly points out the difference between their conduct and that of the bullion speculators holding large notes, who, when their turn came to be paid in specie, " ran " to the bank in crowds to draw gold, in the hope of making their profit out of the transaction,—proving that, however small note holders may be accused of *panic in time of panic*, the large note holders are the dangerous men to the banks in ordinary years.

By the Act of 1819 one pound notes had been doomed to withdrawal in the year 1824 ; but as this decision had been come to upon some finely spun theories of Mr Ricardo, which events proved to be fallacious, the distress of 1822 compelled the Government to pass the Small Note Act of that year, permitting their continuance until 1833. In the following year the joint-stock mania began to develop itself, having received its first impulse from the lowering of the interest on £215,000,000 of national debt ; such a reduction in their income leading many to look for a still lower rate, and exciting a feverish anxiety for any scheme, however absurd, which might allow of a higher profit being earned. When making payments on this account, the Bank of England was so ill-advised as to issue its notes in large quantity, in the face of an *adverse exchange*, thereby adding to the confusion. Mr Henry Ayre, in his " Financial Register," says :—" Attempts have been made to shew that the country bankers were the primary cause of these disasters, but an examination of the facts *prove* incontestibly that this assertion has no foundation in fact." Lord Liverpool, in his violent speeches against the country bankers in 1826, asserted that their issues shewed a very large increase in the three years preceding the panic, giving as his reason for believing so that they had paid *a larger*

sum to the stamp office for note stamps than usual! He
could scarcely have taken a more delusive means of calculating their circulations. The returns of stamps of the
three Scottish chartered banks at the same period are most
unequal, and bear no proportion to their circulation, such
as would enable the reader to judge of the increase. There
is another reason for the rise in the stamp duties, which
does not appear to have been mentioned or thought of by
his lordship. Chiefly through their own neglect of good
engraving, the British banks were almost at their wits' end
at the time to devise proper checks against the numerous
forgeries of their notes. Again and again, particular banks,
at great expense, were compelled by some attempted forgery
to call in all the notes of a certain issue, and as there was
no hope of the Government refunding the stamp on the
back, the old notes were simply burned, and new ones
stamped in their place, without the stamp office knowing
anything of the reasons for the change. In this way very
large sums of duty went to swell the stamp revenue, having
absolutely no connection with increased circulation, although,
with peculiar shortness of vision, no other possible reason
could be seen by Lord Liverpool.

When at last the real amounts of the circulations were
got, it was found that they were actually smaller than they
had been for some time, except in 1825, when they were
somewhat higher. But the discovery did not in the least
affect the Prime Minister's decision,—he had made his
assertion, arrived at his conclusion, and saw no necessity
for altering his proposals.

One important cause of the increase of country circulation in 1825, will probably be found in the action of the
Bank of England, who called in all their small notes,
amounting to nearly £7,000,000, in 1824-25. Such an issue,
circulating as it did over a considerable part of England,
could not be permanently recompensed by the gold paid by
the bank in exchange, as, from the constant determination
of specie to the capital, the provinces were in a very short
time deprived of seven million pounds of their daily cur-

rency. Yet because the country bankers were almost compelled, by national requirement for a currency, to issue their notes in larger amount *to replace this withdrawal*, Mr Tooke, and other writers, use their action as an argument against them, and assert that they added seven million pounds to the currency, solely for their own speculative customers, and that this small note paper produced the panic of 1825. If so, why was Scotland so completely exempted from the scourge? or why does Mr Tooke elsewhere *admit*, that the issue of one pound notes by the Bank of England stopped the distress? In his work on "The State of the Currency," the same writer states that the Bank of England was saved from a "run" by the contraction of the country currency; when the real fact was, that that contraction, being caused by the failure of the country banks, *produced* a run on the bank, which was *only stopped by their again issuing one pound notes* to replace those of the failed banks.

The foreign loans floated at this time amounted to £48,000,000 in five years, to which hundreds of millions fall to be added for other projects. In all this the small note circulation had almost no place, the transactions being carried on by other forms of credit. Of necessity, as prices rose, the purchasing power of notes fell, thereby increasing the demand for currency by the people, who required the same amount of commodities, but now needed more notes to purchase them with. The Bank of England and the country banks were both compelled in this way to increase their issues, though not nearly in the same proportion as the rise in prices. The bank shews an increase of £4,000,000 compared with 1823. During the restriction period, it had been the excessive issues of notes which raised prices, but in 1825 the high prices were the primary cause of the increase in notes. The bank directors were shrewd enough to see the coming danger, and contract d their own issues by refusing discounts; but unfortunately their attempted remedy was ludicrously absurd, when they called on the Government to recall the Act of 1822, and exclude small notes at once from circulation. Prices, which had run up to fabulous amounts, suddenly came toppling down.* Failure followed failure, until the notes of the country banks were completely discredited. London bankers came next, and the bank itself was severely run upon. By the irony of fate, it fell to the poor, despised, *one pound note* to be again the salvation of England. Messrs Gurney & Co., of Norwich, placed a pile of Bank of England small notes on their counter, and they were troubled no more. The Bank of England, which had stopped the issue of these notes, by mere chance found a box containing nearly £700,000 ; and, according to the testimony of Mr Harmer, one of its directors,—"They worked wonders, and it was by great good luck that we had the means of doing it ; because one box containing a quantity of one pound notes had been overlooked, and they were forthcoming at the lucky moment. As far as my judgment goes, *it saved the credit of the country.*"

Before glancing at the remedies proposed by Lord Liverpool, it may be well to point out two of the principal reasons for the unconquerable aversion exhibited by the Bank of England to the one pound note.

Prior to 1797 there had been no such aversion, the probable reason for their not being issued lying in the fact that the bank was a Government bank, or a bankers' bank, but not particularly a *national bank* in the sense that the large Scottish banks are. A gold currency was always fairly plentiful in London, and the provinces, so far as the bank was concerned, were left to look after themselves. Small notes, from their *number*, were both expensive and troublesome to prepare and keep in circulation ; so that as the bank had abundant other means of getting rid of its capital in advances to Government, there was

	1824.	1825.	1826.
* Cottons, .	9d.	1s. 6½d.	7¼d.
Coffee, .	58s.	88s.	50s.
Saltpetre, .	20s.	36s.	23s.
Silk, .	11s. 6d.	17s.	11s.
Tobacco, .	2½d.	6½d.	3¼d.

T

no inducement to make a profit off these notes, which,
in addition, were supposed to be the first portions of a
currency affected by a "*run*" or rumour of panic.

While this was the state of things up to 1797, after that
year the bank had no objections to launch out a small note
currency of seven millions, for which it could not be called
upon to pay coin, and accordingly a large profit was made.
"Runs" were impossible ; numbers would be lost and
burnt, all adding to the profit ; so that, had other things
been equal, the one pound note might possibly have had its
life spared.* But unfortunately a weak spot was discovered
in the bank's armour, by the criminal classes of England
who made their ignorant countrymen their prey. Supposed
to be merely a temporary expedient, no care had been
taken, in preparing the notes, to make them of a character
difficult of imitation. On the contrary, they were as bald
and simple as the old notes which illustrate the previous
chapters ; the engraving was poor, the printing unequal, and
even the paper did not present the beautiful appearance
it now does.

In 1818 the Royal Society of London took up the
matter, and invited communications from the London
engravers. One of these, Mr Beaumont, says :—"Forgeries
of Bank of England notes are so frequent, because they are
so easy of imitation. They are of inferior workmanship to
common engraved shop bills. An apprentice to a writing
engraver, of two years standing, by three or four days work,
is able to copy a bank note plate so that ordinary judges
cannot tell the genuine from the spurious. There are not less
than ten thousand persons in this country who are able to
engrave successful imitations of Bank of England notes,
and nine-tenths of these are in needy, and many of them
in distressed, circumstances." Similar testimony was given
by all the other witnesses regarding the small note

---

* It is surprising how the Bank of England did not discover what
evil things small notes were, until the resumption of cash payments
forced it to pay them in gold.

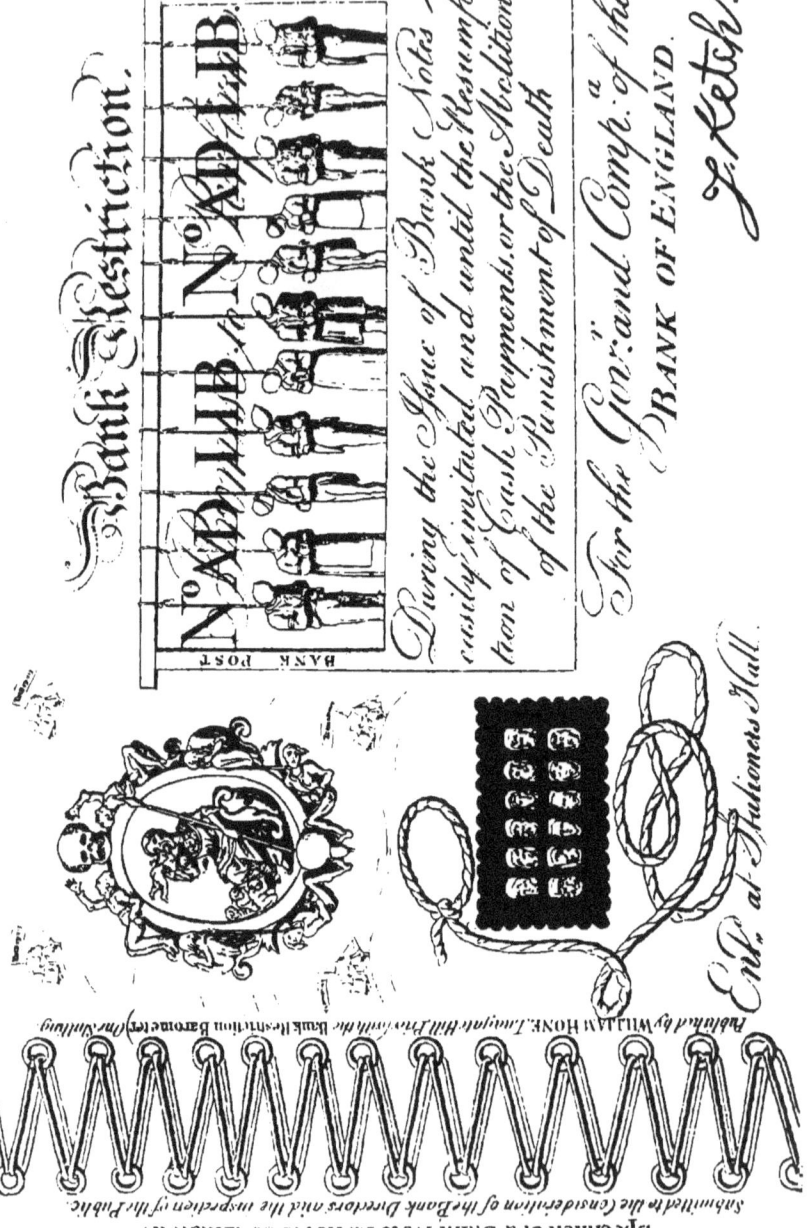

Bank Restriction.

During the Issue of Bank Notes ~ easily imitated and until the Resumption of Cash Payments, or the Abolition of the Punishment of Death

For the Gov.r and Comp.a of the BANK OF ENGLAND.

J. Ketch.

Ent.d at Stationers Hall.

Published by WILLIAM HONE, Ludgate Hill Price with the Bank Restriction Barometer One Shilling.

Submitted to the Consideration of the Bank Directors and the inspection of the Public.

BANK RESTRICTION NOTE

Specimen of a Bank Note ~ not to be imitated.

circulation of the Bank of England; and, let it be remembered, that this was at a time when it was greatly improved from what it had been in 1797, when its roughness first attracted the forger's attention. The checks proposed, consisted of a finer style of engraving, the general opinion being that there should be a combination of vignette and engine-turned work, in place of the *written note*. To these suggestions the bank paid no attention, allowing the forgeries to go on, and trusting solely to Jack Ketch to solve the difficulty by suspending the perpetrators.

Opposite we reproduce George Cruikshank's famous "Bank Restriction Note," which literally stopped the hangings, creating the most intense excitement amongst the public, and corresponding annoyance to the bank directors. The ghastly picture justly pourtrays the scene witnessed by the artist himself, as one day he passed Newgate on his way to the Royal Exchange, a whole row of unfortunates, among whom were two women, being executed for forgery of one pound notes. The bitter irony of the sketch,—Britannia on the right devouring her own children, Newgate Gaol window surrounded with a roped pound £ and crammed with the faces of the victims ready to take the places of those already on the gallows, the grim promise of the latter to perform "ad lib," and the transports crossing the main to Botany Bay,—all reveal the wrath which must have been stirred within the kindly heart of the great artist. His delight, when he heard that the police had to clear the crowd away from William Hone's shop in Ludgate Hill, where the notes were being sold, can only have been exceeded by the satisfaction of knowing that, more than any man in England, he had given the final blow to execution for forgery.

The number of forgeries of one pound notes, compared with other denominations, is certainly alarming, could it not be accounted for by their miserable workmanship. During the six years prior to 1797 only one capital conviction was obtained for note forgery; during the four following years there were eighty-five. In 1801 the bank

attempted to improve matters by printing with paper
having a better watermark,—always a dubious expedient
with notes circulating amongst the middle or lower classes,
who at that time were very illiterate.   From 1797 to 1817
there were 710 convictions, from which there were more
than 300 executions.   The year 1818 was the worst, no less
than thirty-two individuals being hung in twelve months
for this crime.   From 1812 to 1818 107,238 one pound
notes were refused at the bank as spurious, the number of
large notes in the same period being 24,123, equal to, at
the very least, £120,615.   In the two following years, 1819
and 1820, 49,333 small notes were refused.   From 1797 to
1818 the total expense to the bank for prosecution of
forgers was £148,370. 9s. 3d.   Large as this sum may
seem, it bears no comparison to the profit realised by the
bank on its small note circulation during these twenty-two
years ; it was upon an average about £5,000,000 per annum,
which at £3 per cent. yields £150,000 yearly, or £3,300,000
when accumulated for that number of years.   With the
withdrawal of the one pound notes the crime almost
entirely ceased ; and from this coincidence an argument has
been drawn by the enemies of the one pound note which
entirely leaves out of sight other important factors in the
case, for in thus stating the facts as against small notes, the
peculiar circumstances of the time must be taken into
account.   War had dislocated trade, throwing thousands
out of employment, and, as if to aggravate the distress,
corn laws for the protection of landlords, added famine to
the general suffering.   Misery, discontent, and crime
invariably go hand in hand, and undoubtedly had much to
do with the strange epidemic of forgery.   Mr Beaumont's
statement, before alluded to, as to the number of *engravers*
in poor circumstances, is very important, as at such a time
their calling would have little honest employment for them,
and the simple Bank of England notes afforded temptingly
easy returns for dishonest skill.   It may also be observed,
that though in *number* the small note forgeries greatly
exceeded the large, the latter considerably exceeded the

small in *amount*, a fact which does away with much of the argument against small notes ; and, further, if it is asserted that forgery ceased with the abolition of small notes, it should not be forgotten that it ceased just as the resumption of cash payments and an established peace, were bringing back *prosperity* to the country and *employment* to the poorer classes.

The expenses of engraving at that time were serious, as from the large number of notes required, the copper plates wore out very rapidly, and had to be renewed at no little cost ; but in considering the modern applicability of small notes to England, this argument cannot be urged by any bank, as under the new hard steel plate process, or by electrotypy, there is only one cost of engraving, the first plate lasting an indefinite number of years, and giving much greater security to the public than the successive copper plates, each issue under the new system being absolutely identical with its predecessors.

In the event of one pound notes being again adopted, it would be found that the advance in education amongst the lower orders would be a considerable security against forgery. When reading and writing were the privileges of a few, the common people stood at the mercy of designing men of superior attainment. The most dreadful results were predicted, when teaching the poor how to read and write was first spoken of, none of which have transpired. On the contrary, the *wider* the ability to understand and distinguish caligraphic characters, the greater will be the difficulty for any but forgeries of the very finest description to pass current without detection ; and such forgeries, it need not be added, are only attainable by a few, and at such expense, that the artist probably would and could earn a livelihood in a more honest way. The progress in this respect in the condition of the people of England has been great, and gives ground for belief, that the same advantage could not be taken of them now, as was the case in 1812 or 1818. The difficulty forgers would have in turning out work so good as to defy detection, would proportionally compel many of them to abandon their designs, if once begun.

The greatest difficulty to be faced with the Bank of England, would be their inveterate refusal to recognise *two* parties as interested in the immunity from forgery. All bank notes should be so constructed, as to give equal security, first, to *the holder;* and, second, to the bank. Almost the constant rule of English law, in mercantile matters, has been *caveat emptor*, and the bank has carried a somewhat similar rule into their manufacture of notes. They have been provided with many checks and private marks, known or recognisable *only at the bank;* but they are devoid of such character as makes an imitation easily *discoverable by the public*, whose casual observation is more directed to the *general impression* of the printing, than to peculiarities of paper or watermark. This general impression is very easily imitated in a Bank of England note ; and whether owing to the paper, or defective inking, the printing is seldom identical, a comparison of a few of its notes shew-ing certain lines thick in one note and thin or blurred in another ; while, side by side with other bank notes, the difference is obvious. If the one pound note is to come safely into use, the bank must recognise the principle of *public detection*, as well as detection at its own offices. They were compelled in 1820 to own that the old doctrine of mere punishment was of no use, and that it was as much its duty to hinder the easy commission of the crime, as it was of the Government to punish the criminal. The former principle is simply an extension of the latter, and, having been honestly faced by nearly every bank in the kingdom, there is no reason why the Bank of England should decline to adopt it. A fair specimen of their arrogant caution may be seen in the Act, which makes it criminal for any one to adopt such waved lines as are used for the watermark of their notes.

The elaborate system of registration of their notes adopted by the bank, involving cancellation on their first return to office, and consequent checking of numbers *et cætera* by other banks, would entail a serious increase of work if a small note issue were established; and possibly the best way out of the difficulty, would be for the bank to abandon its registration system as regards small notes, and re-issue them until worn out, adopting the simple method of record followed by the Scottish banks. The intricate English plan is little check upon theft, as the bank is bound to pay notes when presented by a *bonâ fide* holder, even when there is proof of their having been stolen; a stop payment having as little effect against notes as against stolen sovereigns. It is true that the notes might be traced back from the holder to the thief, but even this is uncertain, and is becoming every day more so from the innumerable ways in which notes can be got rid of.

Returning to the remedies proposed by Lord Liverpool in 1826, let us see what lessons he and his ministry had learned from the history of English banking, of which we have endeavoured to give an epitome.

Here is his summing up, placed somewhat unjudicially at the very beginning of his statement :—" The principal source of the recent distress is to be found in the rash spirit of speculation, supported, fostered, and encouraged by the country banks;" the English system of banking is "an unsolid and delusive system." In his first conclusion he was almost totally wrong. To assert that the 624 new companies, with nominal capital of £372,000,000, were floated through the support, fostering care, and encouragement of the feeble country banks, is so manifest an absurdity, that it scarcely requires the refutation given to it by Mr Palmer, the Governor of the Bank of England. The great plenty of the few previous years, the accumulation of capital after the cessation of the war, the reduction of interest on national debt, all combined to put the nation in a ferment of speculation, with its new found wealth, which would have gone on if no bankers had existed. Indeed, so strong was the mania, that it would have *created* bankers to carry it on, had they not already been there. They were there, however, and without admitting that they carried on all the companies, this brings us to Lord Liverpool's second contention, in which he was quite correct. Banking in England was " an unsolid and delusive system," and therefore all the more dangerous if required to bolster up numerous new companies, legitimate or·otherwise. But whose fault was it that it was " unsolid and delusive ? " How long had it been so ? and what means had been adopted to make it otherwise ? It has been shewn whose fault it was, and how long it had existed, and that any attempts to alter the *status quo* had been in the direction of making it still more " unsolid and delusive." The law of 1708, the monopoly of the Bank of England, prohibition of large banks, and the dependence of the bank on the Government,—had all, with one accord, united in making the *one* strong institution unwieldily strong and arrogant, leaving the nine hundred weak institutions more helpless and dependent. Correctly admitting, as he did, that paper credit must be regulated, Lord Liverpool's only idea of regulation consisted of amputation or abolition. If some unfortunate were cramped in close confinement, until lack of air and liberty weakened his nerves, unstrung his muscles, and unhinged his brain, what would be thought of a physician who, instead of ordering instant freedom and exercise, could prescribe amputation of a limb as a remedy ? Yet this was precisely Lord Liverpool's performance, in his capacity of currency doctor for England, and would equally have been his practice for Scotland, had the patient not determinedly refused his prescription. He partially saw the evil, but utterly failed to realise its importance, or to see the true remedy. He only saw an unreliable class of bankers, and lacked boldness to deal effectively with the *system which had prevented any other from coming into existence.* True to his preconceived notions, of their speculative tendencies, and egged on by the Bank of England's dread of forgery, his first step was to abolish notes below £5,—this he called "regulation of the currency." Having accomplished this feat, he permitted, for the first time in English history, the establishment of those joint-stock banks which alone could issue notes of any kind with

a fair measure of security for their payment on demand, and
with certain assurance of ultimate convertibility. If one
part of the circulation of the country banks was bad, the
whole was evil, and ought to have been swept away ; but
instead of adopting this radical measure, and allowing
regulated circulation of all the notes to the new joint-stocks,
he preferred tinkering still further the decaying system of
private bankers, creating a new monopoly in the sacred
sixty-five radius, and leaving an entirely unlimited system
of issue to the new banks. In his endeavour to prevent
speculation, as every one knows, he has not been very
successful, while his ignorance of what really constituted
a " *regulated paper currency* " should be held responsible for
the panics occurring prior to 1844 ; for while he allowed
joint-stock banks, he assigned no limits to their circulation,
or to the amount of gold to be kept in reserve. With this
semi-free banking, and total want of experience, the joint-
stock banks issued their large notes so extensively, that, in
combination with other usual causes, all the evils and distress ensued which had before been wholly assigned to the
influence of the one pound note. In England, it may truly
be said that panics have been more frequent and regular
since the abolition of the one pound note, than they ever
were during its existence.

In 1826 a remarkable instance was afforded of the
appreciation of small notes by the English people, which
also strongly marks the inconvenience attending their
abolition. In December of that year a return was given to
the House of Commons of a memorial from the principal
" gentry, land occupiers, merchants, manufacturers, and
tradesmen " of Cumberland and Westmoreland, to the Lords
of the Treasury, respecting the circulation of Scotch notes
in these counties. On the decision of Government becoming
known regarding small notes, the Scottish banks at once
proceeded to restrict their issues within the limits of Scotland, and notified " to their correspondents the necessity of
closing all accounts on the south side of the border within
a few weeks." The memorial proceeds to say, " that from

the contiguity of this district to Scotland, and from the constant intercourse existing between the two kingdoms, a large part of our money transactions has been negotiated in Scotch paper, which has freely circulated among us nearly half a century.

"An Act of Parliament limited the number of partners in our English banks to six at the utmost, while the absence of any such limitation in Scotland gave a degree of strength to the issuers of notes, and of confidence to the receivers of them, which several banks established in our counties have not been able to command.

"The natural consequence has been, that Scotch notes have formed the greater part of our circulating medium, a circumstance in which we have reason to rejoice, since, in the course of the last fifty years, with the solitary exception of the Falkirk bank, we have never sustained the slightest loss from one acceptance of Scotch paper ; while in the same period the failures of banks in the north of England have been unfortunately numerous, and have occasioned the most ruinous losses to many who were little able to sustain them.

"Our local banks cannot therefore be strengthened ; and our Scotch circulation is about to be withdrawn suddenly, and before the meeting of Parliament, when these difficulties might be removed. Thus a vacuum is about to be created, which cannot be filled up so rapidly as the Scotch notes are withdrawn ; and in this case we shall be exposed for some length of time to the appalling evils which, it is known, must result from a deficient circulation. We have the honour to enclose a copy of a representation which the urgency of the case has induced us to send to the Scotch banks."

The memorial was strongly supported by the two Members of Parliament for the district, Sir Philip Musgrave and the well known Sir James Graham of Netherby, the latter of whom, while not desiring the permanent continuance of Scotch currency, deprecates any sudden change until they should be able to establish a sound bank of their own, " consisting of more than six partners, and subjected, as we hope, to a limited responsibility." The Treasury gave due attention to the matter, and ordered their secretary to "acquaint Sir James Graham, that my Lords, having bestowed their most careful consideration on these representations, their Lordships do not feel that they could with propriety attempt to use any interference with the Scotch banks in the measures which they may think it necessary to adopt,"—thereby affording ample proof of the ability of their lordships to avoid one awkward question, by returning an answer to another which had not been asked. Sir James Graham's proposal, that the Bank of England should establish a branch in Carlisle, was passed on to the board of directors, with a request that their " serious consideration " might be given to the subject. What was the result of this consideration is not definitely known, but it is needless to remark, that the " Old Lady of Threadneedle Street " has not yet set foot in Cumberland.

" The issue of paper representative money is beneficial to *all parties*, provided that it be conducted upon a sound method of regulation," says Professor Jevous. What hinders then? or why should the most useful paper money be declared the most dangerous? It has been shewn that the one pound note *never had a fair chance* in England ; but notwithstanding the difficulties through which it passed it was most beneficial, again and again saving the country in time of panic ; while to its powerful help, more than to any other financial agent, is it due that England passed so easily through the twenty-two years of the restriction. Without the seven millions of small notes, stoppage of cash payments would have forced the nation to resort to a barbarous system of barter, if indeed that could have been found possible at all. We have also endeavoured to shew that none of the evils popularly attached to the one pound notes can be truly traced to their influence, as *all* these evils have been seen in even greater form since small notes ceased to exist, with the one exception of forgery, against which the bank provided no check by fine engraving or elaborate engine-turning.

With the date of their abolition, the first *modern* talk of bi-metallism was begun in 1827, with silver at 5s. 2d. per ounce, now selling at 4s. At the present time, when the necessity for an additional currency is becoming stronger in England, the unprecedented fall in silver has injured the bi-metallic proposal in public esteem, without revealing any other way out of the difficulty. It raged in the London financial papers a few years ago ; but in view of recent facts has somewhat changed its form, and in its place the idea of a small paper currency is again being mooted. Mr Childers' proposals for renewing the gold currency brought the whole question to the front, from the heavy loss to the nation by the wear of its coin, not to speak of the waste in coining gold, much of which is merely exported to other countries, to be melted and recoined there. Of the £90,000,000 sovereigns and £20,000,000 half-sovereigns estimated to form our metallic currency, fully *one-half* is understood to be light in weight. The expense of recoining is estimated at one halfpenny per coin, amounting on £110,000,000 to £270,833,* equalling annually £18,749 ; while the *annual waste of gold* by wear amounts, according to estimates by Professor Jevous and the Master of the Mint, to the large sum of £42,000,—making the total expense for England's gold currency £60,749 ; while the interest upon the principal sum amounts to £3,300,000 at 3 per cent., *at least one-half of which might be saved.* Of these expenses Scotland is compelled to pay her proportion, without any corresponding relief on account of her more economical habits.

If one pound notes were adopted in England, the great part of the *waste* would be saved, while the mint expense could be still further reduced were the banks allowed to keep uncoined bullion as part of their reserve, say in £1000 blocks, with the mint stamp impressed to ensure weight and fineness. It would also be found that one pound notes

---

* Sovereigns have to be renewed every eighteen years ; half-sovereigns every ten years.

circulated more rapidly than gold, and would be hoarded less. They would consequently effect more payments, and it would probably be found that their amount in the hands of the public was less than that of the gold they had replaced.

Mr Childers' proposals were dropped, because of the many practical difficulties seen to be in the way,—first, the danger, upon general principles, of debasing £20,000,000 of the gold coin, which in turn would give illegal manufacturers a clear profit of one-tenth on the amount they could coin. The reserves of the banks were another difficulty. Would the Bank of England give £20,000 of new sovereigns for 40,000 half-sovereigns, nominally worth £20,000, but really worth only £18,000? or could its issue department give credit to its banking department for the full issue, if £20,000 of debased half-sovereigns were offered by the latter in exchange for the same amount of notes? Further, would the Scotch and Irish banks be permitted to count at their nominal value any half-sovereigns forming part of their reserve? It was seen that truly to answer these questions involved so many others, that it was deemed best to drop the proposal, with the result that the country is again slowly surging towards a lack of currency and depreciation of its coinage. Gold is becoming scarcer year by year, as other countries adopt a gold coinage ; the mines of Australia and California no longer produce the ingots of virgin gold which enriched the country in years gone by, the metal being now obtained, slowly, laboriously, and at serious expense, by the crushing of the quartzose rocks in which it lies entombed. For years past, prices have been falling, with apparently no prospect of rising, *one of the surest signs* that gold, the universal medium of exchange, is becoming dearer; for if the mint price of gold be *fixed* at £3. 17s. 9d. per ounce, any scarcity of gold must have the effect of lowering the prices of other commodities, seeing that, according to British law, it cannot raise its own price. France, Germany, Italy, and other countries have thrown their silver on the market and adopted gold currencies, widening the gap between the two metals, and carrying the prospects of bi-metalism still further into the future. Although the objections to this remedy were said to be serious, yet it is certain that the question was not raised without cause. There is seldom smoke without fire, and one of the causes, alike of the bi-metallic schemes, Mr Childers' proposals, and the recent fall in prices, may be found in the increasing demand for gold in place of silver.

For nearly twenty years from 1860, a period of extraordinary commercial development in Europe, the United States of America conducted their affairs with a depreciated and inconvertible paper currency, and, in consequence, the amount of gold released - materially assisted in maintaining a plentiful supply for the wants of Europe. When this supply was stopped, through the resumption of cash payments compelling the United States to collect gold, the abrupt change began slowly to make itself felt across in Europe. In the course of these two decades, how vast have been the changes on the eastern shores of the Atlantic! In Britain the legislature has chosen to enact, that while an individual is liable to his last pound for all his debts, ten or twenty individuals in the form of a limited company do not require any such responsibility to keep them in the paths of prudence. Along with this absolution from debt to a company, the utter want of stringent punishment for speculative bankruptcies, headed up in the abrogation of imprisonment for debt, has opened the way for an increase in production on speculation hitherto unknown. Had Britain been the factory for the world's trade as truly as she was so in 1800, there would have been ample room for the expansion ; but, synchronous with the increase at home, a similar expansion also occurred on the Continent, where, since the revolutionary period of 1848, industries have expanded in such volume as not only supplies their own requirements, but enables them to export their wares at a profit to the very country which formerly supplied them with everything. The recent depression in the profits of various branches of trade in this country, is almost entirely outside of the question of Free Trade *versus* Protection ; and it is to be hoped that the Royal Commission presently considering these matters, will make it sufficiently plain, that foreign bounties and protective tariffs only affect the merest fringe of our trade ; and if it is true that our exports to the Continent are not increasing as in former years, it is due to the vastly more serious causes,—that foreign nations are now working for themselves, that their toilers are content to work during longer hours for smaller wages,and to live more economically, than their *confrères* in Britain. Any attempt to remove these difficulties by a return to protective duties, under the new name of Fair Trade, cannot but be a very inadequate remedy, if it be one at all ; and if they are to be faced and overcome, it can only be done by a widespread intelligence, which will convert the "working-man" again into the "craftsman," and lend its impulse to every home in the kingdom, —an intelligence which will teach industry, temperance, and ingenuity to the workman, economise the material and machinery of the manufacturer, and give foresight to the merchant to discover new markets for his merchandise. That the trade of Great Britain is at present in a critical position, is a fact which there is no use in Britons disputing ; the period is one of transition, and the future largely depends on the new markets and new measures of the commercial world. In these circumstances, it is for Englishmen to consider, amongst other economies, the necessity for a more economical currency, which would so far prevent the scarcity of gold from affecting prices in the degree that it lessened the demand, and therefore the appreciation, of that metal for purposes of current use.

In a letter to the "*Times*" newspaper by " F.," upon Mr Palgrave's paper on one pound notes read before the Institute of Bankers in London, the writer strongly advocates their use and application to England, but recommends that at least £40,000,000 of gold should be retained against the issue of the small notes, the balance to be covered by Government securities, thereby releasing

ناnearly £60,000,000 for other purposes. He says, "If at
this moment we substituted for the gold currency, notes of
one pound, secured one-third by gold and two-thirds by
securities, we should call £60,000,000 into useful existence.
It is not enough to say that we lose interest on that amount,
and have on much of it lost interest and compound
interest for sixty years. Who can measure what we have
lost, by having for sixty years in this country a mass of
useless gold, instead of useful and productive commodities?
Our loss by wear of gold and by mint charges is as nothing,
compared to our sacrifice of all this working capital. If
one pound notes were gradually substituted for the gold,
the difficulty of withdrawing the light coins would at once
be done away with." The "*Times*" thought the proposal
revolutionary and unsafe, and made certain criticisms on
the subject, which produced a letter from Mr William
Fowler, M.P. for Cambridge, in which he states :—"I have
long advocated the issue of one pound notes on principle,
but I have never thought of forcing gold out of circulation.
I have merely said, that I thought the public would prefer
notes to gold in England, as they do in Scotland, Ireland,
and America." He then mentions an instance of a country
banker, who, having sent £15,000 of gold to London for his
credit, was charged £160 by the Bank of England for light
weight, a grievance which would be largely done away with
were one pound notes introduced.

Making allowance for possible defects in " F.'s " scheme,
there could be abundant safeguards provided under an Act
somewhat similar in its provisions to that of 1844, whereby
the issuing banks were granted a fixed circulation, upon
which the Scottish system might be grafted, allowing an
increase beyond the limit upon *gold being kept as reserve*,
not necessarily in *coin*, but partly in bullion stamped by the
mint. The proportional reserve method would be a much
more elastic one, and is thought desirable by many.
Germany has a still better method. The Imperial Bank
there, and such other banks as are in conformity with the
law which regulates the Government bank, have a right of

issuing to a certain fixed quantity, unbacked by gold ; beyond this amount each may increase their circulation upon deposit of gold. Up to this point the procedure is the same as guides the issuing and banking departments of the Bank of England ; but in Germany, to provide against those ruptures of Acts of Parliament which the panics of 1847 and 1857 forced on our bank, there is a provision whereby even that limit may be exceeded on payment of a tax of 5 per cent. In this way, while no bank can profit by its 'over-issue, yet, in time of sudden emergency, an elastic limit is provided, which might be of great public utility.*

To dispense with the unnecessary expense and danger of carriage, some public repository could be opened in London or elsewhere where such reserves as were not actually required for current requirements might be retained in safe custody,—under the same rule as is in effect at Melbourne, where the banks unite in having one common safe, with separate compartments for the specie of each bank, a committee being appointed of several bank managers, who all require to be present before the doors are opened or any transfer made.

Above all, refuse permission to issue small notes to all banks or bankers who do not publish a regular state of their affairs, and curtail their existing circulation by every means consistent with reason. Allow none but joint-stock banks to have the right of a one pound note issue ; and of them, only those whose paid up capital reaches £500,000, with at least three times as much uncalled, but subscribed for ; increasing the number of partners from its present extremely low limit, and allow no bank to commence business with fewer than one hundred partners.

By these means the adoption of a small note currency might be effected, with the least possible alteration of existing systems. The monopoly of issue of the bank for

---

* In Germany the 5 per cent. is levied as a *tax* or *fine;* and to make the same method safe in England, we should probably require an 8 or 9 per cent. tax.

the sixty-five mile radius might or might not be left to it, on its agreeing to issue safe one pound notes. Its greatest evil has been negatived by joint-stock banks having a regulated right of issue in the provinces ; but much may be said in favour of the total suppression of the bank's monopoly as concerns the note issue. With proper precaution for the limits of *uncovered* circulation, there need be little fear of speculation from the change. That danger arose chiefly in the olden time from *the total want of regulation*, and the arbitrary fluctuations of Government policy, which, affected by circumstances, *gave* certain rights, withdrew them, and then *granted* them once more, only to be again withdrawn without any sufficient reason in a few years,— changes which, easily made as they were by the Government or its bank, were productive of the most serious distress throughout the country. If, instead of this harassing interference with private duty, southern legislators had endeavoured to inaugurate a national exchange of notes, they would have been less exercised with so-called inflation or over-issue. Unfortunately, from the large number and local character of banks in England, this is no easy matter, owing to the difficulty in maintaining the exchanges without a considerable amount of agency; yet complex as it may appear, if earnestly attempted through some of the associations of English bankers the difficulties would vanish, and, in comparison with the railway clearing-house, a national note exchange for England would soon be simplicity itself. The measure would be "twice blessed," for as a "small note" issue would economise the gold capital, through fewer notes doing the work of a larger quantity of gold, so an exchange would economise the note issue, thus giving bankers a two-fold margin of accommodative power presently allowed to go to waste.

Free banking would have led to the extinction of those numerous small banks, whose perpetual failures over nearly a century imbued the English mind with a sense of insecurity, and induced that panic feeling whose traditions have still so much strength. Any soldier can tell, that continual and harassing alarms, however petty, demoralise and dishearten a force much more certainly than one great repulse ; and so it seems to have been with English banking in the past, though each day will lessen the evil, as the great joint-stocks—such as the National Provincial Bank —instil a feeling of confidence hitherto unknown. The same traditionary dread still hovers around the question of forgery, no notice being taken of the immense strides made in engraving and note security since 1800 ; the notes at that period being little if any better than the simple Scottish notes, which have been reproduced in this work specially to shew the extremely easy work forgers had to imitate. George Cruikshank's bank restriction note admirably caricatures the bald Bank of England note, which, even yet, could be *engraved* by almost any apprentice in the country.

Hitherto it has been assumed that regulated *private issues* would be the best means of launching a small note currency ; but it cannot be forgotten that a State, or Bank of England, issue, is the great desideratum of our leading politicians. It has been said of one of these, and could be said with equal truth of nearly all, that he knew neither more nor less about the currency than he learned from Sir Robert Peel ; so that as long as these opinions or prejudices are current, it is not probable that private issues of one pound notes will be permitted, no matter how useful they may be proved to be, as the whole tendency of modern statesmanship is to assert the same right over the paper currency, as it asserts over that of specie.

To one bank of issue, there appear to be a number of objections, so serious as to counterbalance the possibility of greater security. It would require to be simply a State institution, existing for no other purpose than the issue of notes. To conjoin ordinary banking with it, would be to make another huge monopoly, and increase the confusion already existing.

Banking, to be " free and unrestricted," in quite another sense than that used by Sir Robert Peel in 1844, must give

the same rights and immediate command of banking neces-
saries to one bank as to another ; but a State issue would
give an advantage to those banks who, being near the source
of supply, could accommodate their demands to their
daily requirements ; while others, more remote, would be
compelled to keep a much larger stock of notes on hand,
which would have to be paid for with gold or securities.

London banks, from their vicinity to the bullion and
consol markets, would have the further advantage of at
once making any profit they could, out of superfluous
reserve uplifted from the issue office ; and, conversely, the
further a bank was placed from the centre of issue, the
burden would be proportionally increased,—so that in the
remote and thinly populated districts of country, where
banks find it most difficult to maintain a footing, a decrease
of banking accommodation and an increase in charges
would be a necessary result.   Mr Somers points out
another objection in event of a number of State issue offices
being opened throughout the country, that even though the
banks in these favoured towns might reap some advantage,
they would still have to go to London for the gold they
required to lodge in security ; while consols, being only
transferable in the Bank of England, at London, would
place the same difficulty in the way of their sale or
purchase.

The absorption of such a mass of moveable capital
would retard the action and freedom of the banks, most of
whom keep as much of their funds in consols now, as they
would do under the proposed system, while at present they
have the advantage of being able to utilise their stocks in
any way they choose.

In measure, a considerable part of the difficulty could
be got over, were the State office to issue notes specially
appropriated to each bank, with its name printed upon it,
as in America, charging only for the *circulation ;* because if
this were not done, and a uniform currency established
throughout the country all payable in London, there would
be a continual flow of notes to the capital.   London money

is always of use to provincial bankers ; and to those with whom State notes accumulated, there could be no better remittance to London than these notes. The provinces, thus denuded of their currency, would look to the banks for a further supply ; and those banks who had issued all the notes they had received, without receiving an equal number in return, would be forced to make perpetual purchases of notes in London, to an extent two or three times the value of those they would have required under their own issues, as under these, there was practically no expense, except *on the actual circulation.* By these various forced sales and purchases, both the bullion and consol markets would be subject to more sudden and violent daily fluctuations than they have hitherto experienced.

To entrust the management of the national debt and public money to a State bank as some propose, would not be more economical than the present arrangement, and on general principles would be objectionable. Two memoranda appear in the appendix to the Bank Act Report of 1858, by Lord Monteagle and Mr Arbuthnot, which are well worthy of attention in connection with this question. The objections there urged may be classed briefly under two heads, namely, the difficulty under which a State bank would labour from having no mercantile connection, such as the Bank of England enjoys; and the liability of a State establishment to abuse, by a powerful and extravagant government, in time of war or financial pressure. For example, under existing conditions, when the dividends on the funds are being paid, the circulation of the Bank of England is but slightly increased, as the greater part of the dividend is merely transferred in the bank's books from public deposits (kept in its function as the bank of the Government) to private deposits (in its ordinary mercantile business). Were these dividends paid by a State bank, millions would go out in notes, which would immediately come pouring back through the mercantile banks into which they would be paid by the stockholders, causing a great expense and waste of time by the unnecessary friction.

Difficulties would also arise at certain periods of the year, when, with an empty exchequer, the State bank could not meet the temporary requirements of Government, as the Bank of England can now do by advancing mercantile deposits in the discount of the Government's deficiency bills, to be repaid when taxation is collected. In such a case the State bank would be compelled to sell consols, in a market possibly already overstocked, and as these sales would usually occur at the same season of the year, they might be taken advantage of for speculative purposes by the outside public. An alternative plan would be open to a foolish government, of forcing out, by some means, a temporary circulation, sufficient to tide over the few weeks of vacuum until receipt of taxation,—a little beginning, which might lead to greater operations at a different time. It is unnecessary to name any other difficulties or objections, as they are somewhat foreign to the question at issue, for even Mr Ricardo, in his scheme for a State bank, made provision for one pound notes, so that it may at once be admitted, that whatever impropriety or inconvenience might attend a State issue, there would be nothing in such an issue to prevent it including notes below £5.

Dogmatic writing upon the final adjustment of the currency in connection with the adoption of one pound notes is neither prudent nor necessary, for where such masters of finance as Jevons and Levi tread cautiously, ordinary mortals may not rush in with ill-advised theory But it can at least be said, that there are no axioms applicable to the entire paper currency, which are not of equal force regarding small notes, so far as their safe issue in England is concerned. The select committee of 1858 practically admitted this in their report, although their inveterate prejudice would not allow them to adopt Earl Gifford's proposed motion :—" That your committee have been unable to discover any difference, either in principle or in practical consequence, between the notes of a denomination of £5 and upwards, and those of a lower denomination now in use in Scotland and Ireland ; . . . that such a currency performs, in a perfectly satisfactory manner, all the purposes of circulation which could be performed by gold coin ; and moreover, that during the runs upon the banks in Scotland and Ireland last year, it was for deposits mainly, and to a very small extent for notes, that a demand for gold took place."

But after making due allowance for all honest and reasonable objections of a scientific nature, it remains a fact, that the two greatest foes in England of the one pound note, are as utterly mean and ignoble as they are absurd and unreasonable.   The dread of forgery, and the supposed liability of the small note holder to sudden and mysterious panic, are the two spectres which must be exorcised before any progress can be made.   They have been shaken in the face of the public for the last sixty years, and brought with almost childish iteration before every banking committee since 1810.   Capable of being proved to be mere phantasies, and having no basis even in the experience of England, save as distorted traditions of a period whose conditions' are happily passed away, they are nevertheless dragged in and held up in awful warning whenever the question of small note currency is mooted.   The committee reports of 1858 and 1875 may be searched through in vain for a single good reason in support of these delusions, yet they appear in every chapter, asserted, with apparent sincerity and with much wagging of heads, by their grave propounders, not one of whom, however, attempts to render a reason for the faith that he holds.   Absurd as they seem, it is absolutely necessary that they should be faced, for they are held with all the stubborn tenacity that characterises the race; and, as all the world knows, there is no position, military or logical, from which it is so difficult to rout a sturdy Englishman, as one in which, according to science, he ought to be able to make no defence at all.   In the course of the present century public opinion has ripened upon certain questions with amazing rapidity, while others have required long years of exposition before the national attention could be aroused ; but once this has been accomplished, the final

blow has invariably been both swift and complete, so that
if the few remaining years of the nineteenth century are to
witness the removal of England's inherited antipathy to the
small note, it is now full time that the cry again went forth,
—" Agitate, agitate, agitate ! "

The Acts of 1844-45, unpractical as they may have
proved for Scotland, placed English issues on a much safer
footing ; and the legislation of 1826, although apparently
ringing the knell of the one pound note, really brightened
its prospective hopes, by destroying another portion of that
monopoly which had so long prevented its healthy circulation by joint-stock banks.

The difficulties in the way of a simpler system of banking
in England are very great, and, until these are removed, no
note issue can have the effect in that country that it has
had in Scotland.   Glancing briefly at the various kinds of
banks, there are :—First, Banks of issue, subdivided into the
following classes :—

> Bank of England, issuing notes throughout England ; legal
> tender.
> Private provincial banks,   ⎫ Who cannot open offices within
> Joint-stock banks, limited,   ⎬ sixty-five miles of London
>   „   „   unlimited, ⎭ without giving up their issue.

Second, Banks who cannot issue notes :—

> Private bankers, within the sixty-five mile radius from London.
> Joint-stock banks,   „   „   „
> Private, or joint-stock banks in the provinces, which did not
> issue notes prior to the Act of 1844.
> Of these again, some are limited and others unlimited.

Third, Invading banks, empowered to issue notes in
another country, but not in England ; as, for example, the
Scottish or colonial banks.

This list exhibits the various divisions created at one
time or another, by an interfering legislature,—divisions so
flimsily constructed, that two of the most important classes
of banks (the great London joint-stock and the Scottish
banks) have obtained a footing within the charmed radius,
entirely by a chance omission in the letter of the law, an

omission which subsequent legislation would fain have interfered with had it dared. The mutual jealousies of these banks, in event of a small note issue being thrown open to some but not to others,—as, for example, given to joint-stocks and denied to private banks,—would be difficult to encounter and allay, except on principles of equality and freedom, which would entirely revolutionise the English law of banking.

To effect such a change is no child's play, and will not be accomplished in one sitting of Parliament. Englishmen are tenacious of their beliefs, or prejudices, as foreigners may design them, and the evidence led before the Committee of 1875 brought out a heavy weight of opposition, not to speak of the more active hostility of those who can see no flaw in Lord Liverpool's performance of 1826. Foreigners (Scotchmen included) may formulate theories to their heart's content, and wonder, as a great foreigner once did, at "these stupid English." Their formulæ have no effect upon John Bull, save upon his temper, which injudicious interference is apt to arouse. He does not, and never will budge, until he sees, or thinks he sees, it to be for his advantage to do so. Fortunately, there are not wanting signs that he is cogitating,—casting the matter over in his capacious mind, taking a secret look at it now and again, afraid lest any one see him donning his new raiment. Some of the leading economists are on the side of the one pound note ; while newspaper articles and letters signify a change of opinion, the influence of which cannot but be felt sooner or later. But stronger than any of these in forcing a settlement of the difficulty, will be the future production of gold. Another California or Australia would put the one pound note hopelessly into perspective. Should nature, however, persist in concealing her treasuries for a few years longer, popular opinion—that tremendous force before which statesmen and hobbies are alike compelled to bow—will slowly form and gather power. At present the question is not a party one with politicians, both Mr Gladstone and Lord Iddesleigh sharing Peel's opinions; but strongly opposed as these statesmen are to an extension of private issue, even their great influence and talents would be unavailing against the national will.

In the meantime it behoves those happy countries which have been blessed with the small note for so many years, to be prudent and cautious, giving no opportunity for the accusations of the enemy. Fate's irony is gradually forcing wealthy England to copy the wealth - making establishments of her once impoverished sister, and there seems small reason in adopting these without also using the INSTRUMENT which has most advanced their prosperity. If Scotchmen are "guiding with conspicuous success" many of England's large banking companies, their influence will not be thrown away ; and the time may not be so far distant as some may imagine, when we shall again read of the one pound note in the homes of Merrie England.

Index.

EDINBURGH CO-OPERATIVE PRINTING COMPANY LIMITED.